The Political Economy of International Financial Instability

The Political Economy of International Financial Instability (1986) discusses international financial problems as a global issue, concentrating on systemic interactions. The interrelations among nation states, international organizations and market forces provide the framework for analysis. This global perspective emphasizes the interaction between political and economic elements.

The Political Economy of International Financial Instability

Pier Carlo Padoan

Routledge
Taylor & Francis Group

First published in 1986
by Croom Helm Ltd

This edition first published in 2025 by Routledge
4 Park Square, Milton Park, Abingdon, Oxon, OX14 4RN

and by Routledge
605 Third Avenue, New York, NY 10017

Routledge is an imprint of the Taylor & Francis Group, an informa business

© 1986 Pier Carlo Padoan

Publisher's Note
The publisher has gone to great lengths to ensure the quality of this reprint but points out that some imperfections in the original copies may be apparent.

Disclaimer
The publisher has made every effort to trace copyright holders and welcomes correspondence from those they have been unable to contact.

A Library of Congress record exists under LCCN: 86002664

ISBN: 978-1-032-95470-7 (hbk)
ISBN: 978-1-003-58508-4 (ebk)
ISBN: 978-1-032-95475-2 (pbk)

Book DOI 10.4324/9781003585084

_The Political Economy of_____

INTERNATIONAL

_FINANCIAL____

_INSTABILITY____

_PIER CARLO PADOAN_____

CROOM HELM
London • Sydney • Dover, New Hampshire

© 1986 Pier Carlo Padoan
Croom Helm Ltd, Provident House, Burrell Row,
Beckenham, Kent BR3 1AT

Croom Helm Australia Pty Ltd, Suite 4, 6th Floor,
64-76 Kippax Street, Surry Hills, NSW 2010, Australia

British Library Cataloguing in Publication Data

Padoan, Pier Carlo
    The political economy of international financial
    instability.
    1. Economic history – 1971-   2. World politics
    – 1975-1985
    I. Title
    330.9'048   HC59
    ISBN 0-7099-4003-3

Croom Helm, 27 South Main Street,
Wolfeboro, New Hampshire 03894-2069, USA

Library of Congress Cataloging in Publication Data

Padoan, Pier Carlo
    The political economy of international financial
instability.

    Bibliography.
    Includes index.
    1. International economic relations. 2. Debts,
external. I. Title.
HF1411.P25   1986   332'.042   86-2664
ISBN 0-7099-4003-3

Printed and bound in Great Britain by Mackays of Chatham Ltd, Kent

CONTENTS

TABLES AND FIGURES

Tables

Figures

PREFACE

International political economy and the financial instability hypothesis are the two elements on which is based the view of international financial problems discussed in this book.

The financial instability hypothesis maintains that, in financially sophisticated systems, endogenous forces are present that will transform a state of tranquillity into financial distress and, eventually, collapse.

The financial instability hypothesis has been developed by Hyman Minsky over a number of years. His work represents the last product of a line of thought which dates back, at least, to Bagehot and includes Irving Fisher, Keynes, Kalecki, as well as part of the marxist tradition. These authors, although distant in their political beliefs, share a view of the capitalist system which is centred upon the interaction between capital accumulation and financial phenomena.

International political economy is an emerging field. Its aim is to combine in one approach the analysis of political and economic aspects of international relations. In this respect a political economy approach contributes to pull the economic profession out of one of its favourite hiding-places: the idea that the solution to most (if not all) problems of our society is fundamentally a political one and that, as a consequence, the economist should defend his "scientific neutrality" by remaining one step behind.

The perspective taken up in this book is global in the sense that it discusses international financial problems concentrating mainly on systemic interactions. The interrelations among nation states, international organizations and market forces provide the framework for analysis.

This approach may seem ambitious. It is our strong belief, however, that progress toward the understanding of the international system requires such a perspective.

A global perspective which emphasizes the interaction between political and economic elements puts one largely outside mainstream economic analysis which allows for only one global framework, the purely competitive general equilibrium model.

The search for alternative paradigms may require heavy costs. One is the loss of elegance ("rigour") at least in the early stages of investigation. We know, however, that a rigour-relevance trade-off exists. We propose to pick a different point on such a trade-off.

This book would have never been written if I had not enjoyed the opportunity to collaborate on research with the Istituto Affari Internazionali in Rome. Stimulating intellectual exchange with researchers, and friends, of the Istituto has convinced me of the usefulness of an interdisciplinary approach when studying international relations.

A particular thank is due to Paolo Guerrieri with whom I have discussed many of the arguments treated in chapters 1, 2, 3, and 11. I would also like to thank the University of Rome for financial support.

Chapter One

INTRODUCTION

In the summer of 1982 the international
financial system was threatened by the risk of
insolvency of the two most heavily indebted
countries, Mexico and Brazil. A wave of panic swept
the international banking community and for several
months fears of a generalized bankruptcy were more
than just the creation of some imaginative financial
journalist. Since then the emergency has been
temporarily called off thanks to the formulation of
short term rescue plans for the most urgent
situations by the International Monetary Fund (IMF).
The overall picture is far from reassuring, however.
Rescheduling of debt, although quite costly for both
banks and the populations of the indebted countries,
is in some cases continually rediscussed and no
stable solution to long term insolvency problems
seems to have been reached.

Recent experience, as well as lessons from
history, suggest that financial crises cannot be
cured with economic recipes alone and that an
analysis of financial instability, whether national
or international, cannot ignore other aspects of the
matter in addition to the purely economic or
financial ones. This statement is in contrast with
most of the existing literature on the topic which
is either strictly descriptive or highly technical
and often follows a purely mechanical approach.

In recent years students of international
relations have produced a growing number of
contributions which are leading to the development
of a new field of research known as international
political economy (Frey and Schneider 1982, Frey
1984). Its ambition is to give a description, and
possibly an explanation, of international economic
problems assuming a close interaction of political

and economic processes. It aims at providing an
economic base for political decisions and an
explanation of economic choices which also takes
account of political variables and political
behaviour. Such an approach is particularly powerful
when one has to deal with international financial
problems (1). Although many contributions have
appeared treating different aspects of international
relations, very few deal explicitly with the problem
of debt (2). The aim of this book is to provide a
contribution to help fill the gap.

The rest of this chapter is devoted to a brief
description of the transformations which have
occurred in the international system since the
collapse of the Bretton Woods agreements, which
represent the last attempt to provide an
international order, a set of rules through which to
govern international relations. It constitutes the
general framework in which the political economy of
international financial instability has developed.

From hegemony to oligopoly

International financial relations have undergone
profound changes over the past decade. The
widespread instability which affects them represents
a deep behavioural modification with respect to what
has been called the "long decade" of the Bretton
Woods system (Keohane 1982). The fact that
instability has reigned for so many years suggests
that it has deep roots which still have to be
eradicated. These roots are to be found in the very
forces which led to the collapse of the Bretton
Woods system. In other words, to look for the
reasons of the still ongoing instability requires a
short investigation of the causes of that collapse.

The end of the Bretton Woods system has produced
a number of "reaction mechanisms" on the part of
both private and institutional operators, both
national and international. They represent the
reactions to the breakdown of a generally accepted
set of rules which constituted the framework of the
system itself. However, although over the past
decade the role of the single agents, be they
individual market agents or nation states, has been
greatly emphasized, a "systemic" approach has to be
adopted in the analysis of international relations
since it is the interaction of the behaviour of the
single agents which is crucial to the understanding
of international financial instability. This is

Introduction

particularly true, paradoxically, since nationalistic attitudes have mounted thus leading to a much higher degree of conflict.

Economic theory still has to provide a satisfactory analytical framework for the overall comprehension of international financial and monetary phenomena. We do, however, dispose of a large number of contributions pertaining to different aspects of the matter which allow us to make some headway in that direction. We are now in a position to try to make some progress in the construction of a new approach to international economic and financial problems following an international political economy approach.

In what follows we shall briefly discuss the most important transformations of the international financial system in order to provide a minimal background for the analysis of international financial instability from a political economy point of view.

A first point deals with the very structure of the international monetary and financial system. This structure has shifted from an hegemonic to an oligopolistic framework (3). The former structure, i.e. the Bretton Woods system, was based on one hegemonic country which was able and willing to monitor the behaviour of the whole system. The remaining countries accepted the hegemon's choices since this brought benefits to them.

The second type of structure, which has been developing over the past decade, includes a (small) number of nation states which are able to influence the behaviour of the international system. As in industrial oligopoly, however, no single agent is able to impose on the others its solution to conflicts which eventually arise but it is only able to prevent others from doing so. It follows that such a system will operate successfully, i.e. without conflicts, only if "rules of the game" are agreed upon among the oligopolists. To put it differently, an international oligopoly will be a stable system only if a cooperative solution is reached among the oligopolists.

The past decade has witnessed the emergence of a number of nation states, in addition to the US, which are able (but not necessarily willing) to influence the behaviour of the international system, thanks to their economic and political weight (4). Not all countries have of course reached such a position and this means that, in the present system,

Introduction

interstate relations present both oligopolistic and
domination (5) features. This means that present
international relations are also characterized by an
articulated hierarchical structure.

A second element, closely linked to the first
one, is the increase in interdependence (6).
Interdependence has been a topic deeply investigated
by international political economy students; what
interests us is the role of monetary and financial
policies in a highly interdependent system. This is
a crucial aspect for our purposes if we consider
that an international monetary system actually
exists only as long as "rules of the game" on the
appropriate policy behaviour are in operation and
are generally accepted by its members.

A recent assessment of international monetary
interdependence (Bryant 1980) classifies countries
according to their size in an interdependent system.
In the Bretton Woods years countries could be
roughly divided into two groups. There were the
"large closed economies" which were able to
influence the international system without in turn
being influenced by it; this group included only the
US. The remaining economies were all classifiable as
"small open economies" which, symmetrically, were
influenced by the operation of the system with no
power to influence it. A well known implication of
such an approach is the "small country assumption"
in monetary models of the open economy which asserts
that international prices and inflation rates are
given for the single country and hence that, in
equilibrium, each country must be in line with those
magnitudes.

Over the past decade, however, a new group has
emerged, which has been labeled the "intermediate
interdependence" group. As the expression suggests,
countries belonging to this group are both
influenced by the international system and have
enough power to influence the system itself, at
least partially. A schematic representation of the
intermediate interdependence structure is shown in
fig.1.1.

Increasing interdependence, the emergence of
intermediate interdependence countries and the
growth of oligopoly are closely linked phenomena.
Oligopolistic countries present a typical
intermediate interdependence structure. Hence one of
the most relevant features of the oligopolistic
system of the 70's is the growing interdependence of
national economic and financial policies. It is easy

4

Introduction

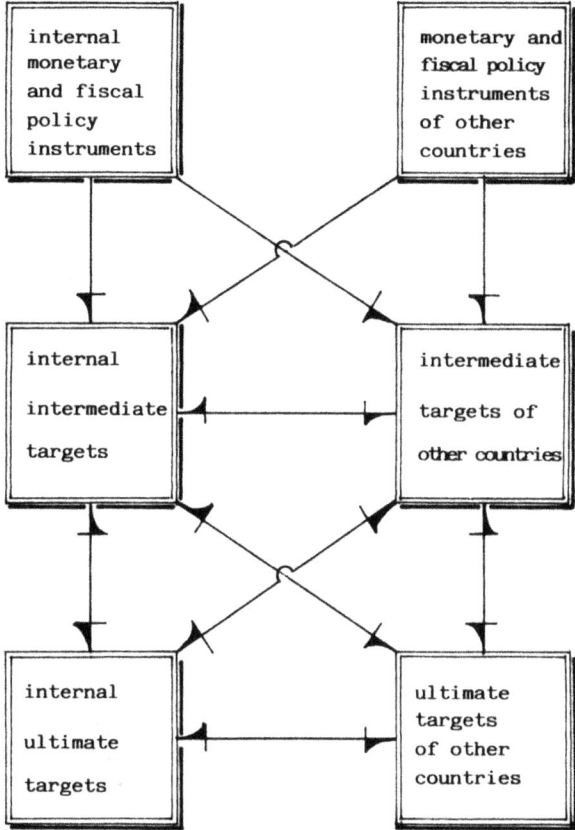

internal
monetary
and fiscal
policy
instruments

monetary and
fiscal policy
instruments
of other
countries

internal
intermediate
targets

intermediate
targets of
other countries

internal
ultimate
targets

ultimate
targets
of other
countries

Fig. 1.1 The "Intermodiate Interdependence Economy".

to understand that it is much harder to define
"rules of the game" for such a system than for an
hegemonic one. Or, to put it differently,
international cooperation is much harder to achieve,

Introduction

and, therefore, international stability is a much
costlier (public) good in an oligopolistic system
(7).
    The shift from an hegemonic to an oligopolistic
structure has produced a large number of
transformations in the behavioural mechanisms of the
system itself. These transformations, in turn,
reflect the fact that the international economic
system has undergone a profound crisis over this
period.
    It is not the aim of this work to analyze the
crisis of the international economic system. However
we must briefly discuss the "real roots" of
financial instability. This necessity arises from
the fact that, contrary to the prevailing view (8),
we maintain that financial crises arise, quite
often, when destabilizing forces are at work in the
"real" economic system. In other words, an analysis
of international financial instability must rest
upon some view of international economic instability
in a more general sense.

A general "disproportion" crisis
    We may consider the economic events of the
seventies as the result of a "crisis of
disproportions". According to this view (Ciocca
1981) the exceptionally high and stable growth
experienced by industrial countries from the end of
the '50s to the end of the '60s was possible mainly
because crucial relative prices and quantities
(proportions) were kept stable . As successive
events have shown, however, this (apparently) stable
growth produced built-in mechanisms which later led
to fundamental alterations in relative prices and
quantities. A number of them may be recalled.
    In the first place, high growth in the
industrial (exposed) sectors of the OECD economies
produced excess demand pressures in labour markets
which deeply altered industrial relations. As a
consequence "new industrial relations" brought about
deep changes in the distribution of income among
wages, profits and other income shares while the
rate of growth of productivity declined considerably.
    High growth was due mainly to an export push (9)
and to increasing government expenditure in
accordance with Keynesian and "welfare state"
doctrines. The role of the state has in fact
increased in size and scope while deteriorating in

6

efficiency (Cameron 1978). Consequently the "exposed" sector's share of the national product has declined relative to the "sheltered" sector's quota, thus decreasing the growth of the system's overall productivity.

Crucial proportions have also been altered in the context of North-South economic relations. The rise of the real price of oil is the most evident example of a "price shock", but relative prices of other commodities have also been affected, though to a lesser degree. The primary commodity shock has produced both price and quantity alterations contributing to the stagflation process of the past decade. The facts we have just summarized are well known and do not represent an original interpretation of the economic crisis of the seventies. The relevant element in this interpretation is a different one.

A general "disproportion crisis" occurs not just when relative price and quantity shocks break out but when mechanisms (both market and non-market) are lacking that will enable the system to restore original proportions. This in turn does not imply that the general economic crisis is due to "rigidities" occurring in the price mechanisms (e.g. real wage rigidities) as a neoclassical interpretation of the crisis would suggest. We assume instead that market mechanisms, both price and non-price, are not able to restore equilibrium once this has been displaced by major shocks. In the real world there is no such thing as a "pure" market mechanism. To be operational any economic mechanism needs to be embedded in an institutional framework, a "regime" which provides rules of conduct for the economic agents involved. The crisis of the seventies has been so severe and long lasting mainly because market disruptions (at both the national and international level) have produced regime (institutional) disruptions as well. The recent history of the international economy is full of examples in this sense. Monetary and trade relations, just to mention the most obvious, were regulated both by market mechanisms (e.g. price movements) and by institutional rules (intervention rules of monetary authorities, trade agreements). The relative efficacy of economic variables to "clear" the markets heavily rested on the robustness of institutional rules. The dramatic changes in some economic variables eventually produced the collapse of the institutions which had previously allowed

Introduction

them to operate with apparent smoothness and
efficacy.

   On the other hand, if we recognize that old
adjustment mechanisms have definitely failed this
does not mean that no regulating mechanisms are at
work (10). On the contrary, in response to the
crisis, new regulating mechanisms have been produced
as a reaction. Some of them have strengthened
   themselves, others have been replaced in their
turn by different institutional arrangements giving
rise to an interaction between market behaviour and
institutional modifications which seems far from
having reached a stable equilibrium.

   A first regulating mechanism may be considered
the shift from an adjustable peg to a managed float
regime in international monetary relations. The most
violent exchange rate fluctuations have taken place
among a relatively small number of currencies of
leading industrial countries while most developing
countries have tried to peg their currencies to one
leading currency (or to a basket of currencies)
(11). Consequently, the regime of generalized
floating operating during the '70s should better be
defined as a float among currency areas. This in
turn may be considered the exchange rate aspect of
oligopolistic relations. As we shall see in more
detail below oligopolistic relations and regional
currency areas have been sustaining one another.

   A second regulating mechanism may be considered
the transformation of international reserve
instruments. The collapse of the Bretton Woods
system at first led to a demonetization of gold and
later to a new role for it as a major component of
international reserves (12). Special Drawing Rights
seemed to assume a leading role when the dollar
reached its low peak in 1977-78 and the Substitution
Account was proposed. The initiative was abandoned
when the dollar revalued at the end of the decade
(Micossi and Saccomanni 1981, Gowa 1984). The
implementation of the European Monetary System has
introduced the ECU (European Currency Unit) onto the
financial scene. Its present success, however
(Triffin 1983), is entirely due to market
preferences since official decisions about its
future role as a full status currency have been
postponed for the moment.

   From the point of view of reserve instruments,
however, the most important phenomenon has been the
increasing role of national currencies other than
the dollar as international reserve instruments and

8

as international private monies (13) The most
important international currencies are the
deutschemark (Brown 1979), the Japanese yen, the
French franc and the British pound. The renewed
strength of the dollar at the beginning of the
present decade has somewhat arrested this
diversification. However, the highly unstable
behaviour of international monetary relations and
the absence of a full-fledged payments regime
suggest that the possibility of a return to currency
diversification is to be considered as an open
possibility.

A third regulating mechanism is the shift from a
balance of payments "adjustment regime" to a balance
of payments "financing regime" (Cohen 1982) and is
associated with the expansion of private credit
markets on the international scene. This aspect will
be dealt with at length in the rest of the book and
shall not be further discussed here. What we wish to
stress is that the increasing role of private
financial markets in international relations should
not be investigated as an isolated phenomenon but as
one of the outgrowths of the global crisis which has
affected the international system since the
beginning of the last decade (14).

A fourth regulating mechanism, which in a sense
includes all the others, is the explosion of
inflation as an international phenomenon.

There is a very large number of studies on
international inflation (15). The interpretation we
will follow is an application to the international
system of the "demand and supply approach to
inflation" (Gordon, 1975)). According to this
approach observed inflation may be considered as the
result of a demand for and a supply of inflation.
Inflation is demanded by economic agents willing and
able to "fix the price" of the goods and services
they sell. When downward inflexibility prevails, any
attempt to alter relative prices will produce an
upward pressure on prices and factor rewards. This
will lead to inflation if such pressures are
financed or "accommodated", i.e. if the supply of
inflation meets demand.

The supply of inflation depends on the creation
of liquidity both by public and by private
mechanisms. This emphasis on the effect of liquidity
creation on the inflationary process should not
convey the impression of a monetarist approach.
Contrary to monetarist assumptions, this approach
maintains that the process of liquidity creation is

9

Introduction

not independent from the demand for inflation. Two
simple examples will clarify the matter. Monetary
policy is not independent from political business
cycle considerations, (16) i.e. account will be
taken of the costs -for example in terms of higher
unemployment- of lower money growth. Credit creation
by the private banking system in both domestic and
international markets is deeply affected by the
demand for loans by the economic agents.

The inflationary process will be enhanced as
long as disproportions persist since economic
agents, both private and public, will try to impose
new proportions, i.e. alter terms of trade in their
favour, by raising the prices of the goods and
services they sell.

This way of looking at inflation also has some
other political economy implications. It has been
argued that international inflation may be
considered the result of a conflict which arises
when asymmetry of power characterizes the
international system (Kehoane 1985) and that
inflation is likely to increase when the
distribution of power among leading actors is
altered. In this respect international inflation may
be considered the result of persisting
disproportions not just among economic variables but
also among political variables such as power. In
other words, this way of looking at inflation is
consistent with the view that the shift from
hegemony to oligopolistic interdependence is the
consequence of a major shift in the distribution of
power in the international system (17).

The regulating mechanisms we have mentioned
mutually sustain one another and have contributed to
the transformation of the international system from
an hegemonic to an "oligopolistic interdependence"
one. Exchange rate fluctuations have interested
mainly the currencies of the oligopoly leaders, and
it is among such currencies that one has to look for
the new international reserve instruments. The
increasing role of private international financial
markets has produced a growing interdependence both
among national markets and among national monetary
policies (Herring and Marston 1977, Swoboda 1983).
Increasing conflicts which characterize the
oligopolistic system have found in international
inflation a most powerful channel if one considers
the fact that conflicts over terms of trade is one
of the most striking phenomena of the economic
crisis of the past decade.

Introduction

The elements we have mentioned so far should
have helped make one major point. Although
international financial problems may be studied as a
separate topic in international relations, a
"systemic" approach is needed if one wishes to
investigate the political economy aspect of
international financial instability. A political
economy approach is needed if we accept the view
that adjustment mechanisms which have developed over
the past decade involve changes in both markets and
institutions and, therefore, that a satisfactory
analysis of these events requires that both be
considered in a unified framework.

An outline of the book
The main idea which will be discussed in this
book may be expressed as follows. The growing
financial instability which has characterized the
international system over the past decade and which
has led to the debt crisis of 1982-84 may be viewed
as the result of the interaction of two elements: 1)
the increasing role of private (and unregulated)
financial markets in providing intermediation
between saving and investment decisions and 2) the
(almost) permanent state of conflict among the major
industrial countries in monetary and financial
affairs (18) in the absence of a set of agreed upon
"rules of the game".
The next three chapters are devoted to the
analysis of the transformations which international
political and economic relations have undergone
since the collapse of the Bretton Woods system. The
following two chapters (5 and 6) provide a
description of the events which have led to the debt
crisis of 1982-84 and how the international system
has managed it. Chapters 7 and 8 provide a framework
for the analysis of international financial
instability. Chapters 9 and 10 discuss the present
state of the theory of international debt and the
operation of the international system. Chapter 11
discusses the present state of international
financial relations and its perspectives.
Chapter 2 discusses the roots of the present
instability. It argues that this stems largely from
the fact that the forces which have led to the
collapse of the Bretton Woods system are still
partially at work. It stresses that that system was
not just a monetary arrangement but it involved
financial as well as trade, strategic and political

regimes and that the policy behaviour of member
nations in that regime was influenced by a number of
issue linkages. It also argues that the elements
which can explain the success of the system - the
seignorage enjoyed by the United States and the
export-led (neomercantilistic) growth enjoyed by
other industrial countries - eventually developed
into obstacles to its orderly operation and became
the causes of final collapse.

The chapter also discusses the most popular
interpretation of the instability of the Bretton
Woods system, Triffin's dilemma (Triffin 1960) which
is restated in a different interpretative framework
deriving from an application to the international
system of the financial instability approach
developed by Minsky (Minsky 1975, 1982a).

Chapter 3 outlines an analytical framework for
the international economic policy behaviour of
nation states. It is argued that national policies
are fundamentally neomercantilistic in the sense
that they systematically pursue balance of trade
surpluses. A brief review of the main benefits of
such a policy for the national economy is provided
drawing mainly on post-Keynesian economic
literature. Neomercantilistic goals spark persistent
conflicts in international relations which may be
overcome only if a suitable international regime
exists. The existence of an international regime, in
turn, may be considered a public good. The problem
then arises of which country (or countries) will be
willing and able to provide such a public good (the
United States was the main supplier of this good
under the Bretton Woods agreements). In
oligopolistic interdependence a trade-off arises
between neomercantilistic policies and the supply of
public goods by the single countries.

The final part of the chapter is devoted to a
brief analysis of monetary relations in an
oligopolistic setting. The theory of group behaviour
is used to describe these relations, and to explain
why, without explicit cooperation, an oligopolistic
setting cannot reach a stable equilibrium.

Chapter 4 is devoted to the analysis of the
position of the United States in the international
system after the collapse of the Bretton Woods
agreements. We discuss how US foreign economic
policy was at first aimed at governing the
international oligopoly by disinvesting (i.e.
consuming) the power which the US had accumulated in
the previous decade and the reasons why this attempt

failed. These reasons may be found partly in the
lack of cooperation from the other oligopolists
(mainly Germany and Japan).

The aim of this chapter is not to review the
history of the past decade but rather to investigate
how growing financial interdependence has modified
the behaviour and increased the constraints of US
economic and monetary policy.

It is investigated how political business cycle
management has been modified by increasing openness
(both commercial and financial) of the US economy
and by the lack of a well established international
system. It is also discussed why and
to what extent the US (and not the IMF) may be
considered the true lender-of-last-resort of the
international financial system.

Chapter 5 provides a brief description of the
build up of international financial instability
which dramatically exploded in the summer of 1982
(Mexican and Brazilian debt crises). It does not aim
at providing new evidence, rather it uses that which
exists in abundance in order to show how financial
imbalances have mounted for single countries and for
the international financial system as a whole.
Empirical evidence is used to show how the
interrelation between real, monetary and financial
variables mentioned in this chapter have developed.

Chapter 6 discusses the debt crisis of 1982-84.
The problem of the insolvency of Mexico, Brazil,
Argentina as well as of other borrowers and how it
has been managed so far. This crisis can be
considered a very interesting case study of the game
going on in debt rescheduling. The actors involved
are: the US, indebted countries, private banks, and
the IMF. It is discussed why effective bankruptcy
has not materialized after a state of technical
bankruptcy had been reached for the majority of
borrowing countries. It is also an example of how
the turning points of the "financial instability
cycle" need not come out in a deterministic way as
different outcomes are possible. In this chapter the
characteristics and the consequences (for both
borrowers and banks) of the rescue plan devised by
the International Monetary Fund are also discussed.

Chapters 7 and 8 are devoted to interpreting the
facts described in chapters 5 and 6. The
interpretative framework is based on the financial
instability hypothesis developed by Minsky (1975,
1982a). In chapter 7 this framework is briefly
discussed for the closed economy basically rerunning

Introduction

Minsky's ideas. The framework is then reexposed for
an international economy. This represents a
development of Minsky's original framework since, in
the international setting, new agents are introduced
(e.g. nation states rather than single firms). The
chapter ends with a discussion of the unsatisfactory
aspects of the financial instability framework which
can be traced mainly in the incomplete explanation
of the "critical points" i.e, the turning points,
upper and lower, of the financial cycle. It is also
argued that Minsky's model does not give rise to a
traditional cycle but rather provides the
description of the mechanisms which eventually lead
to financial crises (19) and, in this respect, it
provides more insight than traditional cyclical
models.
    Chapter 8 tries to provide a more satisfactory
explanation of the critical points by applying
results derived from financial crisis
investigations. The mechanics of financial crises
may be divided into two qualitatively different
aspects: the economic forces which lead to the
"technical insolvency" of the indebted unit, and the
strategic interplay among the actors involved
(debtors, creditors and intermediaries) which
eventually lead to actual bankruptcy. This second
stage of analysis involves the discussion of the
behavioural patterns of the actors involved
(countries, banks, international organizations). The
results about the role of the US as an international
lender-of-last-resort reached in chapter 4 are
reconsidered in this new framework.
    Chapter 9 discusses the political economy of
country risk and the state of the growth-cum-debt
literature. Traditional country risk analysis has
been centred on the monitoring of a number of
economic and financial variables in the attempt to
provide "leading indicators" of bankruptcy risk
(Padoan 1980, Saini and Bates 1984). This approach
is criticized by showing how increasing
interdependence has enhanced politico-economic issue
linkages in international relations. Hence the
analysis of the "propensity to repudiate debt"
(Eaton and Gersovitz 1981) needs to be carried out
keeping in mind not just economic and financial
variables but also political and strategic ones.
    The chapter also briefly reviews the existing
literature on growth and debt. The aim is not to
provide an exhaustive presentation of the wide
production on this topic but rather to discuss how

present approaches are generally not sufficient to
deal with all the aspects involved in international
financial instability, although for different
reasons. A class of these models provides the
equilibrium conditions for a growing economy with
external debt and states how an economy should
behave in order to repay the debt. Another class of
models incorporates the interaction between banks
and borrowers in order to evaluate how the amount of
credit obtained is determined. This second group of
models discusses one crucial feature of the
international credit system, the interdependence
between the parties involved.

Chapter 10 is divided into two parts. The first
part reviews the different approaches to the
analysis of global international problems. The
chapter initially outlines the traditional view of
North-South economic relations which was developed
in the past decade and which rests on a Bretton
Woods fixed exchange rate system. A review of
alternative frameworks for the analysis of
post-hegemonic international relations follows. A
neoclassical, a traditional Keynesian, a
post-Keynesian and a Marxist perspective are
discussed. The second part of the chapter presents
what we have called an "agenda for research" into
global politico-economic interrelations. A stylized
model of an international economy is presented. The
fundamental economic variables, pertaining to trade,
monetary and financial relations in oligopolistic
interdependence are discussed and linked in a
framework in which major international political
economy relations are present. This framework
provides some tentative suggestions for the
construction of a global politico-economic framework.

Chapter 11 discusses the present state of
international financial relations. International
financial instability is viewed as the outcome of
the interaction between the two main factors we have
discussed in the previous chapters: policy conflicts
among oligopolistic countries and the role of
private credit markets in the world economy. The
chapter argues that the policy followed by the US
administration since the turn of the the decade has
increased the propensity to pursue neomercantilistic
policies on the part of all actors involved and that
the problems posed by the behaviour of the dollar in
the international economy requires a much larger
amount of cooperation among nations, institutions

and market operators. The chapter also argues that
the strength of the dollar cannot be interpreted as
a return of the United States to an hegemonic
position. This conclusion is reached through an
application of a modified version of the the theory
of hegemonic stability.

No conclusion is presented. The facts we discuss
in this book suggest that international financial
relations have not reached a state of tranquillity
even if success in the management of the debt crisis
of 1982-84 has led many observers to think that the
international system is finally back on the road to
stable growth and widespread welfare.

NOTES

1. A pioneering analysis is contained in
Kindleberger 1970.

2. A few exceptions exist. See the
contributions in Wionczek 1979 and Fair and Bertrand
1983. For a political economy approach to the
problem of debt see Lipson 1981.

3. The first one to discuss the oligopolistic
structure of international monetary relations was
Lord Balogh. A description of the hegemonic and
oligopolistic (multipolar) systems is contained in
Cohen 1977. See also Kindleberger 1970 and McMahon
1978.

4. The question here arises of the links
between size and power. A wide literature exists on
the topic. See Kindleberger 1970, Hart 1976. The
question of financial power will be taken up again
in chapter 11.

5. A difference should be drawn between
hegemony and dominance. As the matter is rather
complex we may limit ourselves to note that only in
the first case small size nations consent to the
position of the leading power.

6. The obvious reference for the analysis of
international interdependence is Cooper 1968. A more
recent assessment is contained in Bryant 1980, see
also Padoa Schioppa 1981.

7. See Cohen 1977, Bryant 1980 and for a more
formal approach Hamada 1976 and 1979 who, however,
does not use the concept of oligopoly.

8. This view has been particularly emphasized
by Friedman and the monetarist tradition. See
Friedman 1959. A contrary view is held by Minsky.
See for instance Minsky in Kindleberger and
Laffargue 1982.

9. This aspect is discussed at some length in chapter 3.

10. The term "regulating mechanisms" has been introduced by French economists to take account of not only the standard market mechanism but also institutional mechanisms which interact with the former. The emergence of new regulating mechanisms thus implies institutional as well as economic changes in the behaviour of the system. On this see, for instance Benassy, Boyer, Gelpi 1977 and Boyer, Mistral 1983.

11. Developing countries have followed different policies. On this problem see Moon 1982.

12. Proposals have been made to restore some form of gold standard as a recipe against international monetary instability. For a critique see Parboni 1981.

13. The requisites of national currencies as international monies is discussed by Krugman 1982. Although one should keep separate the private and the official roles of international monies historical experience shows that they have developed, and declined, together (see Aliber 1982).

14. It is well known that the expansion of euromarkets dates well before the first oil crisis.

15. Literature on this topic abounds. See for instance Krause and Salant 1977 and Biasco 1979.

16. This is extensively discussed in the political business cycle literature. Little attention has been devoted, so far to international influences on the domestic policy cycle. For exceptions see Tufte 1978 and Thompson and Zuk 1983.

17. And it is therefore linked to the theory of hegemonic stability on which we will return in chapter 11.

18. At the beginning of the present decade increasing trade and protectionistic conflicts have characterized the international scene. Although they are strictly related to monetary and financial affairs they will only be marginally considered in this book.

19. For a stimulating discussion see the essays in Kindleberger and Laffargue 1982 and Kindleberger 1978a.

Chapter Two

THE ROOTS OF INSTABILITY

The roots of the present international financial
instability have to be sought in the very forces
which produced the unprecedented period of
international stability known as the Bretton Woods
era.

Reams have been written on the evolution of the
Bretton Woods system and on its crisis. This chapter
is devoted to a very brief reexamination of the
issue but with a particular target in mind. We will
argue that the mechanisms which first allowed the
system to function with apparent smoothness and
subsequently brought it to its final collapse are
the same forces which should be considered as
responsible for the present state of international
financial instability.

Mention of the "crisis of the Bretton Woods
system" always brings to mind its official close:
the proclamation of the dollar's inconvertibility in
August 1971. Analyses of the crisis often do not go
beyond its purely monetary and financial aspects. In
so doing the very expression "system crisis" is
betrayed. The collapse of the post-war international
monetary order is the outcome of the interplay of
monetary and financial as well as economic and
political forces.

As is well known, the Bretton Woods system may
be classified as an "hegemonic" system. In such a
system the hegemonic country guarantees, through its
policy, the stability and well-behaved performance
of its mechanisms. The remaining countries, because
of their economic and political power are not able
to oppose the hegemon's choices. They benefit,
however, from participation in the system while
sustaining its costs only in part. The hegemon
supplies a "public good" represented by the system

18

itself. The remaining countries exploit this public good and eventually act as free riders.

The stability of the hegemonic system is based on the mutual convenience of the hegemon and of the other countries in keeping it in operation: the former by supplying the public good, the latter by accepting the rules of the game which this entails.

The system's collapse is the signal that mutual convenience has vanished.

As a first approximation it can be said that the advantage of the hegemon in supplying the public good lies in the exploitation of seignorage. The advantage of the other countries is to be found in the fact that the existence of such a public good allows them to pursue neomercantilistic policies to the greatest advantage.

The role and scope of widespread neomercantilism as well as its economic justifications will be discussed in the next chapter. Here it is sufficient to recall that the hegemonic policy of the United States was the necessary condition for widespread neomercantilistic policies to be successful without generating unbearable tensions within the system itself.

Seignorage

The (narrow) definition of seignorage links (Wijkman 1981) the advantage of the hegemonic country to its role of reserve currency country. For such a country, it is generally maintained, there is no balance of payments constraint. By exploiting seignorage, the hegemon acts as a "residual country" in the international system, thus allowing for the compensation of strains emerging from conflicting policies.

Such statements are widespread in the literature on the subject and they undoubtedly contain some truth; however they need further specification in order to understand their role in the evolution and crisis of the international economic system.

Seignorage should not be considered as an end in itself. Rather it is the instrument which allows the hegemon to achieve a number of goals, the simultaneous attainment of which justifies its participation in the system, i.e. its supply of the public good. For convenience we may list these targets as follows.

a) politico-strategic goals. The United States have borne (Olson and Zeckhauser 1966) a

19

proportionally larger share of the cost of the NATO alliance compared to other countries. This was
possible also because of the reserve position of the dollar but, what is more important, it was accepted by the US because it proved to be the necessary condition for the very existence of the western military alliance. In other words the US was willing to shoulder a proportionately larger economic burden because the benefits received from the existence of this public good were greater than the costs.

On the other hand, the remaining countries were willing to bear the (economic) cost of participating in the alliance as their participation cost was proportionally inferior. Since benefits exceeded costs their propensity to free ride was minimized.

b) economic goals. Seignorage allowed for the financing of the international expansion of North American industry, and in particular the increasing outflow of direct investment abroad.

c) financial goals. Seignorage associated with the reserve position of its currency allowed the US to act as the world banker thus reaping substantial benefits for its banking system (De Cecco 1976).

d) monetary goals. The pursuit of the above mentioned goals, allowed the US to provide a public good additional to the military alliance, i.e. the public good represented by the currency area (1). As we shall see in more detail later, the succesful pursuit of economic and financial goals allowed the US, thanks to seignorage, to carry out the two roles which are required for the stability of a financially complex monetary and financial system: the autonomous source of effective demand and the international lender of last resort (Minsky 1979).

The fulfillment of these two conditions made the currency area represented by the Bretton Woods system a public good which was acceptable to the other countries (and thus minimized free riding problems). Substantial effective demand push made the Bretton Woods system far more expansionary than the previous hegemonic system: the Gold Standard centered on Imperial Britain (De Cecco 1975). Financial stability, associated with expansion, led to the development of a system in which availability of finance was not necessarily accompanied by the risk of financial crisis (2).

The existence of a soundly centered monetary system reinforced and was in turn sustained by the progressive opening to free trade through the GATT

agreements. As has been widely noted it was one of
the most important US foreign policy goals to
maintain and expand an "open international system"
based on free trade as this was considered the basic
economic prerequisite for the political stability of
the western world.

In sum political, strategic, economic, financial
and monetary goals merged in determining the
hegemon's foreign policy.

The role of the US as the "residual country " of
the Bretton Woods system must then be considered as
that of the supplier of the public good represented
by such a system. A definition which is far richer
than the somewhat mechanical one often adopted in
the analysis of international relations.

The close of hegemony. Triffin's dilemma

Nixon's decision to suspend official dollar
convertibility in 1971 was a political decision to
give up the role of residual country in the above
sense, that is to say to stop supplying the public
good of an "international system". It would,
however, be wrong to consider the crisis of the
Bretton Woods system as the result of a unilateral
decision on the part of the US administration as
this would imply, among other things, that only for
the US the costs of participating in the system had
exceeded the benefits. On the contrary, the crisis
must be understood as the consequence of the choices
of all the leading western countries. In addition
this crisis cannot be considered as the purely
mechanical breakdown of some economic or
institutional mechanism. Rather it should be
considered as an example of resolution of a deep
rooted politico-economic conflict within the western
alliance.

The most celebrated analysis of the instability
of the Bretton Woods system is the one associated
with "Triffin's dilemma" (1960).

A reserve system based on a national currency,
itself linked to gold, oscillates between a
liquidity shortage, if the reserve country does not
expand sufficiently, and instability if the supply
of the reserve currency with respect to gold in the
centre country becomes too large. This second
possibility undermines the base which makes the
reserve currency acceptable to other countries. In
other words both upper and lower limits exist to the
"equilibrium" values of the gold reserve currency

The Roots of Instability

ratio (Kenen 1960).

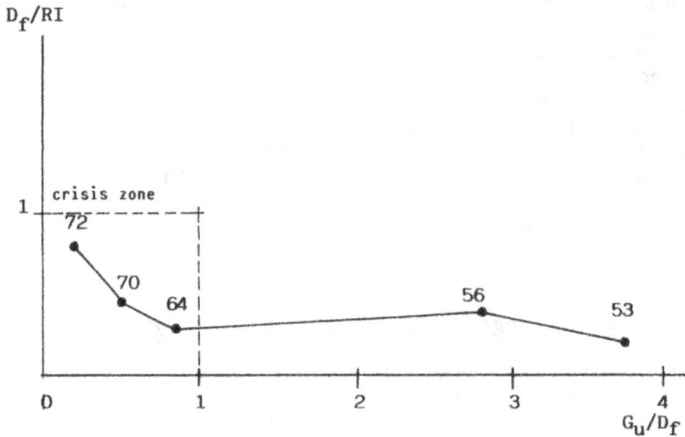

Fig.2.1   The Gold Exchange Standard and the "Crisis Zone"

According to this view, the Bretton Woods system entered the "crisis zone" when the US started exploiting its seignorage power in order to pursue policies (such as the Vietnam War) requiring financing support incompatible with the international position of the hegemon country.

Figure 2.1 (from Alessandrini 1976) shows the time path of the ratio between dollar liabilities and gold reserves in the US (Gu/Df) during the Bretton Woods period and its final entry into the "crisis zone" (Df/Ri is the share of dollars in international reserves).

This analysis offers two interesting insights. First , the fact that a national reserve currency system must fulfill some conditions in order to make this currency acceptable to other members of the system. Secondly, the (implicit) emphasis on the link between financial and political elements in the mechanics which lead to the crisis of the system.

What, on the contrary, is not entirely convincing in this view is the idea that the strength of the hegemonic system lies, in a much too

22

mechanical way, on the "equilibrium" value of the
gold dollar ratio. It is doubtful, to say the least,
that such a ratio can offer an appropriate synthesis
of the interdependence among real, monetary,
financial, strategic and political elements which
characterizes the operation of an international
payments system.

A second shortcoming is that this model of the
hegemonic system links the excess supply of dollars
to the balance of payments of the central country
and it neglects the role of the (changing) structure
of the balance of payments itself.

The traditional view, as embodied in Triffin's
dilemma, may however be fruitfully complemented
with a contribution by Officer and Willet (1969) in
which the authors, while accepting the main argument
in Triffin's analysis, develop its political economy
implications follwing a public choice approach.

Officer and Willet draw attention to the fact
that when the system enters the crisis zone, that is
when the gold dollar ratio passes beyond a critical
value, a "confidence problem" arises (Kenen 1960) as
the willingness of the participants in the system to
support it is put to proof. The crisis could have
been overcome by a mix of a change in US financial
policy and a round of exchange rate adjustments of
the main currencies in relation to the dollar and or
of the latter in relation to gold.

To put the matter in terms of Hirschman's
celebrated approach, (1970) at this stage the
participants in the system will use "voice" rather
than keep "loyal" or even "exit" out of the system
(3).

In so doing the authors (implicitly) draw
attention to the fact that in any "financial crisis"
(that is in any crisis in which a confidence problem
has to be solved) the mechanics of the crisis itself
may be divided into two separate phases: the
technical phase, which occurs when the debtor (the
reserve country in this case) is technically
insolvent, and the decisional (or strategic) phase,
when the confrontation between debtors and creditors
produces the effective outcome of the crisis, i.e.
final bankruptcy or rescue.

Officer and Willet note that ten years after the
formulation of Triffin's dilemma (1960) the
political decision of keeping the system in
operation (i.e. the strategic phase) was no longer
only in the hands of the United States but it was
shared by a number of industrialized coutries which

had gained some control over the international
financial scene. This is equivalent to recognizing
that the hegemonic system had been replaced by an
oligopolistic structure in which strategic
descision-making is in the hands of a small number
of leading countries.

The authors judged this evolution positively as
far as the survival of the system is concerned. They
maintained that the Bretton Woods system could have
easily continued to prosper if the leading
participants had been willing to resort to
substantial parity realignments although they did
not enter into the matter of the amplitude of such
realignments nor into the problem of the dollar
price of gold. The authors felt that the European
countries would have been willing to continue to
bear the costs of dollar seignorage if the US had
accepted a susbtantial devaluation of the dollar
with respect to gold. (The US was instead interested
in a revaluation of the strong European currencies
with respect to the dollar while keeping the
dollar gold parity unchanged).

If such a resort to "voice" had produced a
cooperative solution to the pending conflict the
supply of the public good of an "international
system" would have continued.

Successive events have shown that Officer and
Willet's optimism was ill-founded. However, their
analysis confirms that, at the end of the decade,
the transformation of hegemony into oligopoly had
almost been completed. The demonstration lies in the
fact that the resolution of conflicts could not be
pursued by unilateral action of the hegemon anymore
but that a cooperative solution had to be
implemented.

Hegemonic instability: another view
We will now reexamine the role of the US as a
residual country following a different analysis
developed by Minsky (1979).

This interpretation maintains that the key role
of the hegemon in the international payments system
is to be found in its position as the world's
banker. The strength of the system thus depends on
the success of the US in acting as a "bank". This in
turn rests on the acceptability of its liabilities
(dollars) by the other countries.

The amount of confidence which lenders have in a
bank depends on the ability of the latter to use its

liabilities to finance profitable activities. As was
mentioned above, US monetary expansion and
seignorage financed both the expansion of the
international economic system and the expansion of
American industry on the world market. Confidence in
the US "bank" therefore depends on the ability of US
"industry" to make profits. This is, according to
this view, the crucial condition for the smooth
functioning of the system.

If we consider the US economy as a whole this
amounts to attaining and maintaining a surplus in
the foreign trade balance (Kalecki 1934). Such a
surplus allows for the financing of the expansion
both of US investment abroad and of US foreign
policy (i.e. military and aid outflows). In other
words, the existence of a trade surplus is the
necessary condition for the hegemon to sustain the
costs of the supply of the public good of an
international system. The trade surplus represents
the most important deterrent against "voice" rather
than "loyalty" being raised on the part of the other
countries, for instance, in terms of a generalized
request for conversion of dollars into gold.

Seignorage will be a bearable cost for US allies
as long as it allows the expansion of all western
economies, including the American one.

With this view in mind, the US's role as a
residual country can be restated as follows. An
overall US balance of payments deficit makes the US
a "center of effective demand" for the international
economy which boosts other countries' growth. A
trade balance surplus, insofar as it meets the
"confidence problem" of the reserve country,
supports confidence in the bank's liabilities
(dollars) and, in addition, makes US monetary
authorities de facto responsible for the
international lender of last resort function needed
to keep the international system viable.

To conclude US foreign economic policy covers in
the international system the dual function which is
carried out by government expenditure and the
central bank in a closed system (Minsky 1982a).

According to this view the stability of the
hegemonic system does not depend on the relation
between US liabilities to the rest of the world and
its gold reserves as in Triffin's analysis. It is no
longer the amount of gold which "gives value" to the
dollar (one might argue for the opposite) but it is
the economic thrust of the centre country which
gives value (international creditworthiness) to the

reserve currency. This is precisely what is meant
when one talks of the Bretton Woods system as a
dollar standard rather than a gold exchange standard
system.

Such a dollar standard, in addition, is not
based on an international currency but rather on an
international credit mechanism. This last point can
be further clarified if one recalls that credit is a
"two-dimension" good defined both by its "quantity"
and by its "quality" i.e. the creditworthiness of
the borrower involved. While the overall deficit of
the US balance of payments determines the quantity
of finance available to the system, its structure
(i.e. the existence of a trade surplus) determines
its quality.

To be fully acceptable such a view of the
hegemonic system's operation needs a theory which
links real phenomena (accumulation and profit) with
financial ones (credit and interest). Unfortunately
such a theory is not yet available in full form. In
spite of this an attempt can be made to advance
suggestions for filling the gap.

In the "equilibrium years" of the Bretton Woods
system the US balance of payments presented a
deficit in long-term capital movements, generated by
the expansion of the US economy abroad, and in
unilateral transfers (military expenditures and aid)
generated by US foreign economic policy. This was
contrasted by a surplus in goods and services which
reflected the superior thrust of the US economy with
respect to the other industrialized countries.

The Bretton Woods system collapsed between 1968
and 1971 when the deficit financed Vietnam war
increased military expenditure outflows and (in
1971) US trade balance runs into defict for the
first time since the beginning of the century. Thus
an overall balance of payments deficit was no longer
sustained by a trade surplus. Following Minsky's
view we may interpret this as a signal that the US
"bank" was financing an "industry" which was no
longer profitable. As a consequence a confidence
problem arised since the bank's liabilities are no
longer acceptable, from a technical point of view,
by the bank's creditors, i.e. the other western
economies.

What we need, at this point, is a theory which
explains the long run behaviour of a country's
balance of payments. Such a theory should explain
how long run accumulation forces produce changes as
dramatic as those experienced by the US economy in

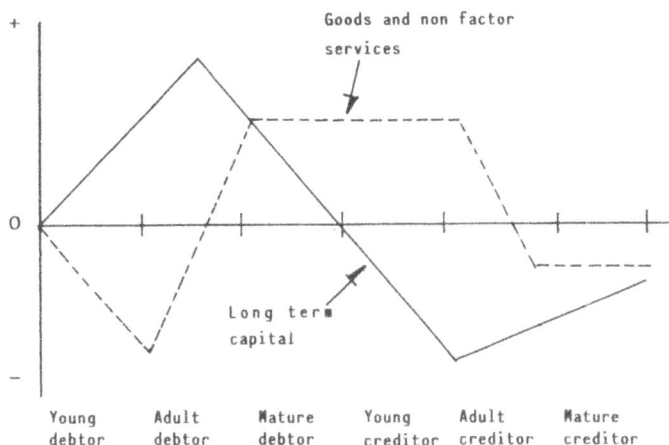

Fig.2.2   Stages of the Balance of Payments

the post war years.

As our investigation does not aim at explaining
the accumulation process on a world scale we may
limit ourselves to recalling a conceptual framework
which we will take as nothing more than a
provisional starting point. This is "the balance of
payments stages hypothesis" (4).

According to this hypothesis the components of a
country's balance of payments change sign (from
negative to positive and vice versa) over time,
producing changes in the structure of the balance of
payments itself (see fig 2.2). Different structures
correspond to different positions of the national
economy vis-à-vis the international system.

According to this classification, at the end of
the sixties, the US economy passed from a "young
creditor" to an "adult creditor" position. This
evolution of stages corresponded to the full
development of the role of the US as a world banker.
If we go back to fig. 2.1 we may see that the entry
of the Bretton Woods system into the crisis zone
corresponds to the period in which this change in

27

the international position of the US took place.
    Simple observation cannot provide any more
insight than this. The stages hypothesis does not
explain why the stages occur, i.e. why a country's
economic system produces different balance of
payments structures. Since this hypothesis is
related to long run phenomena all this amounts to
saying that we need a theory of accumulation in an
open economy. We have to look at long run
accumulation forces in order to explain changes in a
country's structural competitiveness as well as
changes in the direction of long term capital flows.
    It is clear that once such a theory is fully
worked out the analysis of international systems
will rest on a much stronger economic base. Just to
give an example, the erosion of hegemony could then
be linked, although not mechanically, (also) to the
structural change in the economic system of the
hegemon vis-à-vis the other countries.
    Assuming, however, the "stages hypothesis" as a
useful starting point we may proceed by noting the
correspondence between the evolution of the
hegemon's balance of payments and the balance of
payments of the "rest of the world" (5). In the
expansionary period of the Bretton Woods system the
balances of payments of the rest of the
industrialized countries moved from a position of
"adult debtor" to one of "mature debtor" as the
trade balance improved considerably while the
capital account remained in surplus. This was also
an outcome of the expansionary policy pursued by the
hegemon which had financed the growth of the
European (and Japanese) "firm" to the point of
making it profitable, that is to the point of
generating positive net exports.
Such a policy in turn allowed Europe to pursue a
policy of neomercantilistic expansion. As long as
the US was able, through the exploitation of
seignorage, to guarantee the general expansion of
the system, Europe's neomercantilistic growth could
proceed at an unprecedented rate and, what is more
relevant, without generating unbearable conflicts.
When the weakening of US economic growth undermined
the "real" (as opposed to monetary) foundations of
hegemony, and the system slipped into the crisis
zone, and seignorage was greatly eroded. As a
consequence the autonomous expansionary power of the
hegemon was severely slowed down, its ability (and
willingness) to act as a residual country came to an
end, and with it, the possibility of sustaining

28

generalized neomercantilistic expansion while
keeping conflicts at a minimum level.

Triffin's dilemma restated

The loss of competitiveness which brought the US
trade balance into deficit for the first time in the
century may be viewed as the other side of the coin
of growing European competitiveness which
consolidated during the years of tranquil
neomercantilistic expansion. This suggests that what
may be termed the "necessary" conditions for the
crisis of the hegemonic system - the end of the
hegemon's external profitability - were rooted in
the same mechanism which had produced its success:
Europe's neomercantilistic growth financed by the
seignorage of the US bank.

This analysis leads to a first conclusion. The
stability of an international (hegemonic) system
based on a credit creation mechanism requires a
mutually consistent structure of the balances of
payments of its members and, what is more important,
a mutually consistent development of the phases of
these balances. If the long run evolution of the
international economic system does not allow for a
maintenance of the appropriate structure of the
balance of payments then the economic basis of the
system is bound to be eroded.

As we have already said it is not our intention
to push this argument further. We will conclude this
discussion by proposing a reformulation of Triffin's
dilemma which may be expressed as follows. If the
hegemon does not use its seignorage power to finance
the (neomercantilistic) growth of the other
countries, they will not accept the costs that the
exploitation of seignorage imposes on them as the
system will prove too deflationary. If the
expansionary policy of the hegemon is, however,
pushed too far, this will eventually erode the real
base of seignorage, i.e the capacity of the
hegemon's economic system to produce net exports and
a net outflow of long term capital movements.
Consequently the other countries will not accept
participation in the system as this will prove too
inflationary.

During the sixties the US fell into the second
trap, also because this was required by the
fulfillment of the strategic and political goals of
the system. As the economic theory of alliances has
shown (Olson and Zeckhauser 1966) the US had to

finance a more than proportional cost of western
rearmament in order to prevent other countries from
increasing their free riding tendencies thus
undermining the existence of the alliance itself. As
a consequence the supply of the public good of a
"military alliance" would have fallen below demand.
In other words the need to fulfill strategic and
political goals led to a weakening of controls over
the evolution of the economic conditions necessary
for the survival of the system.

With time, the same factors that had made it
advantageous for both parties (US and Europe) to
participate in the system grew increasingly
burdensome as costs eventually came to outweigh
benefits. Europe's growth and its increasing
competitiveness threatened American export potential
and thus the "overall profitability of the US
economy". This eroded the confidence on which US
seignorage was based but, at the same time,
convinced the US that the costs of continuing to
play the role of residual country had become
unsustainable (Odell 1982).

The complementary evolution of the phases of the
balances of payments of the US and of Europe, both
in the expansionary and in the crisis period of the
hegemonic system, suggests that part of the
explanation of the phases themselves could be found
in the different roles that are played by different
economies in an international system and by the fact
that any international system evolves as a result of
the transfer of wealth among its members.

The evolution of the US economy from a young to
an adult creditor position and the corresponding
shift of the European economies from adult to mature
debtor positions may be considered the necessary
conditions for the outbreak of the crisis. We must
now examine the "sufficient" conditions, that is the
political choice of putting an end to the system.

The emergence of oligopoly
The official end of the Bretton Woods system is
usually considered the result of a unilateral
decision taken by the US administration (Odell
1982). This episode should however also be viewed as
an example of the failure to cooperate in an
oligopolistic setting.

Officer and Willet (1969), in their
contribution, had evidenced what to them appeared as
the sufficient conditions to ensure the

30

The Roots of Instability

strengthening of the international payments system
once this had entered the crisis zone. One element
was the recognition of the emergence of oligopoly in
place of hegemony; the survival of the system no
longer depended on the decision of one single
nation, albeit still by far the most important one,
but on the agreement of the leader countries of the
system.

The second element was that it was reasonable to
believe that the strong European countries would
have continued to accept de facto inconvertible
dollars as the necessary price to pay in order to
continue enjoying the existence of the public good
of an international system. In other words these
countries would have considerably increased its
share of the aggregate cost of supplying this public
good.

Both these conditions amount to assume that a
cooperative solution to oligoplistic conflict had
been reached and that a new form of public good
"production" had been arranged. If we look at these
conditions fifteen years after they were formulated,
however, we may reach the conclusion that the
existing system was actually ripe for replacement.
The emergence of oligopoly after hegemony implied
that the decision-making mechanism in the
international system had been deeply altered and
that it was now much more difficult to take crucial
decisions since they had to be the result of a
bargaining process and existing rules of the game
could no longer provide an adequate guide to the
monitoring of the system (Bergsten, Keohane and Nye
1975; Hirsch and Doyle 1977).

The evolution of the hegemonic system towards an
oligopolistic structure was accompanied by an
increasing "politicization" of international
relations: that is, by an increased propensity to
negotiate the "rules of the game" and to establish
conflicting issue linkages in international
relations (6).

In the "equilibrium years" of the hegemonic
system these elements were already present. Issue
linkage operated in the direction of conflict
resolution as conflicts arising in single areas were
positively resolved through the unification of
strategic, political, financial, trade and monetary
goals which the US was able to achieve through
seignorage, and to which other members of the system
consented. Increasing politicization of
international relations may be considered as the

31

result in the shift of power relations between the
hegemon and the other leading countries which
occured (also) as a result of the successful
mercantilistic policies pursued by the latter (7).
Such a shift in the distribution of power did not
occur evenly among the other countries, rather it
benefited those countries, such as Germany and
Japan, which had been most successful in their
neomercantilistic policies. It is not surprising
therefore that financial as well as political
conflicts were most pronounced between the US and
these countries. The shift in the distribution of
power encouraged the emerging leaders of the
international oligopoly to use their power to modify
"the rules of the game" as the existing ones were no
longer perceived as acceptable given the state into
which international relations had evolved.

The shift in the distribution of power resulting
from successful neomercantilism had also increased
the propensity of the US to pursue such a more
nationalistic oriented policy itself as a reaction
to increased American weakness. Even if the US had
lost the power to act as the residual country it was
certainly strong enough to act as an oligpolist.

NOTES

1. Hamada (1977) clarifies in what sense a
currency area is a public good. It is a "spurious"
public good since its benefits -which arise from
greater monetary stability- are limited to the
members of the currency area itself.

2. For an analysis of the interaction between
financial crises and institutional arrangements
under the Gold Standard see Hawtrey 1928.

3. Students of international relations (Johnson
1972, De Cecco 1979) have maintained that one of the
conditions for the take-off of the exceptional
post-war economic growth was an exchange structure
which favoured european competitiveness with respect
to the US.

4. For a discussion of this hypothesis see
Halevi 1981, Fisher and Frenkel 1974, Onitsuka 1974.
All of these contributions are based, however, on a
standard neoclassical approach which bear a risk of
excessive mechanicism as the stages of the balance
of payments are considered as the adjustment to an
equilibrium path.

5. We are not considering here the role of
developing countries in the overall distribution of

balance of payments' surpluses and deficits. For a more general discussion see Biasco 1984.

    6. The best known example is perhaps the link between dollar convertibility and the burden of financial support of Nato which both France and Germany lamented in the sixties.

    7. Neomercantilistic policies wll be discussed in the next chapter.

Chaphter Three

FOREIGN ECONOMIC POLICY AN INTERPRETATION

We will now discuss in greater detail the
assumption that industrial economies pursued
neomercantilistic policies in the post-war years and
will offer arguments for a modern interpretation of
mercantilism (1).

Economic basis of neomercantilism
Economic justifications for neomercantilism may
be found essentially in Keynesian literature (2).
They do not make up a full-fledged theory of
neomercantilism .They offer, however a number of
complementary arguments which may represent a useful
starting point.
A first argument is found in Keynes' General
Theory (1936). In chapter XXIII Keynes argues that
an inflow of liquidity from abroad which results
from a positive current account (3) will stimulate
investment if, given the level of the marginal
efficiency of capital and the level of the money
wage, it produces a fall in the interest rate. A
partially related argument is the following (De
Cecco 1968). If prevailing monetary conditions are
generally restrictive, exporting firms will force
their sales abroad in order to obtain domestically
scarce liquidity. Both these arguments suggest that
export growth is a major channel for improving
liquidity conditions at both the macro and the micro
levels. They are also strengthened by considerations
on policy behaviour advanced below.
Another justification for neomercantilistic
policies stems from the idea that (Schmitt 1979) the
export producing (exposed) sector of the economy is
characterized by a higher rate of technical progress
and innovation and hence higher investment and

34

productivity growth. It follows that an expansion of the exporting sector increases the growth potential of the whole economic system. If such an expansion is successful it will eventually produce the virtuous circle "export-productivity-investment" associated with the works of Kaldor and which is the main justification for export-led models.

This second justification has been advanced by Schmitt (1979) as a major argument in favour of neomercantilistic policies. It has however been criticized by Vines (1980) on the grounds that the necessary condition for the virtuous circle is competitiveness in exports and not a trade surplus.

Increased competitiveness need not produce a trade surplus. On the contrary, it is quite possible that export-led growth will produce an increase of imports so large as to give rise to a negative trade balance. If a trade surplus does show up in export-led economies (as in the cases -recalled by both Schmitt and Vines- of Japan and several European economies in the post-war years) it is to be considered as the result of deflationary economic policies and cannot be considered as the product of export-led growth itself.

On the other hand, as Vines himself recognizes, an economic policy targeted at defending a trade surplus has good reasons to be pursued by the authorities. A tendentially deflationary policy is a necessary condition for the successful defence of a country's growth potential in an international economy and that for a number of reasons. We will consider the fixed exchange rate case first.

A first reason is that a restriction of the growth of internal demand checks the penetration of foreign firms into the domestic market, both because of fewer outlets and because of lower domestic inflation (and hence higher competitiveness). Low internal absorption in addition forces domestic firms to seek foreign outlets and thus increases domestic competitiveness.

Secondly a successful export-led mechanism improves the performance of the accumulation mechanism of the domestic economy both on real and on financial grounds as a positive trade balance increases the share of profits in the economy. The demonstration is due, as is well known, to Kalecki, and it rests on the relation which links net investments and exports to earned profits (4). Hence, as long as policy authorities wish to support domestic accumulation they will try to increase the trade surplus, i.e. they will try to maximize the country's share of foreign demand.

A positive trade balance, in addition, enhances the "creditworthiness" of the economy in international financial markets (Ciocca, Vito-Colonna 1978). This improves the access of domestic firms to international financial markets as the amount of credit they obtain credit is (also) a function of the country they operate in (country-risk) (5). A good creditworthiness also improves the access of monetary authorities to international financial markets. This provides an incentive for neomercantilism which concerns the immediate interest of policy authorities and not just the indirect benefits they might obtain through the improved performance of the economic system. A country enjoying a persistent trade surplus will be most suited to act as an international financial centre since, as we have seen in the previous chapter, its financial assets will enjoy the "guarantee" represented by the profitability of the economy as shown by the trade surplus (Ciocca, Vito-Colonna 1978; Minsky 1979).

Other reasons in favour of a neomercantilistic policy may be considered from a political economy viewpoint (6). A positive trade balance increases the international prestige of the government (Johnson 1972, McMahon 1978, Frey and Schneider 1982) and its international power. Greater international power is also associated with increased domestic power since a positive trade balance provides the room for an expansionary policy which will provide internal support for the government. Greater domestic stability is thus pursued at the expense of international stability if a neomercantilistic policy increases international conflict.

This last result must however be confronted with our previous statement that the pursuit of neomercantilistic goals requires a tendentially restrictive policy. What is called for here is a "neomercantilistic" version of "fine tuning". Policy must oscillate between the restrictions necessary to defend the trade surplus and the amount of expansion which will allow the country to enjoy the benefits of such a surplus.

Figure 3.1 provides a synthetic representation of a neomercantilistic economy in which all the elements discussed above are combined.

36

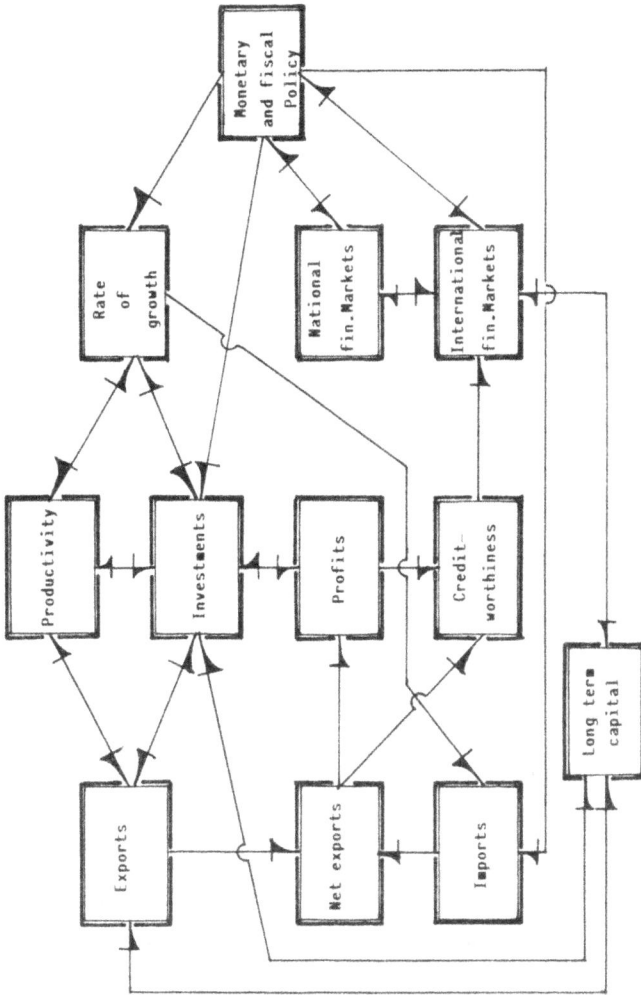

Fig. 3.1   The Neomercantilistic Paradigm

Limits of a neomercantilistic policy
    The major difficulty associated with a
neomercantilistic policy consists in maintaining a
surplus over time. From the point of view of the
international system as a whole this is obviously

37

impossible for all countries simultaneously (8) This
is certainly true as an ex-post identity but it is
also the less interesting aspect of the matter. A
system-wide analysis of neomercantilism has to be
put in an ex-ante perspective and it has to be
integrated in the structure of the existing
international system. To put it differently the
investigation of international neomercantilism is
misleading without an explicit consideration of the
institutional setting in which it operates as
different international organizations are bound to
produce different outcomes to the same policy
attitudes of single nation states.

The discussion of the role of the US as a
residual country developed in the previous chapter
has already introduced the matter. The hegemon had
to be strong enough with respect to other countries
in order to fulfill two conditions at once: a) allow
a generalized expansion so as to minimize the
conflicts implicit in a generalized
neomercantilistic behaviour and b) finance this
expansion through the imposition of seignorage on
other countries. Conflicts in the hegemonic system
were thus present both between the hegemon and other
countries to the extent that the pursuit and the
maintenance of a trade surplus was vital for both
(although justified on different grounds, i.e. the
justification of seignorage and neomercantilistic
benefits respectively) and between the remaining
countries for the acquisition of shares of world
trade. Generalized expansion guaranteed by a
successful residual country function weakens the
second type of conflicts but eventually exacerbates
the first if the result of such an expansion is a
loss of the relative competitiveness of the US with
respect to Europe and Japan. In conclusion the
success of neomercantilism of any single country is
directly proportional ceteris paribus to the
robustness of the hegemonic system.

A crucial role will be played by capital
movements. In the initial phase of an export-led
growth mechanism an inflow of capital (be it under
the form of direct investments or aid) will finance
the build-up of domestic industry (9). But once this
is well under way an outflow of capital will ease
the pressure on the exchange rate which a persistent
trade surplus would produce. Consequently during
this phase it might be in the interest of policy
authorities to allow for an outflow of capital in
order to avoid an undesirable revaluation. Such a

policy might also meet the interests of the business
community to increase real and financial investment
abroad as the initial development thrust of the
economy begins to lose momentum and as deflationary
policies might lower further opportunities for
domestic investment (10).

Widespread neomercantilism also provides an
explanation for the so-called "asymmetry in balance
of payments adjustment" which was a characteristic
of the Bretton Woods period. As is well known, the
burden of adjustment inevitably fell on deficit
countries given the resistance of surplus economies
to absorb excess exports through expansion as this
would have run against their own neomercantilistic
interests.

Asymmetry of adjustment could be maintained as
long as surplus countries were able and willing to
finance the deficits of unsuccessful mercantilists.
As differences between these two groups increased
and became a sort of permanent feature a new
internal strain hit the Bretton Woods system as
divergences between the two groups tended to widen
rather than to be absorbed.

Untenable strains. The dilemmas of oligopoly

As it developed, the hegemonic system fueled
conflicting tendencies within the system at
different levels: between the hegemon and the other
countries, among the latter as a group, between
surplus and deficit countries. It is not surprising,
therefore, that the Bretton Woods arrangements
eventually collapsed. It is also easy to understand
why an oligopolistic structure replaced hegemony
during the seventies.

This may be considered as a natural outcome of
the centrifugal forces which had produced the
collapse of the previous arrangements.

This also partly explains why the strong
countries emerging from the collapse of hegemony,
the leaders of oligopoly, enjoyed an increase in
their power. This was the result of the increase of
the hegemon's relative weakness (Lake 1984).

The years of oligopoly are also the years of
increased exchange rate instability. The change in
the exchange rate regime, however, affected
neomercantilistic attitudes in form but not in
substance.

Under managed flexibility neomercantilistic
behaviour is enhanced from a double point of view.

Foreign Economic Policy

In the first place, as the US is no longer acting as the residual country, the redundancy problem is not automatically solved. Secondly, managed flexibility provides national policy authorities with an additional policy tool (Kreinin 1979).

The implications of the first point will be discussed in the next chapter. We may just note here that the fact that the US was not <u>willing</u> to act as the residual country anymore implies that it pursued nationalistic goals, or to put it differently, that it ceased to supply the public good of an international system as it had under the Bretton Woods arrangements.

In an oligopolistic setting the public good of an international system cannot be provided unilaterally as the very definition of oligopoly implies. Such a public good can be provided only if a cooperative agreement is reached among oligopoly leaders. The question then arises whether or not such a cooperative solution will be reached. This is a fundamental issue in the political economy of international relations and to provide a conclusive answer is extremely problematic.

We will, nevertheless, extend to international relations a result reached by group theory (Olson 1965, 1982) and which has also been applied to international monetary relations (Hamada 1976, 1977, 1979). According to collective action theory the larger the number of participants in a group, the number of oligopolists in our case, the smaller will be the supply of public goods generated by the group. The larger the number of members who have to agree on a new set of "rules of the game" the lower will be the probability that such rules will be set up (11).

A further difficulty is that the interests of western nations involved more than one issue area. Hence with the breakdown of hegemony issue linkages and hence conflict areas increased considerably thus decreasing the probability of finding a cooperative solution to conflicts.

In such a situation oligopolists interact with each other at two different levels. At the "cooperative" level they bargain for new rules of the game, at the nationalistic level they pursue their own, neomercantilistic goals and hence they increase conflict. The two levels interact with each other as a country wishing to impose its design rules of the game might use its power in order to force the solution. On the other hand each country

40

will design new rules so that their implementation will maximize its own neomercantilistic goals.

In an oligopolistic setting, as a consequence, a trade-off exists for each country between the pursuit of neomercantilistic goals (which imply a tendentially deflationary and beggar-my-neighbour policy) and the supply of public goods (12) -i.e. the definition and support of new arrangements-which implies a tendentially expansionary policy in order to be accepted by other members of the group (i.e. in order to minimize free riding problems) especially "second level ones" (13).

This trade-off may be more clearly understood if we recall that the costs of the supply of the public good of an international system are represented by the loss of neomercantilistic benefits, while the costs associated with neomercantilistic policies stem from a generally lower level of effective demand (exogenous to the single country). This results from the shortage of supply of public goods and thus increases the difficulty of pursuing such policies successfully.

In such a situation the resort to a managed float may be considered also as the temporary solution to the new conflictual scenario.

Managed flexibility, oligopoly, and mercantilism
Two separate aspects should be considered in discussing the role of managed flexibility. A first one relates to the reasons why fixed rates had to be abandoned in favour of a less rigid monetary regime. These reasons have in part been discussed in the previous chapter and need not be repeated. Other reasons (14) may of course be mentioned but we shall not discuss them here.

The second element which is of greater relevence to us, relates to the fact that, once fixed exchange rates were abandoned, they were not replaced by other monetary arragements. In other words abandonment of fixed exchange rates implied that, from a formal point of view at least, national policy authorities had achieved a greater degree of freedom.

This last point needs some qualification. Managed flexibility involves an interaction between market forces and policy interventions in the determination of the course of exchange rates which is extremely difficult to disentangle. Recent empirical research has shown in what bad shape exchange rate theory currently is (Meese and Rogoff 1981, Shaffer and Loopesko 1983). In particular it is increasingly difficult to single out the role of "fundamentals" in determining the driving forces behind exchange rate movements. Hence a more acceptable road to follow in assessing exchange rate behaviour under managed floating may be the following.

The exchange rate is the price for foreign currency, hence it is determined by the excess demand for this good on its own market. No single variable should be considered as the main determinant of excess demand for currency on a priori grounds. Rather all variables concurring to determine the behaviour of the balance of payments (and hence the currency market) play a role in the determination of the price of the foreign currency (Kouri 1983).

One implication is that the definition of a long-run "equilibrium exchange rate" loses much of its relevance at least on empirical grounds. Another implication is that we must admit that policy intervention plays a role in the determination of exchange rate movements which is at least as important as that of any other market variable. This statement is perfectly acceptable once it is recognized that policy authorities are one of the decision-makers in the economic system (15).

One of the consequences of oligopoly is that currencies may be divided between "leaders" and "followers". This division goes along with the tendency towards a multi-currency system which we mentioned in chapter 1.

Currencies belonging to the two groups entail different policy constraints for the authorities in charge of their management. Smaller economies did try to drive the course of their currencies given the constraints imposed by the behaviour of leader currencies. This eventually led to the formation of regional monetary arrangements.

The crucial point then is the determination of the exchange rates of leading currencies vis-à-vis each other In this case too the prevailing exchange rate theory is not of much help. Consider as an example the most celebrated model of exchange rate determination, the asset market model. This model emphasizes the role of capital movements in the determination of exchange rates in the short run and it is based on the assumption that financial markets clear much more rapidly than goods markets, hence in

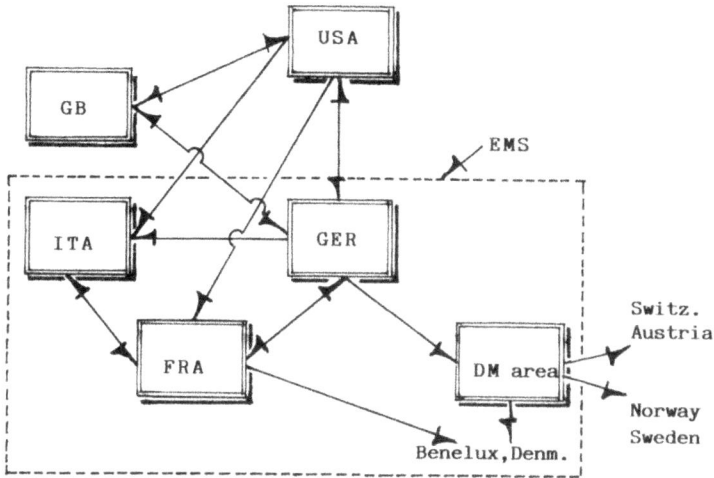

Fig. 3.2   Hierarchical Currency Relations

the long run "real" forces as well as relative
inflation rates determine the exchange rate
equilibrium value. Recent empirical investigation
(Horne 1983, Gandolfo and Padoan 1984) has shown, on
the contrary, that real and financial capital
markets adjust much more slowly than goods markets.
Hence accumulation forces should be considered as
the most relevant ones in the long run in the
determination of exchange rates. To put it
differently the fundamental forces driving the
external value of a currency should be sought in the
accumulation mechanism of the underlying economy (as
the balance of payments stages hypothesis
maintains).

If we accept this view some implications follow.
Accumulation requires the formation of long run
expectations. In an oligopolistic setting policy
options are crucial in the determination of
expectations (both short and long term). Hence they
determine exchange rates through their effect on the
long run behaviour of the economy.

We can sum up as follows. In the post-Bretton

Foreign Economic Policy

Woods economy relative exchange rates of leader
countries are heavily influenced by the interaction
of policies both in the short and in the long run.
This policy interaction determines the general
framework in which second level countries and
currencies make their options. (See fig.3.2) Within
this framework second level countries have continued
to pursue their neomercantilist goals (as the
trade-off between neomercantilism and the supply of
public goods may considered to be very weak for
them). What is crucial to the understanding of
monetary and financial instability under oligopoly
is, therefore, the policy course of the oligopoly
leaders.

As we have already mentioned, one of the
consequences of the collapse of the Bretton Woods
system was the exacerbation of the division between
surplus-prone and deficit-prone economies. Under
managed flexibility this eventually led to the
formation of vicious and virtuous circles:
depreciating currencies building on, and being fed
by, higher inflation and revaluing currencies
building on and being fed by lower inflation
respectively.

However, if we accept neomercantilism as a
unifying policy guideline for all countries the
"viciousness" of the behaviour of an economic system
cannot be inferred simply by looking at monetary
variables. If accumulation comes in to the picture
(Aglietta, Orlean, Oudiz 1981) then it is no longer
necessarily true that, for example, a revaluation is
virtuous. An overvalued currency produces lower
inflation but can depress the growth process as long
as it depresses profits and the ability of the
economy to compete in the world market over the
medium run. In other cases, however, revaluation can
stimulate investment in more advanced sectors (where
price competition is less relevant). In the first
case the trade balance will worsen while in the
second the opposite might occur. Virtuousness will
thus have to be considered to the extent in which
the exchange rate movement allows the attainment of
neomercantilist goals.

A similar argument can be made for inflation and
devaluation prone countries. An inflation
devaluation spiral might be the price a country has
to pay for the maintenance of a trade surplus. This
may be achieved, for example, if an inflationary
spiral allows for higher business profits and
investment which improve the country's growth

44

performance.
    Since neomercantilistic goals can be achieved
either through a devaluation or through a
revaluation, if different accumulation mechanisms
are accounted for, opposite currency trends under
managed flexibility may be viewed as the consequence
of the new form assumed by a preexisting common
(neomercantilistic) policy behaviour.

Oligopolistic reaggregation

    Monetary relations in the post-Bretton Woods
period are characterized by centrifugal impulses
which may be considered as the most evident
consequence of the transition period characterizing
the end of an international "order" without its
substitution with new arrangements (Aglietta 1982).
    It would however be incorrect to consider such a
period as characterized only by increased
instability and stress. One of the peculiar features
of oligopoly is that it encouraged a reaggregation
of national economies which may be described as
follows.
    With the collapse of the hegemonic system the
supply of the public good of monetary stability
falls largely below demand. Increased instability
and the failure to cope with inflation successfully
bring about a growing disillusionment with the
benefits of flexible rates. This increases the
demand for monetary stability especially from
second-level countries. Exchange rate and hence
monetary stability is sought through the so-called
"strong currency option mechanism" (Thygesen 1979,
Moon 1982). Smaller economies peg their currency to
that of a leader country (or sometimes to a currency
basket) and, by so doing, they give up freedom in
domestic policy in exchange for increased monetary
stability. The leader country may be tempted to
increase the supply of this public good by pursuing
a policy which also takes into account the needs of
smaller economies. A sort of regional and limited
hegemonic system is thus set up (16).
    Examples of this kind of arrangement include
cases in which no hegemonic policy is pursued by the
leader (17) and other cases in which such an
arrangement explicitly exists (18). In these latter
cases the leader finds a convenience in pursuing a
"limited hegemonic role" by increasing the supply of
the public good to satellite economies since the
larger the number of economies forming the currency

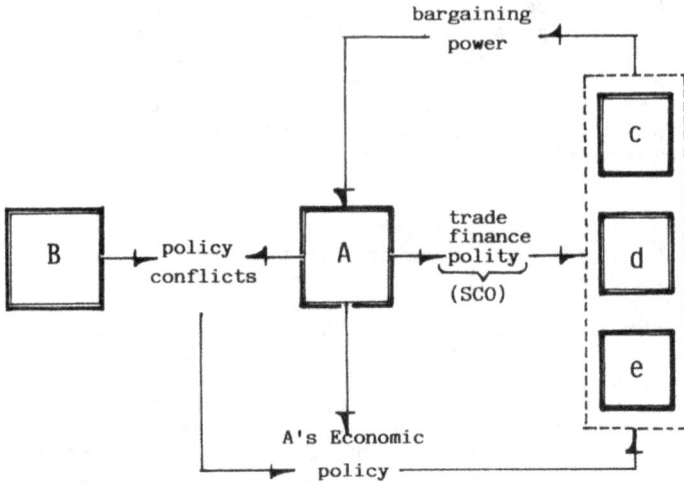

Fig. 3.3   The "Strong Currency Option"

bloc the greater will be the bargaining power the
leader enjoys vis-à-vis the other leading economies
(see fig. 3.3).

Oligopoly and strong currency options thus
sustain each other. The larger the supply of the
public good by the leader the greater the
attractiveness of joining the bloc. The stronger the
bargaining power of oligopolists vis-à-vis each
other, the more difficult it is to reach a solution
to emerging conflicts and hence the greater the need
for a defense against instability (Strange 1979a).
The interaction between demand for greater stability
by smaller countries and the advantages that a
leader enjoys by acting as a regional hegemon offers
an example of the trade-off between the supply of
public goods and the pursuit of neomercantilistic
goals (19).

The trade-off we have just mentioned, however,
pertains to a public good (monetary stability) which
is different from the one represented by a high and
stable rate of growth. Given the deflationary
tendency present in an oligopolistic structure this

46

second public good assumes a much greater relevance than the expansion of effective international demand. However, the fact that successful neomercantilism requires foreign demand to grow at some positive rate monetary stability may come into conflict with expansion. In this respect the "regional hegemon" faces a new trade-off between expansion and restriction and its choice on the matter will influence its attractiveness to smaller economies.

The problem then arises of why the aggregative impulses of an oligopolistic system do not lead to the end of oligopoly itself. Why, in other words, can the strong currency option not be extended to the whole system. The application of group theory to intercountry relations provides insight into the question.

The larger the number of participants (countries) in the group (monetary arrangement) the lower the group's efficiency in producing the public good of "monetary stability". This implies that there will be some resistance on the part of the group's participants to accept an increase in membership beyond a certain limit. We may also add that the conflicts which arise between group leaders require that a common (agreed upon) response is produced by the group members. This decision-making process is more difficult the larger the number of the members of the group and the more symmetric is the distribution of power.

The experience of the European Monetary System (Padoan 1985) seems to fit well into the framework we have outlined above. The European "Snake" (Tsoukalis 1977) based its stability on the strong currency option which the Deutschemark offered to smaller European economies. The commercial and financial integration of northern European countries made it possible to supply the public good of "monetary stability " at relatively low costs. The limited number of participants also allowed for easier decision-making on common policies both internal and external.

The EMS not only increased the number of the members of the group but also introduced economies in the group whose size and propensity to inflate made it much more difficult to find a common line of conduct with the leader of the group, West Germany. The costs of the supply of the public goods increased for the leader country because the new entrants increased the demand for an expansionary policy i.e. they tended to worsen the trade-off between neomercantilism and supply of public goods for Germany since in the Snake experience the restrictive policies pursued by German authorities was not seriously challenged by the smaller economies (Basevi and Calzolari 1982, Neumann 1984).

The potential benefits for the leader country in terms of increased bargaining power vis-à-vis the rest of the world (i.e. the US) also increased but they were judged to be too small to account for a change in policy (i.e. toward a more expansionary stance) by German authorities.

This partially explains the German authorities' strong resistance to the implementation of phase two of the European monetary arrangements after they had been, together with France, the strongest supporter of the implementation of the EMS. They feel that the move to a higher degree of monetary integration would entail additional costs for Germany (in terms of decreased monetary independence) which would not be matched by increased benefits.

NOTES

1. Strictly political justifications for neomercantilism will not be considered here; For a recent discussion see Buzan 1984.

2. Mercantilism has a pluricentennial tradition. Its contemporary revival is due to Keynes 1936, Joan Robinson 1965. See also Burbidge 1978.

3. Different authors consider the current account and the trade account as interchangeable concepts as far as mercantilist policies are concerned. As it will be clear below the most appropriate concept is the balance on goods and non factor services.

4. It is sometimes held that this relation should be considered as an ex post accounting identity. This is wrong if we accept, as we should, Kalecki's argument.

5. Country risk analysis will be further discussed in chapter 9.

6. See Buzan 1984 for a further discussion. Buzan introduces the distinction between benign and malevolent mercantilism which is criticized by Guerrieri and Padoan 1985.

7. This could also increase political business cycle management. See Frey 1978.

8. This sheds further light on the role covered by trade deficits of developing countries in the

post war period. See Biasco 1984.

9. The growth-cum-debt literature is discussed in chapter 9.

10. This is in accordance with a mechanism generating stages of the balance of payments.

11. One should assume that only oligopoly leaders are interested in actively seeking a cooperative solution (if any) as the smaller countries have a stronger incentive to free ride. This idea seems implicit in McKinnon's (1982) proposal for a monetary coordination among the major industrialized economies.

12. Both a stable growth rate (Head 1962) and monetary stability are public goods.

13. This partially explains why an oligopolist structure is less expansionary than an hegemonic one.

14. See Biasco 1979 for a survey of the debate on the effects of managed flexibility.

15. The following quotation from Fieleke 1983 seems particularly well suited to assess the issue. "Because we cannot model the "long-run" equilibrium exchange rate it is not possible to test whether the monetary authorities intervene in order to smooth out deviations from that rate" (Fieleke 1983 p. 225).

16. The hegemonic role may be exerted, for example, by intervention in currency markets to sustain the currencies of smaller countries thus preserving the stability of the currency area. In this case the cost for the hegemon would be in terms of a possibly undesired monetary expansion.

17. These include cases of pegging to the US dollar after the collapse of the Bretton Woods system.

18. Such as those in which currencies of former colonies are pegged to the currency of former colonial powers like France and Great Britain.

19. Hamada (1976) demonstrates formally that the larger the economic dimension of a country, the larger the relative weight in the determination (containment) of world inflation and the smaller the relative weight in the attainment of a trade surplus in the preference function of national policy makers.

Chapter Four

US FINANCIAL POLICY AFTER HEGEMONY

As we have said, oligopolistic interdependence
is characterized by the ability of single leader
countries to prevent other leaders from introducing
and implementing new rules of the game without
general agreement on them. The fact that after the
dramatic change in US policy at the end of the
previous decade the US economy seems to dominate the
behaviour of the whole international system does not
mean that we are in a situation of hegemony again.
Oligopolistic interdependence is characterized
either by cooperation or conflict. The former has
seldom been reached after the collapse of the
Bretton Woods arrangements. The latter implies that
someone will eventually win over others.
    The supremacy of one oligopoly leader over the
remaining ones may set the premises for a new
international organization, but this means that a
new public good has to be supplied. This in turn can
be achieved in one of two ways. A cooperative
solution is reached among the leading nations, and
in this case we have a cooperative oligopoly.
Alternatively the winner of oligopolistic conflicts
unilaterally supplies such a public good; in this
case we are in an hegemonic situation again.
    Neither of these two ways out of the crisis of
the Bretton Woods system has materialized until now.
The fact that United States policy has largely
conditioned the behaviour of the international
eocnomy for the past five years is a demonstration
of the fact that the United States may be considerd
the winner of persisting oligopolistic conflicts.
However things have not always been so. In this
chapter we will discuss the evolution of US
international economic policy after the collapse of
the Bretton Woods system as it has developed over

50

the past decade, i.e. in a situation of widespread
oligopolistic interdependence and conflict. In the
final chapter of the book we will discuss how the
position of the United States has changed since the
beginning of the present decade.

US policy in oligopolistic interdependence
Let us consider again the trade-off between
supplying public goods to the international system
and pursuing neomercantilistic (nationalistic)
policies. This trade-off is different for different
contries. Emerging oligopolists such as West Germany
or Japan have a higher propensity towards
neomercantilism than the United States. The US,
however, has increased its nationalistic attitudes
since the collapse of the Bretton Woods system
(Odell 1982).
The unilateral decision to suspend dollar
convertibilty and thus put an end to the Bretton
Woods arrangements may be considered as the sign
that the public good-neomercantilism trade-off had
shifted in favour of the second term for the US (1).
However the peculiar position of the US economy
in the international system does not allow to apply
the neomercantilistic paradigm to its foreign
economic policy without amendments. In order to
discuss this point we need to consider the long
debated issue of the increased openness of the US
economy.
A first point relates to the economic
justifications for neomercantilism. For an economy
as closed as the US system (with respect to other
industrialized market economies) the role covered by
net exports (as discussed in the previous chapter)
is largely supplied by government expenditure and
private investments (Kalecki 1934). Hence for the US
economy the possibilty of pursuing an independent
fiscal policy should be considered at least as
important as the possibility of running a trade
surplus for other countries.
The second point relates to the degreee of
openness of the US economy. Political economy
students have argued that over the seventies
increased openness has imposed new constraints on US
policy (Tufte 1978). This is a major point which
needs some clarification.
The decision to suspend the dollar's
convertibility in 1971 suggests that external
constraints had already been building up during the

previous decade. Discussion set forward in chapter 2 suggests that what really matters as far as this point is concerned is not an increase in international dependence of the US economy (which eventually altered US policy attitudes and options) but rather its qualitative evolution vis-à-vis other industrialized countries which eroded the international creditworthiness of the finacial centre of the world economy. This evolution made it unsustainable for the US to act as the residual country for the international system.

In addition increased openness is usually considered with respect to international trade. We maintain that the crucial point is the increased financial vulnerability of the US economy which produced the major constraints on its policy options and which deeply affected the operation of international monetary relations.

In the third place, after 1971 a dollar policy problem explicitly arises. This does not necessarily mean that US authorities used the dollar exchange rate as a policy tool as some have argued (Parboni 1981). Rather it should be interpreted in the sense that the possibility to let the dollar exchange rate fluctuate if needed became a necessary condition for US policy in the new environment.

If we consider all these aspects jointly we obtain a "US policy function" which is rather more complex than the ones usually implied in discussion of US policy choices after Bretton Woods. In such a framework macroeconomic policy targets must be considered jointly with those relating to the management and support of the US financial system as well as with problems stemming from the control of international monetary relations. Finally, economic and financial policy aspects must be weighted against other foreign policy considerations which the development of oligoplistic interdependence poses to the US.

Defining a dollar policy

US hegemony was eroded when the current account went into deficit for the first time since the beginning of the century. This was perceived, both in the US and abroad, as a structural loss of competitiveness of the US economy. As a consequence, the creditworthiness of the dollar-issuing "international bank" was seriously challenged.

This loss of competitiveness was attributed

largely to an overvaluation of the dollar with respect to the successful mercantilists, mainly Germany and Japan. It is not surprising that top US officials (Odell 1982) considered a devaluation as a means to improve external competitiveness.

The restoration of trade competitiveness was also perceived as a major domestic political problem given the rising concern of leading pressure groups which had become severely damaged by increasing penetration of foreign merchandise. Hence protectionist pressures were beginning to mount (Bryant 1982, Odell 1982).

Commercial weakness was perceived more strongly than financial weakness (Krasner 1978) although, as we have seen, the two should be considered closely connected. Financial problems associated with the devaluation of the dollar were however seriously considered in the administration also on account of the interests of the banking industry which had greatly increased its expansion abroad (2).

From the US point of view an "optimal" dollar policy would have required a revaluation of strong currencies such as the deutschemark and the yen against the dollar so as to increase US competitiveness vis-à-vis these economies while the dollar parity with respect to gold should have remained unchanged so as to defend the financial position of the US currency in the international system.

Such a solution would have met the demands of the business community as well as those of the banking community. Major obstacles came from outside as this solution ran against the neomercantilistic interests of the emerging oligopolistic economies.

At the beginning of the '70s the dollar issue exploded and it continued to represent the major foreign economic policy dilemma for the rest of the decade. This should not be considered an overstatement if we recall that the evolution of the exchange rate is the outcome of overall macroeconomic performance and policy and it is also a major constraint on this policy.

The new dimension of the dollar policy may also be considered from a political point of view. As Calleo (1981) puts it, Nixon's decision to suspend dollar convertibility made America's prosperity (in terms of restored competitiveness and greater freedom of action) dependent upon its external power since it forced onto others a dollar policy which ran against European and Japanese neomercantilistic interests. As Kehoane (1978) suggests, after the turn of the decade the US consumed part of the power they had accumulated during the years of hegemonic stability in order to pursue domestic (nationalistic) goals. Both viewpoints suggest that the US no longer had the power to act as the residual country but had enough power, both on economic and political grounds, to pursue such goals.

This explains why the US was eventually to overcome the resistance of other oligopolists after a decade of conflicts. The power the US was able to exploit at the beginning of the decade was not enough to continue to pursue a hegemonic policy but was more than enough to pursue nationalistic goals in oligopolistic interdependence.

The point to discuss now is how to integrate the "dollar policy" aspect into a more general macroeconomic policy framework.

The consequences of increased financial openness

Macroeconomic policy management has been extensively analyzed using political business cycle models. The main idea behind this approach is that the government wants to maximize its popularity (which implies reelection) given also its ideological preferences (Frey 1978). In this respect the policy rule is to expand just before elections to bolster employment and to deflate immediately after the elections in order to compress the inflation which results from previous expansion.

Much criticism may be addressed to this approach (3). From our point of view the major shortcoming is the absence of international economic conditions (and constraints) (4). The merit of the approach lies in the attempt to integrate in one unified vision the consideration of both political and economic aspects of the economy.

It is therefore necessary to reconsider the political business cycle framework in order to include the influence of increased real and financial openness of the US economy as well as constraints coming from the changed institutional environment, i.e. the emergence of oligopolistic interdependence.

Financial openness must obviously rank high in the policy concerns of a country such as the US. This stems from the fact that the role of world financial centre gives the US banking system a

54

unique position in the international markets. According to some viewpoints (De Cecco 1976) foreign economic policy has been mostly if not uniquely dominated by the interests of the US banking system. In other words this view assigns to the pursuit of financial goals (as defined in chapter 2) the most important reasons for the exploitation of seignorage.

The expansion of a financial system, however, increases (Minsky 1982a) its overall fragility. A major consequence is that even after the collapse of the Bretton Woods system, and possibly more after that event, the dominant financial role of the US implied that a "pure" nationalistic policy could not be pursued by US authorities. Greater financial fragility requires increasing support from the monetary authorities in lender of last resort operations as well as overall surveillance. The financial history of the post-Bretton Woods period (Minsky 1982a, Carron 1982, Woijnilower 1980, Moffit 1983) shows how the Fed increased its support operations for both the domestic and international activities of the banking system.

The economics of financial fragility will be discussed in greater detail in chapter 7. Here we shall concentrate on the policy implications of increased financial fragility and openness.

The expansion of the US banking system, which began well before the collapse of the Bretton Woods system, has proceeded along with the expansion of US business abroad (De Witte and Petras 1979). It was only in the '70s, however, that financial expansion accelerated with respect to business expansion (Bryant 1982).

As long as the dollar was the only true international currency, the expansion of the US banking sytem was equivalent to the expansion of the Eurodollar market. The causes of Euromarket expansion have been analyzed in a very large number of studies and we shall not attempt to review them here. We may however recall that this expansion was so rapid and huge because it met general interests (De Cecco 1974).

The US banking system enjoyed increased market shares as well as an improvement in customer relationship with US multinationals abroad (Fieleke 1977). American multinational firms enjoyed an advantage over domestic firms in host countries as far as sources of finance were concerned. US monetary authorities increased their control over international financial markets. British banks (and later those of other countries) revived their long tradition of international intermediaries by opening the City to offshore banking activities. The monetary authorities of other countries could resort to international financial markets whenever external adjustment proved too costly (Cohen 1982). And of course less developed countries, eager to speed up their development plans and wishing to avoid the costs of official financing borrowed largely from private international banks.

The fact that almost everybody benefited from Euromarket expansion explains why such an expansion proceeded almost free of regulation in contrast with what had happened to highly regulated domestic financial markets.

Expansion of the Euromarkets created a new quality of international interdependence based on the largely uncontrolled action of market forces (Bryant 1982) while laying the basis for a new quality of US dominance in the international system.

This element represents what is probably the most relevant difference of the US economy with respect to other oligopoly leders. The expansion of the US banking system was however not costless to US policy authorities as a new dilemma had to be faced (Hawley 1984) the one concerning the Euromarket regulation issue (5).

The expansion of multinational banking turned out to be a most effective way for the US to reaquire, at least in part, the leadership which the collapse of the hegemonic system had eroded. In order to sustain this expansion, financial innovations have to be introduced so as to exploit market potentials to the fullest. But because expansion of a financial system increases its fragility (De Witte and Petras 1979, Minsky 1982a) regulations must be introduced. A conflictual relationship is thus established between monetary authorities, which must act as regulators and lenders of last resort, and the banking community. Regulations are seen as constraints from the latter's point of view but support operations are invoked whenever fragility becomes too dangerous and the risk of financial collapse materializes. On the other hand, if policy authorities wish to foster the expansion of international banking activities cannot act too tightly on banking firms if they do not want to produce obstacles while trying to avoid moral hazard problems.

56

US Financial Policy

    The balance between these opposing tendencies
cannnot be struck once and for all as regulation and
control of banking requires a large amount of
discretionality.
    International banking activities in addition
pose new problems to regulatory and lender of last
resort (LLR) interventions (Guttentag and Herring
1983) with respect to a domestic environment and
make international banking and finance activities
generally more risky and more fragile than domestic
ones (6).
    The lack of regulation of international markets
and the difficulties inherent in lender of last
resort operations imply that the US monetary
authorities have become the most important lender of
last resort of the international system. This stems
from the obvious consideration that US monetary
authorities act as LLR of the US banking system
which in turn represents the most relevant part of
the international banking system (7).

A conceptual framework
    Students of political economy have produced
several attempts to describe the mechanisms
underlying the operation of US economic policy
before and after the collapse of the Bretton Woods
system. In order to discuss how oligopolistic
interdependence and financial expansion have
modified the preexisting framework we shall start by
recalling what may be considered as the
representative model of the political economy of US
economic policy (Tufte 1978)
    The starting model is Tufte's closed economy
model which may be considered the political economy
counterpart of Bryant's (1980) "nearly closed
paradigm" discussed in chapter 1.
    The model presents the traditional political
business cycle framework. It assumes that the vote
maximizing government uses policy instruments in
order to maximize employment (and inflation) just
before the elections so that the voter's welfare
increases. After the elections the government will
increase unemployment in order to depress inflation
and so be in a position to reflate again when the
electoral mandate is about to expire (see fig. 4.1.)
    In its original form this model assumes that
fiscal policy governs the cycle with no influence
coming from monetary policy. Recent investigations
(Black 1983, Woolley 1983, Laney and Willet 1983)

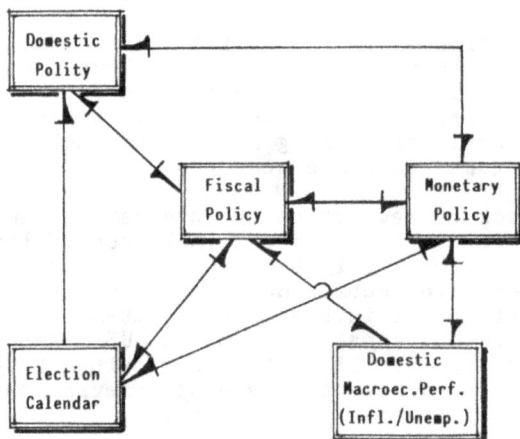

Fig. 4.1   Politico-Economic Interaction in a
            Closed Economy (I)

have however shown that, given the degree of
institutional independence enjoyed by monetary
authorities, they will accomodate fiscal policy or
(at least) will not follow an opposing course with
respect to that chosen by the fiscal authorities
(Gordon 1975).

As we shall see below, to assume that monetary
policy is influenced by political business cycle
considerations has strong implications for our
arguments.

A major modification of the basic scheme deals
with external components entering both the model of
the economy and the objective functions of the
policymaker. Contrary to most political business
cycle models Tufte has suggested that increased
economic interdependence among industrialized
countries has produced an international political
business cycle which could partially explain the
increased synchronization of business cycles among
industrial economies during the '70s (8). Tufte
suggests that, in addition to purely economic
influences, international political considerations

58

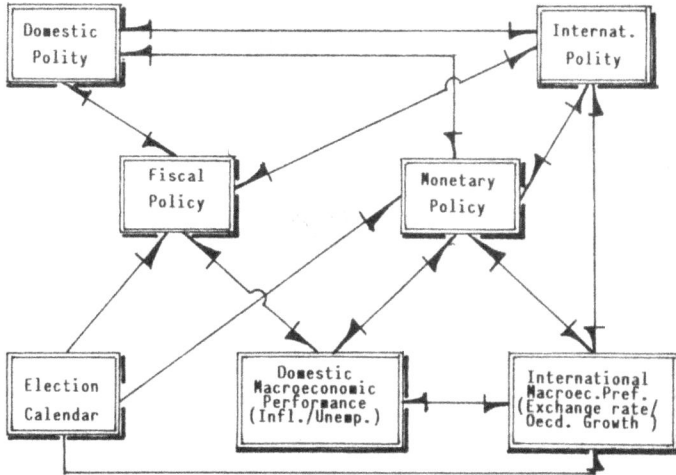

Fig. 4.2   Politico-Economic Interaction in an
            Open Economy (I)

enter into the determination of the domestic policy
options of the US government, especially after 1976.
    The increased international vulnerability of US
economic policy (see fig. 4.2) may be considered as
the recognition that under oligopolistic
interdependence US policy has tried to seek, with
the "locomotive experiment" (Kehoane 1978)
international consensus in addition to the research
for domestic support implicit in the political
business cycle model. In terms of discussion carried
out in the previous chapters this may be defined as
the attempt to supplying unilaterally, the public
good of growth to the international economy.
    This is certainly an improvement with respect to
closed political business cycle models but it still
fails to capture the features of financial
interdependence in the post-Bretton Woods period. In
order to bring financial problems into the picture
Tufte's model must be modified.
    In the first place we must go back to a closed
model and see how the problems of managing a highly
developed financial system modify the behaviour of

59

both monetary and fiscal authorities with respect to the traditional political cycle approach.

Expansionary policies increase employment and inflation but also increase profits (Kalecki 1934) and subsequently increase the overall financial fragility of the system. Financial fragility and inflation interact with each other since, in an expansionary process, firms increase the demand for inflation (Gordon 1975) in order to maintain profit margins and thus earn enough cash flows to validate debt. Insofar as monetary policy validates expansion in order to avoid liquidity problems it supplies inflation as well as increasing financial innovations (Dufey and Giddy 1981).

Deflationary policies cut back employment and inflation but also produce financial distress which may build up on previously built fragility. If risks of financial crises become substantial LLR operations might become necessary and hence a restrictive monetary policy might be at least temporarily reversed. In this respect financial fragility problems might act as a constraint on macroeconomic policies which will not be governed by pure political business cycle considerations.

The converse is also true. Macroeconomic policy considerations might act as a constraint to a sound management of the financial system if general macroeconomic policy goals put excessive strain on the financial structure (Minsky 1981). This also means that conflicts between fiscal and monetary authorities may arise not only as far as ordinary macroeconomic goals are concerned but also because the latter are concerned about the effects of macro policies on the underlying financial structure. Monetary policy should not be considered as merely accommodating the demands coming from both the government and the private sector. Rather one should always admit that a degree of discretionality will be maintained by the monetary authorities (Wallich 1977).

If these financial aspects are adequately taken into account the model described in fig. 1 should be substituted by the model described in fig. 4.3.

The inclusion of the policy of the Fed into the scenario does not involve merely economic aspects. Political considerations come into the picture since the Fed must face possible confrontations with the banking community such as those rapidly sketched above. In periods of stress the banking community wants ready support and LLR operations from the

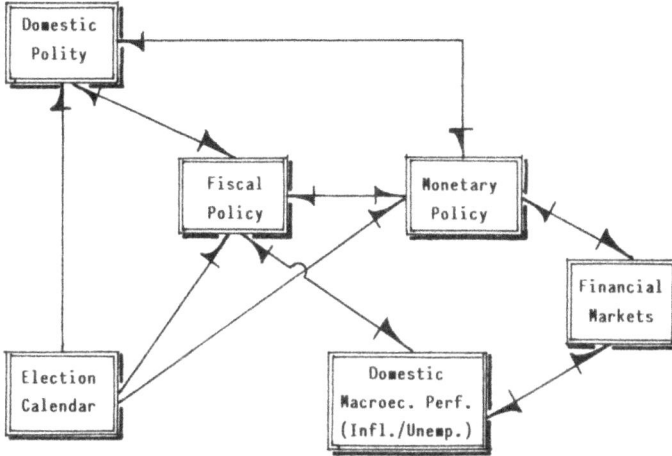

Fig. 4.3   Politico-Economic Interaction in a
            Closed Economy (II)

central bank while the Fed wants to avoid "moral
hazard" problems which may arise from a policy which
may be perceived as excessively lassist. The two
levels interact if we assume that political business
cycle considerations might enter into the behaviour
of the banking community. For example the bankers
know that the Fed will not follow a tight policy if
this goes against political cycle problems (Laney
and Willet 1983, Beck 1984) and hence they will
increase their propensity to take risks. A political
business cycle problem is then interacting with a
structural political economy problem. The Fed has to
respond to its "own" pressure groups and,
indirectly, to those interacting with the government
(Aronson 1979).

We must now consider the modifications of the
model described in fig. 4.2 by extending to the open
economy the consequences of the financial issues we
have just discussed.

This final model describes the political economy
of the US as an international financial centre in
oligopolistic interdependence .This implies

considering also the influences of the behaviour of the dollar on US policy and the interaction of the US "dollar policy" with international lender of last resort operations.

In an oligopolistic interdependence framework US macroeconomic policy is not targeted just at internal goals but also at external ones and the nationalistic-supply of public goods trade-off must be considered. The way in which this trade-off is exploited determines the relative weight of political economic goals.

If expansion is pursued by US authorities, in presence of a lassist monetary policy, the dollar will depreciate and this will increase financial instabilty in the international system. This means that although an expansion provides a public good to the international system it also provides the public bad of financial instability. In addition this decreases the financial penetration of the US banking system as the dollar depreciation encourages international currency diversification. (Minsky 1984).

Financial instability is increased if cooperation among oligopolists on major macroeconomic issues is not reached. If the US reacts to the lack of cooperative agreements with a restriction, the dollar's strength will be restored, however, this will produce widespread financial distress and the need for LLR intervention.

A cooperative expansion on the contrary allows for a generalized decrease of interest rates and a growth in international effective demand (9). Both produce beneficial effects on the financial equilibrium of banks and firms as their cash flows are improved.

It is the lack of a cooperative solution to macropolicy conflicts which increases financial instability in the international oligopoly. A dollar depreciation which is countered by a monetary squeeze in the US starts off a restrictive monetary policy reaction chain (an interest rate war) which increases the fragility of the financial system. The appreciation of the dollar which follows is just as disruptive as the previous depreciation.

Oligopolistic conflicts lead to disorderly currency fluctuations and international diversification away from weak currencies into strong currencies, raw materials, and gold. Regulation and "parental responsibility" conflicts may also arise among central banks when

international LLR interventions are needed
(Guttentag and Herring 1983, Hawley 1984). Once
oligopolistic conflicts break out a negative issue
linkage is also established since macroeconomic
monetary and financial goals interact whith each
other. A cooperative solution is thus increasingly
difficult to achieve. The demand for the public good
of international cooperation rises high above its
effective supply while the trade-off between
neomercantilism and cooperation shifts heavily away
from the latter.

The changing nature of US international power

As we have seen US international economic policy
in oligopolistic interdependence is characterized by
a number of constraints. These are only partially
similar to those prevailing in other advanced
economies as they derive from the peculiar position
of the US economic and financial system in the world
economy. Expansionary policies run against
traditional macroeconomic constraints such as
inflation as predicted by political business cycle
literature, but they also run against excessive
dollar instability which endangers the international
position of the US financial system. In this respect
the external constraint on macroeconomic policies is
rather different from the traditional balance of
payments constraint on domestic policies (which is
however generally ignored by political economy
models).

The evolution of international relations towards
an oligopolistic structure should also be considered
as a constraint on US expansionary policies. This
constraint is not to be understood simply as an
increase in the degree of openness of the US economy
both in its real and financial aspects. The most
important constraint comes from what is usually
termed (Hamada 1976) "strategic interdependence". US
policy cannot be decided and implemented without
taking into account the reactions of the other
oligopolists. When no general rules of the game
exist such a reaction might be generally hostile
rather than accommodating. As a consequence the US
may be tempted to undertake specific actions in
order to decrease this kind of constraint, i.e. to
decrease the power of other oligopolists to
retaliate.

A restrictive policy in the US runs against the
traditional unemployment constraint. The

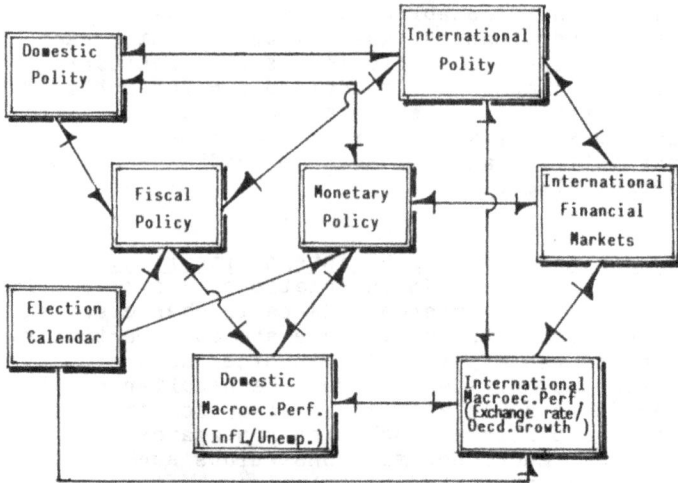

Fig. 4.4   Politico-Economic Interaction in an
            Open Economy (II)

international financial constraint on restrictive
policies stems from the increased fragility of the
international financial system which is mostly US
based. Restrictive policies might run against the
need to operate LLR interventions (Minsky 1980).
Oligopolistic interdependence finally provokes
strategic responses by other oligopolists who, while
complaining about what they may judge as an
excessive restriction, will tighten their policies
as well. International financial interdependence
might then lead to far too heavy restrictions which
may slip out of control of national monetary
authorities even when their intervention power is
relatively large as in the case of the Federal
Reserve (Guttentag and Herring 1983).
      Figure 4.4 summarizes the "full model" of US
economic policy in oligopolistic interdependence.
      This behavioural model has obvious implications
for the international system as a whole. Even though
it is widely held that US power has been eroded
during the past decade a downward trend should not
be assumed too hastily. The growth of US banking

activity abroad and growing financial
interdependence based on US international banking
has in some cases even increased the role of US
policy in the control and management of the
international system.

In addition, the fact that the other leaders of
the system failed to reach a cooperative agremeent,
as they preferred to pursue nationalistic policies,
has increased the capacity of US policy to affect
international relations.

Even after the collapse of the Bretton Woods
system the US has maintained the two roles of
international lender of last resort and of the
ultimate source of international effective demand:
two necessary conditions for the viability of a
highly sophisticated financial system.

The LLR function has been discussed above. The
second element needs some further justification.

After the collapse of the fixed exhange rate
system, the US gradually reaquired the role of
residual economy. This may be justified if we admit
that under flexible rates the exchange rate of the
dollar vis-à-vis other currencies is determined
residually or, in other words, that the US need not
have an explicit exchange rate target. This should
be interpreted in the sense that the US can pursue
an expansionary (restrictive) policy and let the
exchange rate act as a shock absorber of the
consequences of such an expansion (restriction).
This role of shock absorber will be all the more
important if no agreement is reached with other
oligopolists for a coordinated policy.

Since international constraints on US policy
have increased with respect to the Bretton Woods
period the role of ultimate source of effective
demand can be pursued by the US only partially. It
remains true however that the US can pursue an
expansionary policy more easily than any other
nation. The fact that its financial and economic
weakness resulting from the erosion of hegemony
limited this role should be considered a
quantitative and not a qualitative matter.

Under oligopolistic interdependence the role of
international effective demand pull should be
carried out by the group of leading countries. If
this is not possible because no cooperative
agreement is reached then this role will be
underprovided but the US will be the only economy
able to carry it out without the support, or even
against the choice, of others. In this respect the

trade-off between nationalism and the supply of public goods is, for the US, more biased toward the latter than for any other country (Solomon 1982).

Taking account of what we have been saying on the role of the US under oligopoly it is difficult to assess whether its power has decreased or increased during this period.

The collapse of the Bretton Woods system was also a consequence of the decline of US power. Nixon's decision to abandon the system may be considered as an attempt to increase freedom of action in order to regain some of the power which had been lost.

Carter's expansionary policy of the mid 1970s may be considered as a "consumption" of power insofar as it represented an attempt to provide unilaterally a public good (higher growth) to the international system. Its failure may be ascribed also to the inadequate amount of power the US could count on at that moment. The nationalistic policies which followed should, on the contrary, be considered as an attempt to "invest" in (accumulate) power. In this respect the oligopolistic interdependence scenario of the past decade may be viewed as a conflict over power distribution among oligopolists.

Although the dollar's weakness in the seventies may be considered a sign of a further decline in power, the unique role of the US in the international financial system as well as the subsequent turn of the tide which followed the advent of the Reagan administration and the appointment of Paul Volcker as the Fed's chairman indicate that no downward trend in US power may be inferred by the events of the period.
Although no single country has been able to exert complete control over financial flows after the collapse of the Bretton Woods system, the US economy, thanks also to its increasing financial openness, has certainly emerged, or rather reaffirmed itself, as the leading financial power of the international system.

However such a discussion requires a definition of power which has some operative content. We will go back to this crucial point in the final part of chapter 11.

NOTES

1. Lake (1984) discusses the consequences of a decline in the relative position of the Us economy in world trade on the stability of the international system.

2. We shall return to this point below.

3. One criticism is that these models neglect to consider the existence of non political cycles which are produced by "pure economic" forces.

4. For an exception see Willet and Mullen 1982.

5. For two opposite views on banking regulation see Meltzer 1967 and Revell 1981.

6. See Guttentag and Herring 1983 for a detailed survey of this problem.

7. On the willingness of the US to act as LLR of the whole international banking system, and not just of US based banks see De Grauwe and Fratianni 1984.

8. See Thompson and Zuk 1983 for a critical analysis of Tufte's hypothesis.

9. Oudiz and Sachs (1984) provide an analysis of the effects of cooperative macroeconomic policies, they do not, however, consider the effects of international financial instability.

Chapter Five

THE BUILD-UP OF INTERNATIONAL DEBT

The literature describing the build-up of the
international debt problem is immense. The aim of
this chapter is to summarize the main features of
this process in the past decade and to outline its
most relevant characteristics while the following
chapter will be devoted to a description of the
development of the international debt crisis of
1982-84. No attempt will be made here to interpret
this process. An interpretative framework, based on
Minsky's view of financial fragility, (Minsky 1975,
1982a) will be discussed in chapter 7.

After the oil crisis
It is generally assumed that the international
debt problem has its roots in the first oil crisis.
Before that event the most relevant sources of
external finance available to developing countries
were official aid flows and, to a lesser degree,
direct investments (Kindleberger 1978b). It is only
after the first oil shock that the mechanisms of
international finance underwent the major changes
which eventually produced the present system.
It has been argued that the international
payments mechanism has shifted from a balance of
payments adjustment to a balance of payments
financing regime after the collapse of the Bretton
Woods system (Cohen 1982). In our view the relevant
element is the increased privatization of the regime
which shifted emphasis from official financial flows
to international credit flows centred on private
international banks.
It is well known that the offshore activity of
private banks dates well before the outbreak of the
oil crisis. Only after the oil crisis, however, did

private banks take up the role of leading
intermediaries in the international system. This is
a crucial point as one of the aspects of the build
up of the international debt is that it represents
the "solution" to an extremely complex and diffcult
"intermediation problem" in the world economy. In
the face of the excess savings generated by the oil
surpluses there existed an excess investment that
had to be financed. This element represents the
often neglected aspect of the oil recycling problem.
How and why did investment demand soar in a
relatively small group of countries just after the
finance displacement generated by the oil crisis?
    The solution to the intermediation problem
offered by private banks may be considered also as
an aspect of the disproportion crisis view we
discussed in chapter 1. It provides an interesting
example of the chain of causations which such a
crisis produces. The disproportion in the oil market
produces a disproportion in the market for capital
(finance). The reaction of the system is not just a
change in "pure" economic variables -prices and
quantities- but it involves changes in
"institutions". The emerging role of private banks
is the institutional change which allows "pure"
economic variables to find a new equilibrium.
    The "financing gap" was filled to a large degree
by a particular institutional mechanism: syndicated
bank lending. Developing countries were also able to
raise funds in another segment of the market, i.e.
floating rates notes, whose behaviour and mechanics
closely resemble the market for loans (OECD 1980,
O'Brien 1981). Developing countries were, on the
contrary, largely kept out of the other major
segment of the international financial market - the
bond market - as the floatation of bonds would have
required a considerably higher degree of knowledge
of the borrowers by savers. This reflected the
attitude that private banks had towards the new
customers and it also reflected the fact that the
international market was not able to supply in
adequate amount that particular (public) good which
is a necessary input in the credit industry:
creditworthiness. This characteristic of the
international credit market will prove to be most
crucial when the crisis breaks out not later than a
decade. We will discuss this point in some detail in
chapter 8.
    This financing scheme also implied that the risk
involved in the intermediation process was almost

entirely borne by private banks.

The above features of the credit market can also account for another characteristic of the finance mechanism of the seventies: the concentration of both lenders and borrowers.

A widely held opinion is that the behaviour of international credit markets in the post-oil crisis period should be considered as "demand determined" in the sense that the amount of credit allocated depends only on the amount demanded by borrowers at the prevailing price. The absence of supply constraints, contrary to what prevailed before the oil crisis, would be explained, according to this interpretation, by the relative abundance of funds resulting from OPEC deposits in the Euromarkets (Mattione 1985) which put the banks in the position to fulfill any demand for loans if they wanted to face all their liabilities. This is equivalent to assuming a situation of nearly perfect competition among the lenders while a situation of oligopsony (demand oligopoly) prevailed on the borrowers' side.

This view seems too simplistic and fails to understand the mechanisms underlying the international market for funds. It is more convenient to consider the behaviour of the market as resulting from the interaction of demand and supply factors. This should not be interpreted in the obvious way of assuming that equilibrium is reached at the intersection of demand and supply schedules. Rather it should be interpreted in the sense that demand and supply functions are interdependent. The financial instability mechanism outlined in chapter 7 should help to clarify this point.

Another element which is crucial to the understanding of this mechanism is that the way in which borrowers and lenders interact in the credit market is heavily affected by the state of the international economic environment. In other words, the international credit market is largely influenced by the state of oligopolistic relations and conflicts which determine the politico-economic scenario.

Some stylized facts

Aggregate data on the growth of external debt of non-oil developing countries are reported in table 5.1. They show that external debt has been growing steadily over the decade. However the most relevant

Table 5.1. Non-oil developing countries: external debt, 1973-83 (billions of US$)

	1973	1974	1975	1976	1977	1978	1979	1980	1981	1982	1983
Total outstanding debt	130.1	160.8	190.8	228.0	278.5	336.3	396.9	474.0	555.0	612.4	664.3
Short term debt	18.4	22.7	27.3	33.2	42.5	49.7	58.8	85.5	102.2	112.7	92.4
Long term debt	111.8	138.1	163.5	194.9	235.9	286.6	338.1	388.5	452.8	499.6	571.6
By type of creditor											
Official creditors	51.0	60.1	70.3	82.4	98.7	117.5	133.0	152.9	172.4	193.2	218.7
Private creditors	60.8	77.9	95.1	114.8	137.3	169.1	205.1	235.6	280.4	306.4	353.0
By group of borrowers											
Net oil exporters	20.4	26.0	34.1	42.4	53.3	61.2	70.5	79.4	96.5	108.1	129.0
Net oil importers											
Major exporters of manufactures	40.8	51.7	60.9	73.1	85.2	108.1	127.7	145.2	170.6	184.3	212.3
Low income countries	25.4	29.7	33.2	38.3	46.5	53.1	59.5	67.0	73.0	80.1	90.8
Others	25.2	30.6	35.3	41.1	51.0	64.2	80.4	96.9	112.7	127.1	139.4

Source: International Monetary Fund

characteristics are the changes in the structure and
quality of debt.

In the first place the increase of the burden of
debt slows down in the second part of the seventies
and it subsequently shows a strong increase right
after the second oil shock. The average annual rate
of growth is around 19 per cent. This means a
fivefold increase which falls to 2.1 times if
inflation is taken into account (Cline 1983).

In the second place, short term debt was growing
more than long term debt until the end of the
decade. In the first two years of the present decade
there was an upswing in short term debt which has
subsequently slowed down (see tab 5.1).

In the third place, the share of total debt
which is covered by private financial institutions
has been growing rapidly and did not show any
slowdown even in the years immediately before the
second oil shock.

The qualitative evolution of the debt burden may
be appreciated by looking at some traditional
indicators (see tables 5.2 and 5.3). The debt
service ratio, the ratio of total debt to GNP, and
the ratio of total debt to exports show an
increasing trend over the period which has an
upswing after the first year of the present decade.

The evolution of these indicators and the
increasing share of short term debt show that the
quality of debt deteriorated over the period. The
debt burden increased even if inflationary effects
are taken account of. After the second oil shock all
three indicators deteriorated. This was mainly due
to the heavy fall in exports which took place after
the second oil shock both in real terms (due to the
recession) and in value terms (due to the
appreciation of the dollar).

In order to have a better understanding of this
phenomenon we must consider the three elements which
stand out as the most relevant systemic features:
the evolution of the international environment, the
concentration of borrowers, and the concentration of
lenders.

International environment
In the 1970s the international financial
environment became increasingly favourable to
borrowers. In the first place there was the fact
that low interest rates prevailed. Cline (1983)
reports that for 1961-70 Libor on US dollar deposits

Table 5.2. Non-oil developing countries: long-term and short-term external debt relative to exports and to Gdp, 1973-83 (in per cent).

	1973	1974	1975	1976	1977	1978	1979	1980	1981	1982	1983
Ratio of external debt to exports of goods and services											
All non-oil dev. countries	115.4	104.6	122.4	125.5	126.4	130.2	119.2	112.9	124.9	143.3	144.4
of which											
Net oil exp.	154.7	124.9	162.4	169.5	179.3	176.9	144.3	128.4	154.6	179.5	192.2
Net oil imp.	109.4	100.9	115.4	117.5	116.8	121.8	114.1	109.5	118.3	135.1	134.3
Major exporters of manuf.	91.7	88.6	103.3	103.0	99.5	101.1	96.9	94.0	100.6	116.2	114.2
Low income count.	227.9	214.5	226.1	225.1	217.8	226.3	209.8	201.4	231.1	254.1	262.9
Others	96.9	84.7	98.3	104.3	111.6	124.8	115.5	110.9	121.9	138.0	136.6
Ratio of external debt to Gdp											
All non-oil dev. countries											
of which											
Net oil exp.	22.4	21.8	23.8	25.7	27.4	28.5	27.5	27.6	31.0	34.7	34.7
Net oil imp.	26.2	25.2	27.7	32.3	38.5	39.3	37.4	34.0	36.1	44.7	43.5
Major exporters of manuf.	20.2	19.6	22.2	22.7	23.9	25.1	24.8	25.1	29.3	33.2	33.8
Low income count.	20.1	20.1	20.9	24.4	24.9	24.0	24.4	23.6	24.7	26.2	26.5
Others	26.2	25.2	26.2	27.7	28.6	31.5	28.8	30.6	34.1	35.8	35.6

Source: International Monetary Fund.

73

Table 5.3. Non-oil developing countries: debt service payments on
short-term and long-term external debt, 1973-83
(Values in billions of US$; ratios in per cent)

	1973	1974	1975	1976	1977	1978	1979	1980	1981	1982	1983
Value of debt											
service payments	17.9	22.1	25.1	27.8	34.7	50.3	65.0	76.2	94.7	107.1	93.2
Interest payments	6.9	9.3	10.5	10.9	13.6	19.4	28.0	40.4	55.1	59.2	55.1
Amortization	11.1	12.8	14.6	16.8	21.1	30.9	36.9	35.8	39.8	47.9	38.1
Debt service ratio	15.9	14.4.	16.1	15.3	15.4	19.0	19.0	17.6	20.4	23.9	19.3
Interest payments											
ratio	6.1	6.1	6.7	6.0	6.0	7.3	8.2	9.3	11.9	13.2	11.4
Amortization ratio	9.8	8.3	9.4	9.3	9.4	11.7	10.8	8.3	8.6	10.7	7.9

Source: International Monetary Fund.

Table 5.4. US dollar: effective exchange rate (1970=100).

1973	1974	1975	1976	1977	1978	1979	1980	1981	1982	1983
83.6	84.6	84.0	87.6	87.0	79.2	77.1	77.1	87.0	96.0	105.2

Source: OECD.

74

Table 5.5. Summary of terms of trade and world prices, 1973-82
(percentage change from preceding year)

	1973	1974	1975	1976	1977	1978	1979	1980	1981	1982
Terms of trade										
Industrial countries	-1.6	-11.9	2.7	-1.0	-1.1	2.7	-2.6	-7.6	-0.6	1.5
Developing countries										
Oil exporting	11.8	138.4	-5.4	5.8	0.6	-10.7	28.6	41.6	12.2	-5.5
Non oil exporting	6.1	-5.6	-9.0	6.0	6.0	-4.1	-0.3	-4.3	-2.2	-2.0
World trade prices (in US$)										
Manufactures	17.7	21.8	12.3	-	9.0	14.7	14.5	11.0	-5.0	5.0
Oil	40.0	225.8	5.1	6.3	9.3	0.1	48.7	62.0	11.0	-3.0
Non-oil primary commodities (market prices)	53.2	28.0	-18.2	13.3	20.7	-4.7	16.5	9.7	-14.8	-5.5

Source: International Monetary Fund.

Build-up of Debt

minus the US wholesale price increase produced an
average real interest rate of 4.1 percent. This
average was _minus_ 0.8 per cent in the period 1971-80
while it soared to 11.0 percent in 1982.
    Another favourable element was the evolution of
terms of trade. The second part of the decade was
characterized by a slowdown in the increase of oil
prices and by a fall in the value of the dollar (see
tables 5.4 and 5.5). Both benefited non-oil
developing countries. The improvement in terms of
trade was also the result of the expansion of world
demand which pushed up the prices of commodities
exported by developing countries (1).
    Real growth in industrial countries was
relatively high during the 1970s, averaging 3.2
percent between 1973 and 1979, but dropped to 1.2
per cent in 1980-81 and to minus 0.3 per cent in
1982. The behaviour of this variable positively
influenced the developing countries' real export
growth.

Borrowers
    The increase in the amount of total debt assumes
even more striking characteristics if we look at the
concentration of debt. By the end of 1982 21
countries accounted for 84 per cent of outstanding
debt of developing countries while the eight Latin
American countries plus South Korea and the
Philippines held the 66.4 per cent of total debt
(World Financial Markets, February 1983).
    As Sachs (1982) notes, the heavy borrowing
countries such as Brazil, Argentina, Mexico,
Venezuela, and Korea maintained a high rate of
capital accumulation or even increased it in this
period. High investment rates went along with high
growth rates of output and exports (D'Arista 1979).
Export growth however was not high enough to fill
the current account deficit which high investment
eventually produced. As a consequence these
countries resorted heavily to external debt.
    Concentration of debt on a relatively small
number of countries can also be explained using a
case by case approach. Many of these countries
presented peculiar characteristics in their
economies which warranted their relatively high
creditworthiness and easy access to credit markets.
In some cases (Mexico, Venezuela) oil production was
a fundamental element. In other cases (Brazil) a
substantial presence of US and other western

Table 5.6. Largest Ldc borrowers: national banking groups' market shares

June 1983	Total debts to BIS banks, US$ million	US banks	of which (%) UK banks	German banks
Mexico	69797	38.2	12.3	2.9
Brazil	68192	33.7	13.0	4.0
Venezuela	28057	41.7	10.4	5.2
Argentina	27124	34.5	12.9	5.5
Korea	25913	53.9	13.9	1.4
Philippines	15252	44.3	11.0	0.8
Indonesia	14070	30.6	7.2	9.8
Nigeria	12852	15.9	13.5	9.2
Chile	11770	49.7	15.4	4.1
Yugoslavia	10194	22.4	13.7	12.7

Source: American Express Bank.

Build-up of Debt

multinational enterprises attracted multinational
banks also because of the customer relationship
factors discussed in chapter 4 (see tab 5.6).
    In general these countries followed domestic
policies whose effects, if not consequences, were
similar (Cline 1983, Diaz-Alejandro 1984). Most of
the heavy borrowers kept their currency largely
overvalued with respect to soaring domestic
inflation thus producing an increasing loss in
competitiveness. In some cases (Chile) tight
internal policies kept inflation under control but
the fall in the price of crucial commodities (such
as copper) produced heavy trade balance losses. In
addition an inadequate interest rate policy heavily
contributed to an outflow of capital which
subtracted financial resources from the economies
(Diaz-Alejandro 1984).
    Overvalued currencies favoured protectionistic
policies which might have slowed down the beneficial
effects on productivity generated by the high
investment policies.
    In spite of national differences however a
common behavioural pattern of borrowers may be said
to exist. One common element may be found in the
fact that the access to external private debt
allowed these countries to pursue expansionary
policies which would have otherwise been impossible.
According to some analysts (Cline 1983, Sachs 1982)
most of the borrowed funds were, initially at least,
directed to an increase of domestic productive
capacity. In addition domestic saving did not
decline during this period and so no overwhelming
evidence can be produced to support the claim that
external finance was used to increase internal
consumption expenditure. This is a crucial point
because it somehow justifies the willingness of
banks to lend to these countries as the investment
projects to which funds were directed formed in
their view (and in the general view for that) the
fundamental premise for the borrowers to produce
enough future earnings so as to service their debts.
    Concentration of debt in a small number of
selected countries suggests that supply and demand
factors in the credit markets operated with
different intensity in different periods. Supply
factors operated in the first phase when supply
barriers allowed only a few customers to have access
to funds, while demand factors might have prevailed
once borrowers had acquired enough creditworthiness
not to be rationed out of the market anymore. Once

again, however, we must not overstress this point as
it might lead to an oversimplification. Interaction
of borrowers and lenders is a constant feature of
the process and it will be discussed in more detail
below.

Lenders

Concentration is a phenomenon which can be
appreciated also from the point of view of lenders.
A small number of large banks (mostly US) has
produced the majority of loans to large borrowers
and has ended up with an exceptional exposure
towards a very small number of countries.
Concentration of lenders may be viewed as a result
of the behaviour of the credit market.

The international credit market may be described
as characterized by a small number of large banks
who "make the market". The expansion of the amount
of lending and the (apparent) success of borrowers
in repaying their debts, at least in the first phase
of the process, has made international lending an
attractive activity also for medium and sometimes
small banks (Llewellyn 1982, Emminger 1985) who have
entered the market of international syndicated
lending in increasing numbers. As a consequence the
supply side of the market may be said to include two
segments: the large banks and the small ones. A
stylized description of market operations may be
presented as follows.

Entry of borrowers into the markets is subject
to creditworthiness barriers. The assessment of
creditworthiness is in large part carried out by big
banks who actually decide which borrowing countries
will be granted loans.

The assessment is largely accepted by small
banks who will lend to the same borrowers through
syndicated lending. This amounts to saying that
while barriers to entry do exist for borrowers they
are hardly present for lenders as size will not
prevent smaller banks from participating in loan
syndicates.

The amount of control that larger banks are able
to exert over smaller ones has however decreased
with the transition to the "borrower market"
conditions which resulted from the interaction of
two events: the increase of funds resulting from oil
surpluses and the general expansionary conditions
determined by US policy after the first half of the
past decade. This general situation has

Build-up of Debt

significantly shifted the interest of banks toward
international markets.

This shift may be seen as the result of the
perception that sovereign lending was much less
risky than lending to private operators especially
after the Herstatt crash and, later, the failure of
the Franklin National Bank (Spero 1980, Carron 1982,
Moffit 1983). This had produced a temporary drawback
of lending activities which, however, was reversed
shortly afterwards. In addition, the heavy recession
which hit the OECD economies after the first oil
crisis had significantly reduced the demand for
credit while OPEC surplus deposits had greatly
burdened the liability side of the banking system.

To put it shortly, the demand for loans deriving
from high growth developing countries was
entusiastically met by the banking firms, both large
and small, in search of new profit opportunities
(O'Brien 1981). The expanding market for loans
produced increasing competition among banks for
profitable market shares. In many cases small banks
tried to increase their market shares by offering
lower spreads and assuming higher risks than the
large banks (Llewellyn 1982).

Favourable general conditions helped to build
(apparently) sound customer relationships with LDC
borrowers. Easy credit terms encouraged
overindebtedness in the sense that countries
borrowed in excess of their short term requirements
in order to build financial reserves which were
redeposited in the lending banks.(O'Brien 1981).

Small banks, however, were by no means mainly
responsible for the heavy concentration of loans
which, as subsequent events would shown, had greatly
increased the fragility of international financial
relations. As Cline (1983) shows, expansion of bank
loans through syndicated credits had produced
concentration of exposure in a number of big US
banks (2).

As Arista (1979) notes, concentration of
exposure was also a consequence of the fact that
OPEC countries deposited their oil surpluses in a
selected number of large banking firms reputed to
offer the lowest risk opportunities. These large
banks, in addition, preferred to concentrate loans
on a small number of countries which were believed
to offer both the best creditworthiness and the
easiest credit monitoring opportunities.

Both these facts show how fallacious and
misleading the behaviour of credit markets may be.

Table 5.7. Largest Ldc positions with US banks

June 1983	US$ million			As % of capital			As % of US "market" (*)		
	(A)	(B)	(C)	(A)	(B)	(C)	(A)	(B)	(C)
Brazil	14774	4728	3526	48.8	34.0	11.6	64.1	20.7	15.3
Mexico	14494	5523	6623	48.0	39.7	21.7	54.4	20.6	24.9
Korea	8133	3397	2446	26.9	24.4	8.0	31.4	24.3	17.5
Venezuela	8107	1759	1520	26.8	12.7	5.0	69.4	15.1	13.0
Argentina	6051	1930	1371	20.0	13.9	4.5	64.7	20.6	14.7
Philippines	4571	1817	773	15.1	13.1	2.5	67.6	26.9	11.4
Chile	3202	1262	1384	10.6	9.1	4.5	54.8	21.6	23.7
Colombia	2792	1298	631	9.2	9.3	2.1	67.8	31.5	15.3
Peru		740	475		5.3	1.6		24.8	15.9

(*) as a % of all US banks' position with the country.

(A) 9 largest US banks; (B) 15 next largest US banks; (C) 166 other US banks.

Source: American Express Bank.

Build-up of Debt

If we consider the behaviour of single agents their
choices appear rational from a risk minimization
point of view. If we look at the aggregate
consequences, however, they produce an increasing
overall fragility which will eventuallly frustrate
their expectations.

The increasing exposure may be appreciated if it
is confronted with banks' capital (see tab 5.7). The
two largest borrowers, Brazil and Mexico, account
for about one third of the capital of all the banks
and about 45 per cent of that of the nine largest
banks.

The fragility of the banking system is further
evidenced by the exposure of individual large banks
to individual borrowing countries. Data reported by
Cline (1983) show that a number of key banks have a
considerably greater exposure than it is possible to
assess from an aggregated point of view. This is a
crucial indicator of fragility. As history of
financial crises shows (Kindleberger 1978a,
Kindleberger and Laffargue 1982) fragility of
financial systems may be greatly increased by the
presence of a limited number of dangerous positions
even if the overall situation of the system is
apparently sound. Through the domino effect
financial distress is a disease which spreads out
with tremendous force and speed if it is not
adequately countered and if the amount of
interdependence of the system has proceeded a long
way. And this is certainly the case of the
international banking system in the 1970s.

Increasing deterioration

As the end of the decade approached the
internationl debt system showed increasing signs of
deterioration. This was witnessed from all the
viewpoints involved. Deterioration of financial
relations is mainly a qualitative phenomenon
although it is reflected in changes in values of
relevant indicators accruing to the three aspects we
have discussed: the position of borrowers and
lenders and the general economic environment.

The deterioration of the external financial
position of borrowers can be observed by looking at
the relevant debt indicators such as debt service
ratios, debt Gnp ratios and so on (see tables 5.2
and 5.3). These indicators reflect both the
deterioration of foreign currency earnings due to a
fall in export performance and a worsening of

82

Table 5.8. Non-oil developing countries: interest burden and new
borrowing, 1973-82 (billions of US$)

	1974	1975	1976	1977	1978	1979	1980	1981	1982
Total debt (a)	160.8	190.8	228.0	278.5	336.3	396.9	474.0	555.0	612.4
New borrowing net (b)		30.0	37.2	50.5	57.8	60.6	77.1	81.0	57.4
Interest payments (c)	9.3	10.5	10.9	13.6	19.4	28.0	40.4	55.1	59.2
Ratio (c)/(b)		0.35	0.29	0.27	0.34	0.46	0.52	0.68	1.03

Source: Cline (1983).

83

Build-up of Debt

financial terms due to the increase in the amount of
disbursements due. A relevant element is the
shortening of debt profiles and the bunching of
maturities which forced borrowers to try to raise
new loans to meet preexisting commitments (see tab.
5.8).
    This deterioration has a counterpart on the
lenders' side with the deterioration of exposure
positions and capital asset ratios mentioned above.
As borrowers found it increasingly difficult to meet
their payment commitments, banks were pulled in
"involuntary lending" in order to keep credit
relations with borrowers "open" thus avoiding the
risk of (effective) bankruptcies.
    The spread of involuntary lending produced a
qualitative change in international credit
relations. As long as new loans were raised for
balance of payments or even development financing
one could deduce that international credit markets
were working in "equilibrium" conditions in the
sense that the loans granted reflected "normal"
demand and supply behaviour. Once involuntary
lending assumed a relevant part of new credit
operations demand and supply of credit reflected an
increasing state of financial distress in the system.
    The deterioration in financial relations was
accompanied by a tremendous change in general
economic conditions. This is reflected in all major
macroeconomic indicators. Payments capabilities of
borrowers were hit by a pronounced decline in export
volumes, due to a relevant fall in the growth rates
of the OECD economies, as well as in export values
due to the deterioration in terms of trade and in
the value of the dollar which increased both the
cost of imports for developing countries and the
dollar value of their outstanding debt.
    General credit conditions also deteriorated due
to the restrictive stance followed by monetary
policies in the largest OECD countries and in
particular in the US. This increased the cost of new
borrowing while decreasing the amount of new funds
that the banks were willing to supply.
    Finally the balance of payments problems of
indebted countries were further aggravated by the
second oil shock. In this case, however, the effects
on borrowers were different as some indebted oil
exporting countries such as Mexico and Venezuela
benefited from the increase in the price of oil.
    As the rate of growth of exports fell below the

Table 5.9. Export growth rates and interest rates, 1973-82 (percentage changes)

	1973	1974	1975	1976	1977	1978	1979	1980	1981	1982
Libor+1 percent	10.2	12.0	8.0	6.6	7.0	9.7	13.0	15.4	17.5	14.1
Export growth rates										
Non oil dev. count.	---	36.4	1.4	16.5	21.2	17.2	28.9	26.1	5.8	-3.8
Net oil importers	---	33.1	1.6	16.3	21.9	16.9	26.8	24.2	5.4	-3.8
Net oil exporters	---	57.3	0.1	18.9	18.8	18.0	40.4	35.4	7.8	-3.6
Brazil	56.1	33.2	6.1	13.5	19.7	7.2	24.2	29.3	15.7	-13.4
Mexico	26.8	31.6	-0.2	13.3	14.0	39.1	40.2	54.3	21.9	7.3
Argentina	61.6	25.8	-23.9	30.8	43.6	16.3	26.6	13.0	5.1	-15.7
Venezuela	54.4	126.8	-15.7	2.8	5.5	-0.8	50.2	36.4	10.1	-22.0
Chile	49.0	60.1	-21.7	31.7	8.1	13.8	59.0	32.2	-2.6	-3.8

Source: Cline (1983).

Table 5.10. Net inflow (+), or outflow (−) of funds 6 months prior to debt crisis (mid 1982)

US$ million	Total	of which			
		Term debt	Short term	Unused credit	Interest
Chile	+259	+716	+503	−9	−951
Mexico	+2403	+3452	+3825	+281	−5155
Peru	+467	+110	+693	+62	−398
Argentina	−2558	−420	+796	−789	−2145
Brazil	−1588	+2443	+325	+388	−4741
Ecuador	−353	−13	+188	−122	−406
Philippines	−2030	−288	−98	−462	−1182
Venezuela	−2475	+912	−687	−914	−1786
Yugoslavia	−1254	−57	−89	−263	−845

Source: American Express Bank.

rate of interest that developing countries had to pay on their debt their potential demand for loans (see tab 5.9) increased rather than the opposite (3).Interest on debt increased also because banks tried to increase risk insurance as they perceived that the borrowers' ability to pay was decreasing. As a consequence individual risk aversion increased the overall riskiness of the system.

As data reported in table 5.10 show, in the months immediately preceding the crisis (13) all major borrowers witnessed a net outflow of funds, most of which is to be imputed to interest payments, the amount of which could not be met even by a resort to short term credit.

NOTES

1. A more detailed analysis of the behaviour of primary commodity prices is presented in the appendix to chapter 10.

2. US banks were exposed largely towards Latin American countries while European banks were exposed mostly towards Eastern European economies. See Moffit 1983.

3. That is if a well behaved model of growth-cum-debt were to hold. See the discussion in chapter 9.

4. The months preceding the debt crisis differ for different countries involved.

Chapter Six

THE CRISIS OF 1982-84

Between 1982 and 1984 almost all the indebted
countries of the Third World as well as of the
eastern European bloc were forced to declare some
form of debt disruption and to start negotiations
with the IMF and or with the private banks for the
rescheduling of their debts (see tab 6.1). This
state of affairs sharply contrasts with the
experience of the previous decade. As is shown in
table 6.2 since the first oil shock the number of
multilateral debt negotiations had been relatively
small although increasing with the approach of the
new decade. Only after 1982 did the big borrowers -
Brazil, Argentina, Mexico and Venezuela - officially
enter into a situation of debt disruption and open
debt rescheduling negotiations. In this respect the
debt crisis of 1982-84 is mainly a Latin American
crisis (1) and it reflects the concentration of
borrowers and lenders which was discussed in the
previous chapter.
    The situation of distress in which the
international financial system collapsed is also
reflected in the abrupt slowdown in international
lending after more than a decade of very rapid
expansion. The slowdown starts before the Mexican
declaration of suspension of payments in the summer
of 1982 indicating that the banks had already
perceived the state of difficulty into which debt
relations were precipitating. A concise idea of the
slowdown may be obtained from the data presented in
table 6.3 which reports the dramatic drop in the
rate of growth of debt towards the banking system
after 1982 for the Latin American borrowers.
    The situation of widespread financial distress
which emerged at the beginning of 1982 opens a
period of convulsive negotiations and for several

88

The Crisis of 1982-84

Table 6.1. Requests for IMF rescue intervention or
          debt rescheduling 1982-84

	IMF	Debt rescheduling
Argentina	yes	yes
Bolivia	no	yes
Brazil	yes	yes
Chile	yes	yes
Costa Rica	yes	yes
Ecuador	yes	yes
El Salvador	yes	yes
Guatemala	yes	no
Honduras	yes	yes
Mexico	yes	yes
Nicaragua	no	yes
Panama	yes	no
Peru	yes	yes
Dominica	yes	yes
Uruguay	yes	yes
Venezuela	no	yes

months fears of a generalized collapse spread
throughout the international banking community and
the international system as a whole. The rest of
this chapter is devoted to a synthetic description
of the events of the period whose outcome, at the
moment of writing, is not yet clearly defined. We
will not follow a strict chronological order, rather
we will stress the behaviour of the actors involved
during rescue operations and during the recovery
which materialized in the second half of 1984.
Before doing that, however, we will briefly discuss
the change in the economic and financial policy of
the United States in 1979, which was responsible for
the dramatic alterations in the international
environment, and the US policy shift in 1982 which
may be in part considered as a reaction to the
outbreak of the debt crisis.

Changes in United States policy
     In October 1979 the Federal Reserve announced
that it was altering the procedures to control
monetary conditions by setting money supply targets.
The discount rate was raised by a full point while
the marginal reserve requirement in managed

liabilities of banks was increased by 8 per cent.
The Treasury Department also announced that it would
no longer hold gold auctions on a regular basis.
This represented a major change in monetary policy
which, for the past ten years, had been based on the
pegging of the Federal funds rate at a level
believed to be consistent with the desired rate of
growth of the money supply. After October 1979 the
American monetary authorities intended to estimate
the volume of bank reserves consistent with the
money supply targets and then let the market forces
determine the rate on Federal funds.

The immediate effect of the new monetary
measures was an increase in short term interest
rates which rose to positive levels after having
been negative for such a long while (2) and started
making dollar investments more attractive relatively
to investments denominated in other currencies.

The foreign exchange markets also responded
immediately. The dollar regained ground against all
major currencies including the DM, the Japanese yen,
and the British pound. In this respect the new
actions taken by the Fed were different from those
taken almost a year before when massive dollar
support operations were implemented in a moment of
particular weakness of the dollar.

The new course in US monetary policy represented
a major change also because it reversed an inflation
depreciation trend of the American currency which,
although with alternating phenomena, had been going
on for several years after the collapse of the
Bretton Woods system at the beginning of the decade.

This change in policy may be considered
something more than just a switch from a gradualist
policy against inflation to a more aggressive
attitude towards monetary restraint. It may also be
considered as a unilateral reaction of US
authorities to the failure of the attempt to agree
on a joint currency intervention to sustain the
dollar in currency markets with the monetary
authorities of other major countries and of Germany
in particular. It was, in other words, a reaction to
the failure of the oligopolists to reach a
cooperative agreement.

What turned out to be perhaps an even more
dramatic consequence of the policy shift was the
reaction of the US banking system to the new
measures. The effect of the new credit reserve
requirements started a reaction on the part of the
banking firms which introduced an increasing set of

Table 6.2. Multilateral debt renegotiations 1974-82

	1974	1975	1976	1977	1978	1979	1980	1981	1982
Argentina			C						
Bolivia							C	C	
Brazil									
Chile	P	P							
Costa Rica									
Ecuador									
Gabon					P				
Ghana	P								
Guyana						C			C
India	A	A	A	A					
Jamaica						C		C	
Liberia							P	P	C
Madagascar								P	P
Malawi									P C
Mexico									
Nicaragua							C	C	C
Pakistan	A							A	
Peru			C		P C		C		
Senegal								P	P C
Sudan						P		C	P
Togo						P	C	P	
Turkey					A	A C	A		C
Uganda								P	P
Zaire			P	P		P	C	P	

A = Aid Consortia Renesotiations; C = Commercial Banks Agreements;

P = Paris Club Agreements

Table 6.3. Latin American countries: total debt and
rate of change of debt versus private banks 1979-83

	1979	1980	1981	1982	1983
All Latin American borrowers billions of US$	131.3	162.9	196.7	214.5	222.1
% change	38.4	24.1	20.7	9.1	3.6
5 major debtors billions of US$	108.7	139.8	171.3	188.1	195.9
% change	38.2	28.7	22.5	9.8	4.1

Source: Bank for International Settlements.

Table 6.4. Capital asset ratios of US banks 1977-83
(in percent)

	1977	1978	1979	1980	1981	1982	1983
Largest 10 banks	4.17	4.06	3.95	4.02	4.23	4.70	5.41
Largest 25 banks	4.52	4.41	4.31	4.39	4.57	4.98	5.58
Large banks with foreign offices		4.58	4.47	4.49	4.54	4.62	4.48

Source: International Monetary Fund.

financial innovations in the attempt to reaquire
part of the freedom that the new measures had
limited (Dufey and Giddy 1981). As far as the
international debt problem is concerned the short
term effect of the measures of the Fed was not so
much to decrease the amount of lending to sovereign
borrowers but rather to increase the cost of the
borrowing and debt servicing requirements. As we
have seen above, the slowdown in international
lending did not materialize immediately after the
implementation of the new measures. The expansion of
bank credit continued during the following two years
although at a decreasing pace. An abrupt slowdown
did not materialize until the deterioration of the
credit positions emerged in 1982.
The relatively slow adaptation to the new
monetary environment was, however, somehow expected.
The official justification for the shift in monetary
policy was the antiinflationary commitment. This in
turn required, in the logic of the new monetary
strategy, that the markets had to change their
expectations about monetary expansion and hence
their inflationary expectations. It was a general
opinion that change in expectations had to be a long
and painful process on account of the long duration
of the expansionary environment which had ruled for
several years before. A fundamental condition for
the new antiinflationary policy to be successful,
however, was a parallel action toward fiscal
restraint which would have decreased the financing
requirements of the federal deficit. The new Reagan
administration, however, did not reverse the trend
towards a growing budget deficit while the monetary
measures continued to follow the restrictive course
(3). Consequently the tendency towards rising
interest rates was not reversed and the
international financial environment rapidly assumed
the configuration recalled above.
The other fundamental shift in US policy which
we need to consider is the one which occurred in
October 1982 right after the explosion of the
international debt crisis. The discount rate was
lowered in October by half a percentage point. More
importantly the Fed decided to abandon control of
monetary aggregate M1 and to set targets for the
broader monetary aggregates M2 and M3.
The reasons behind this policy shift are
complex. In the first place, the substantial
improvement on the antiinflationary front and the
renewed strength of the dollar had opened the way

for a somewhat easier monetary conduct also taking account of the difficulty of the American economy in picking up a recovery. However this does not fully explain the decision to change the intermediate monetary targets. An additional reason was that the control of M1 had proved to be much more difficult than expected. In the two previous years the trend in M1 had gone out of preset targets on several occasions. This was due both to the fact that money velocity had varied more than expected and to the fact that financial innovations had posed increasing obstacles to the action of monetary authorities (4). The shift to broader monetary aggregates imposed a change also on the philosophy of US monetary policy as the control of these aggregates implies a higher degree of discretion than the control of M1 which was conducted along lines which involved a larger amount of automaticity.

Though official comments and analysis of the 1982 monetary policy shifts do not emphasize the point one of the reasons which led the American authorities to such a change was the disruptive effect that previous monetary measures had produced on interest rates which had soared to unprecedented levels.

During 1982 the Fed became increasingly concerned with the mounting fragility problems that the banking institutions were finding in their lending operations with big sovereign borrowers (5). Capital asset ratios had been decreasing below reasonable safety levels for a number of years. On the other hand, the much higher level of interest rates, the mounting dollar and economic stagnation had started to produce concern about the soundness of these lending operations and, given their size and concentration, the dangerous effects that they could produce on the entire financial system (see tab 6.4).

These stylized facts are not in contrast with the framework we have presented in chapter 4 about the operational guidelines of US monetary and economic policy. A restrictive stance arises when inflation is too high and or when the weakness of the dollar is considered too dangerous for the international financial position of the United States. A more expansionary policy is pursued once inflation and currency behaviour are brought back onto a satisfactory path while signs of distress arise from the financial markets. What these major monetary policy shifts show, however, is that policy

Table 6.5. Mexico: total external debt, 1976-83
(billions of US$)

	1976	1977	1978	1979	1980	1981	1982	1983
Public debt								
Short term	3.7	2.7	1.2	1.4	1.5	10.8	9.3	9.7
Medium-long term	15.9	20.2	25.5	28.3	32.3	42.2	49.5	51.2
Mexican banks	1.6	1.8	2.0	2.6	5.1	7.0	8.0	8.0
Private debt	4.9	5.0	5.2	7.9	11.8	14.9	18.0	18.0
Total	26.1	29.7	33.9	40.2	50.7	74.9	84.8	86.9
Percentage change		13.8	14.1	18.6	26.1	47.7	13.2	2.5

Source: Secretaria de Hacienda y Credito Publico.

Table 6.6. Mexico: selected indicators 1978-82

	1978	1979	1980	1981	1982
Total debt/Gdp (%)	33.0	29.9	27.2	31.2	50.5
Debt service ratio (%)	63.9	66.7	36.1	42.3	52.7

Source: International Monetary Fund.

changes are not just shifts in emphasis of direction
of monetary policy. Rather a qualitative change is
involved in both cases. An additional trade-off with
respect to the traditional expansion restriction one
is involved: that between discretion and automatic
rules in monetary and financial policy.

The collapse of the big borrowers

The October 1982 shift in US monetary policy
closely followed the Mexican declaration of debt
default in August of the same year. During the
following two years the international financial
community, as well as the governments involved,
engaged in an often desperate battle for the
containment of what many feared to be the biggest
financial crash of the century. Although the
international debt crisis of the eighties should be
considered from a systemic point of view we will
briefly review the behaviour of some of the big
borrowers on the occasion as this provides useful
insights on the whole story.

The Mexican experience is particularly
interesting as Mexico, besides being a big borrower,
is also an oil producing country. In this respect it
could be argued (Cline 1983) that the "oil rent"
represented an additional incentive for the policy
of foreign indebtedness followed by Mexican
authorities.

Between 1981 and the first half of 1982 a number
of events rapidly led to the deterioration of
Mexico's financial position, all of which had to be
ascribed to a changing international environment:
the fall in oil prices, the slowdown in
international lending and the rise of interest
rates. These factors increased the difficulties in
foreign exchange earnings which had been produced by
the overvaluation of the peso and the subsequent
deterioration of non-oil trade. The international
banks had already perceived the difficulty of the
Mexican economy to continue on its debt financed
growth process and had started both to decrease new
lending and to shorten maturities. In spite of that
Mexico had collected in 1981 new net funds for over
24 billion dollars which represented an increase of
almost 48 per cent with respect to the previous year
(see tab 6.5). This dramatic rate of increase, which
was largely necessary to service preexisting debt,
was unsustainable and effectively collapsed in the
following year also due to the sharp deterioration

of creditworthiness indicators (see tab 6.6). In
addition the overall situation had been further
deteriorated by increasing capital outflows from the
Mexican economy.

The reaction of the authorities concentrated on
the devaluation of the peso which fell by 68 per
cent with respect to the dollar in a few weeks. As
was to be expected the current account further
deteriorated while domestic inflation soared.
Domestic demand was on the contrary encouraged
through fiscal cuts and wage increases. In May 1982
an attempt to float new loans failed almost
completely as most of the banks refused to subscribe
to the request. After that a dramatic sequence of
events ultimately led to the decision to suspend
payments. A two-tier currency market was established
while forced conversion of foreign currency deposits
of residents was imposed. On September 1 the Mexican
commercial banks were nationalized. Previously, on
August 20, the servicing of foreign debt was
suspended for 90 days while negotiations with the
IMF were started.

It is not possible to discuss at length here the
process which led to the suspension decision. It is
worth recalling, however, that it was later
disclosed that one of the reasons was the attempt of
Mexican authorities to draw the attention of the
United States authorities to the mounting of the
dangerous situation while pressures for unilateral
repudiation were mounting inside the country (6).

Contrary to Mexico, Brazil is an oil importer.
This however has not kept its debt situation from
deteriorating as well (Diaz-Alejandro 1983). In this
respect the Brazilian debt crisis represents a clear
example of how a process of increasing
overindebtedness is not related to a sort of "energy
rent" deriving from oil. Rather it derives from an
industrialization process which required that an
increasing share of resources be devoted to exports
in order to finance growing imports. The rise in the
price of oil in 1979 increased recourse to
international credit markets to finance trade
deficits (although this attempt was not initially
successful and the authorities had to draw down
their international reserves). This policy was also
followed in 1980 when the government increased
foreign borrowing only to service preexisting debt.
In 1981 the situation seemed to improve as the trade
deficit had been reduced (see tab 6.7) thanks to a
negative rate of growth of Gdp of 1.9 per cent. The

The Crisis of 1982-84

restrictive policy adopted by the government had
allowed for a limited pick up in capital inflow. The
following year, however, the beneficial effects of
the restrictive policy on the trade balance had
practically vanished and the balance on current
account had again started to deteriorate. The
tremendous drawing down of international reserves
precipitated the Brazilian economy into what seemed
to be a liquidity crisis but which later turned out
to be an insolvency crisis as the difficulties in
debt negotiations both with the banks and the IMF
would show.

From the second half of 1982 the drama of
Brazilian debt exploded. Between August and
September 1982 the foreign branches of Brazilian
banks suffered heavy deposits withdrawals while
official reserves fell by 2 billion dollars. In
October, although the situation was precipitating,
also on account of Mexican developments, the
government announced that no negotiations would be
started with the banks or the IMF before the
elections which were to be held in November. In
November the request of the Brazilian governor
Langoni for bridge financing was largely ignored
while only major American banks provided new funds
for 600 million dollars. The US Treasury Department
provided 1.2 billion dollars as a bridge finance in
December while negotiations with the IMF started.
Also in December the Brazilian government called a
conference with the major lending banks in an
attempt to implement negotiations without resorting
to IMF intermediation. Although new funds were
obtained from both the banks and the IMF, at the
beginning of January 1983 Brazil announced the
suspension of repayment of public debt while the IMF
received the first letter of intent.

Argentina's story is different again. It
appeared on the scene as a debtor in crisis somewhat
later than the other two big borrowers. The interest
in its case lies in the fact that the new democratic
government which emerged from the general election
following the fall of the military regime after the
Falklands war put an extraordinary effort into
trying to set up a debtors cartel with the other
large borrowers. The Argentina debt crisis
officially broke out in 1984 after the other big
borrowers had worked through the most delicate
moments of their debt negotiations, although debt
rescheduling problems had appeared contemporaneously
with the other borrowers several months before. In

98

Table 6.7. Brazil: balance of payments 1978-82
(billions of US$)

	1978	1979	1980	1981	1982
Current account	-7.	-10.6	-12.8	-11.8	-16.3
Bank loans	9.4	3.6	7.5	10.5	5.0
Other capital mov.	1.9	2.9	1.9	2.3	2.5
Errors and omissions	0.3	1.2	-0.3	-0.4	-0.4
Change in reserves *	-4.5	2.9	3.7	-0.6	9.2

* minus indicates increase.
Source: International Monetary Fund.

Table 6.8. Major rescue operations as of January
1983 (billions of US$)

	Total debt	IMF package	BIS bridge	New bank loans	Bank resched.
Mexico	83.0	3.8	1.85	5.0	19.75
Argentina	39.0	2.2	0.5	1.1	5.5
Brazil	89.0	6.0	1.2	4.4	4.0
Yugoslavia	19.0	0.65	0.5	0.75	1.0
Romania	10.0	0.36			0.86
Ecuador	4.8				1.22
Chile	17.0	0.9			2.8
Cuba	3.0				
Uruguay	3.0	0.4			0.5

Source: Financial Times.

this respect Argentina's debt is partly a result of
the war which had been lost by the military regime.
The new government declared that it would not
recognize debt obligations that had been taken up by
the military regime and claimed a tough standing
with the IMF on the rescheduling of debt which had
fallen due in 1982. In other words the big problem
with Argentina was the political attitude toward
debt more than its economic aspect.

The climax of the debtor club attempt was
reached in Cartagena in June 1984 (7) when the group
of Latin American hard line countries, which include
Bolivia, the Dominican Republic and Ecuador, in
addition to Argentina, failed to convince the
remaining seven governments to form a debtor club to
seek easier debt repayment conditions for the
borrowing countries of the region collectively
considered. The strongest opposition came from
Brazil and Mexico, whose size and bargaining power
were large enough to defeat the attempt. The
Argentinian delegation was recommended that their
government reach an agreement with the IMF as
quickly as possible. As a result of these pressures,
as well as those deriving from the US government,
Argentina changed its attitude and an agreement with
the banks was reached in the following days (8).

Rescue operations: the Fund between borrowers and lenders

The debt crisis into which big borrowers such as
Mexico and Brazil and a number of smaller indebted
countries could have precipitated was at first
avoided, and then slowly steered towards a safer
situation largely as a consequence of the leading
role taken up by the International Monetary Fund
whose rescue operations planned in mid 1984 are
displayed in table 6.8. At the end of 1982 the
International Monetary Fund had taken up a
completely new position in international debt
negotiations with respect to previous years. Not
only its quantitative involvement in credit
concession to borrowing countries had increased or
was due to do so in the years ahead but, what is
more important, its role in debt negotiations had
changed.

It could be argued that the novelty of the role
of the Fund lies not so much in the fact that hard
negotiations had to be carried out with indebted
countries but that hard negotiations had to be

carried out also with creditors and that a policy
conflict emerged vis-à-vis the larger member
countries of the IMF and with the United States in
particular.   The
financial resources the Fund could draw upon to
provide balance of payments financing was limited
with respect to the debt repayment commitments of
the borrowers. Consequently the Fund had to raise
extraordinary loans from financially healthy
countries. In 1983 the Fund negotiatied 6 billion
dollars' worth of new loans, half of which came from
Saudi Arabia and the rest from Europe and Japan
while the United States refused to participate in
the deal and some opposition had also come from the
German monetary authorities (9). The resort to new
extraordinary lending was partly the result of the
difficulties the Fund had faced in raising quotas in
1982, in the middle of the debt crisis, due in
particular to opposition from the United States
Congress which claimed that the US contribution to
the Fund's financial resources (control of which was
not in American hands) had become unbearably high.
Only in mid 1983 did the Fund obtain a 47 per cent
increase in quotas and an expansion of the General
Agreement to Borrow. In those months a debate arose
whether the Fund should resort to more borrowing or
to quota increases in order to bolster its
resources. Although the debate was not settled, the
episode significantly showed how, when the Fund's
initiative was most needed, its institutional
structure, based on quotas, largely limited its
power and reproduced a collective action conflict
within the institution itself (Dreyer and Schotter
1980).
　　The other front on which the IMF was called to
take a stand were the negotiations with the private
banks on the extension of funding to the borrowing
countries. The most difficult problem the Fund had
to face was to convince the smaller banks which had
participated in syndicated lending to sovereign
borrowers to provide new money in order to sustain
the rescue packages. As negotiations with big
borrowers have shown smaller banks were much less
willing than larger banks to participate in
rescheduling programs. Whereas the larger banks had
no choice but to continue financing the insolvent
borrowers given the huge dimension of their
exposure, small banks were much more reluctant on
the grounds that they saw no immediate reason for
"throwing good money after bad" and that if they did

so they would be diverting resources from more profitable opportunities (10).

Smaller banks have been judging negatively their experience in sovereign lending as this had not produced, contrary to what had happened for large banks, any advantage in terms of customer relationship and or ancillary business. Smaller banks saw the request to participate in rescue operations as a form of expropriation of their right to manage their own strategies. Finally the relatively small shares of loans that each single bank had involved in sovereign debt with respect to the total amount of debt of each single borrower encouraged free riding attitudes on the part of the small banks as no one of them would admit that to keep the borrower afloat would depend on its own decision to keep on lending. In convincing small banks to agree on rescheduling programs the IMF was eventually supported by the larger banks who had a much greater interest in keeping the borrowers afloat. In so doing the problem of the IMF was to convince the borrowers to implement adjustment programs which the banks considered the necessary condition for the new loans. This reproduced a phenomenon which is a traditional feature of international banking history, the close relation between financial negotiations and the domestic political affairs of the borrowers. One of the most instructive examples is the role which the approval of a wage law by the Brazilian congress had in starting the flow of new credit from the banks at the end of 1983 after months of convulsive negotiations worldwide.

It has been recognized that one of the positive effects of the crisis was to greatly improve cooperation between the IMF and the banks (11). Before the crisis broke out both sides were much less enthusiastic about cooperation. The IMF was reluctant to pass information on to banks and the banks were reluctant to heed IMF warnings to improve the quality of their loans in a period in which things seemed to be going so well. On the other hand, the borrowers were very reluctant to call for IMF surveillance when the private banks could provide larger amounts of funds at much lower political costs. It was only after the outbreak of the crisis that both parties recognized that much closer cooperation in periods of tranquillity could have avoided much of later troubles and that, in general, the relations which the international

financial markets had built up in the periods of
tranquillity carried the seeds of their disruption.

The IMF, however, has not always been able to
carry out this intermediation role with the banks on
its own. In some cases precious support has come
from the central banks of industrialized countries
and in particular from the governor of the Federal
Reserve, Volcker, even if this was provided with
hesitation due to the different views which
prevailed in the United States with respect to IMF
policy towards the indebted countries. On other
occasions, as in the case of Venezuela's debt, the
IMF was completely left out of the negotiations
which the country undertook directly with the banks.
Even in this case, however, an intermediation role
was necessary and the Federal Reserve exerted strong
pressure on the banks to enter into the deal once a
non-IMF monitored adjustment plan had been approved.

Even if the case should not be overstressed
these episodes suggest that the IMF faces
competition problems with monetary authorities of
larger (oligopolistic) countries and that, although
its role has been greatly strengthened by the debt
crisis, its institutional position is still far from
being precisely defined.

Consequences of the rescue plans: the borrowers
    In the middle of 1984 the international
financial scene appeared to have substantially
improved with respect to twenty months earlier when
the crisis had exploded. Several major debtors had
greatly improved their position thanks to dramatic
changes in their current and trade balances while
economic growth had resumed after several years of
recession (12). The financial climate was also eased
following the progress made by the two major
borrowers, Mexico and Brazil, in meeting their
repayment commitments. Perhaps the most evident sign
that the panic climate had vanished was represented
by the fact that many of the borrowers that had been
in serious difficulty in the previous months (13)
could resort to international credit markets for
fresh lending. The fact that most of the indebted
countries had come out of a difficult position is
also indicated by the new political initiative taken
by the borrowers themselves in the attempt to
stabilize the new relations that had been created
with the international banking community. In March
1984 Mexico, Brazil, Colombia and Venezuela lent

around $300 millions to Argentina to meet its short term requirements.

The interpretation of this event is mostly political. As we have seen, Argentina has been the country which, among the big borrowers had most delayed the agreement of a rescheduling program with the IMF and the private banks and it has been the country that more than any other has pushed for the formation of a debtors cartel which, in turn, has been severely opposed by Brazil and Mexico. The move by the big four borrowers was aimed at establishing a somewhat softer attitude towards lenders while trying to avoid that the political attitude of the new Argentine government could produce undesirable tensions in a still extremely fragile environment. The action of the big four might in fact have been more precious to the banks than to Argentina itself and, in this respect, may be interpreted as an example of oligopolistic cooperation in the supply of a public good for the whole financial community.

The causes of the improvement in the debt situation may be found in the combination of a shift in the policy of the borrowers and the boost provided by the expansion of the US economy (in spite of the increase in interest rates which accompanied it).

The aggregate current account deficits of sixteen developing countries, which together account for about 60 per cent of the total LDC debt, was projected to narrow to about $12 billions in 1984 from about $55 billions in 1981 (14). The biggest improvement was registred by Mexico and Brazil (see tab 6.9). The policy strategy followed by the borrowers centred both on import substitution and on the support of export performance through the compression of internal demand, the devaluation of the currency and severe policies of wage restraint while capital outflows have also decreased. This produced an improvement in short term financial positions which allowed the big borrowers to seek for fresh lending. The costs borne by the countries have however been extremely high, both in terms of the fall in per capita incomes and of inflationary explosions which followed the devaluations (15). Soaring inflation is the result of a reallocation of resources towards the export oriented sectors and it has been accompanied by substantial cuts in the national debt through the compression of subsidies and transfers to the private sector.

The short run success of big borrowers in

Table 6.9. Improvement in trade and current account between 1981 and 1984 (billions of US$) (*)

	Current account	Trade in goods and noninterest services	Interest payments
Argentina	2.7	4.9	-2.1
Brazil	9.5	10.9	-1.4
Chile	2.8	3.1	-0.3
Colombia	-0.3	-0.1	-0.2
Ecuador	0.8	0.9	-0.1
Mexico	16.4	20.2	-3.7
Peru	0.8	0.8	0.0
Venezuela	-3.6	-1.9	-1.6
Subtotal	29.2	38.7	-9.5
Nigeria	5.5	6.3	-0.8
Philippines	0.7	1.8	-1.1
Indonesia	-2.9	-2.3	-0.6
Korea	2.8	3.2	-0.4
Malaysia	0.2	0.8	-0.6
Taiwan	5.9	5.8	0.1
Thailand	0.6	0.6	0.0
Turkey	0.8	1.2	-0.5
Subtotal	13.6	17.5	-3.9
Total	42.8	56.2	-13.4

(*) Negative sign indicates deterioration in current account and trade
    balance or increase in interest payments.
Source: World Financial Markets.

The Crisis of 1982-84

meeting their rescheduling commiments might produce
undesirable consequences in two critical areas.
Internal political stability might be threatened by
mounting inflation and massive income redistribution
to the foreign sector. Import substitution policies
might enhance protectionistic pressures while signs
exist of moves towards new forms of bilateral trade
(16). Both elements may be signs that the short term
success of the rescue plans could be traded off with
heavier medium term costs in national and
international conflicts.

Consequences of the rescue plan: the lenders
The road towards improved performance by the
borrowers has had contrasting impacts on the
international banking community. On the one hand
commercial banks, by slowing down the growth of
their loans and by building up their capital and
reserves, have succeeded in reducing their capital
asset ratios from risk peak levels of 1982. Ratios
of claims on loss to primary capital at US center
banks have decreased considerably from 1982 to 1984
while most of the loans have been succesfully
recheduled. However right in the period in which the
debt situation of big borrowers seemed to have
turned away from the crisis point of 1982 the
international financial community was swept by a
wave of panic as a number of large banks were hit by
clear signs of financial distress which at times
evolved into bankruptcy episodes.
Curiously enough the major cases of financial
distress, which led to the crash of Continental
Illinois after a run on its deposits in early May
1984, were not directly tied to sovereign debt but
rather to loans in the energy sector. The
Continental episode was the climax of a particulary
bad period for American banks. In 1983 more American
banks failed than in any year since 1940 (17).
Shortly after the Continental episode a number of
major banks, most of which were heavily exposed
towards the Latin American borrowers and which
included Manufactures Hanover, Chase Manhattan,
Morgan Guaranty suffered heavy losses in the stock
exchange after rumours of difficulties that they
were facing in their cash operations (18). A typical
phenomemon of banking panic developed. Even if the
debt situation of big borrowers had past its most
difficult point, the market reacted through
increasing panic simply on the basis that the

106

financial fragility produced by the debt situation
might suddenly break out even if no explicit debt
disruption were to materialize. The London Stock
Exchange was hit by a strong fall following the
announcement of the decision of the Bolivian
government to suspend repayments of debt until the
economic situation had not recovered. Comparing it
with the 1982 decision of Mexico to suspend debt
service there was a clear disproportion as Bolivia
is not included among the world's ten largest
borrowers. In those weeks a sort of pre-crash
psychology hit the markets. Transactions seemed to
be determined more by statements of key market
operators than by anything else. The situation of
panic was overcome soon after the major central
banks announced that they would not allow the
difficult position of a number of commercial banks
to spread the disease throughout the market. On May
24 1984 Preston Martin, vice chairman of the US
Federal Reserve Board, announced that the Fed was
prepared to "lend, lend boldly and keep on lending"
(19) to face any other liquidity problems that might
arise. As in 1982 lender of last resort operations
helped to restore tranquillity in the short term
even if on this occasion no major shift in US
monetary policy took place.

    As had been the case for the borrowers, the
lenders found a way out of the crisis through the
help of institutions (which provided the public good
of creditworthiness by their prompt action).
However, as in the case of the borrowers, it could
not be said that the medium term problems had been
overcome. For the international financial community
the big source of trouble had not been dissipated.
Rather it seemed to have been pushed into a
different corner of the financial system and to have
taken on characteristics which may turn out to be
even more disruptive than those associated with the
LDC debt problem. Namely the worrying developments
in the financial position of the United States to
which we will turn in the final chapter of the book.

The need for a general explanation
    A long debated issue is whether the increasing
deterioration of debt relations at the end of the
past decade was the result of irresponsible
behaviour on the part of the borrowing countries, or
even of an excessive easiness of international banks
in pursuing high risk lending policies, while others

stress the effect of the highly permissive
international environment determined by the
expansionary policies followed by the US
administration and the consequences on lending
policies.

To look for one sided responsibilities does not
help much in the search for an overall assessment of
financial instability which mounted in the 1970s and
exploded at the beginning of the present decade. It
is always possible to enucleate single policy
choices of each of the actors involved and show how
different strategies might have eased the situation
and avoided the dramatic events of 1982-84 (see e.g.
Diaz-Alejandro 1984). However the changes in the
international environment which took place after
1979 would probably not have produced a crisis of
the amplitude and depth which occurred at the
beginning of the decade if they had not precipitated
in an intrinsically fragile financial environment.

The debt crisis is the outcome of the
interaction of all actors involved. Such an
interaction, in addition, is more complex than the
one resulting from borrower-lender relations which
is sometimes discussed.(see e.g. Sachs 1982, 1984).
Developing countries and international banks have
built up their credit relations in an international
environment whose evolution was only partially the
result of their direct behaviour. The evolution of
the international environment largely reflects the
behaviour of oligopolistic interdependence among
leading industrial countries. In addition
international institutions such as the IMF have
played a leading role in the management of the
crisis reaquiring a position which previous events
had somewhat weakened.

Sheer recognition of actors' interdependence
however is not sufficent to produce a new assessment
of international financial problems. What is badly
needed is a conceptual framework explaining how a
financially sophisticated system evolves and how it
develops into a highly fragile structure. Such a
framework should be able to account not just for how
such a system reaches some equilibrium point (if
any) but it should also explain why such a system
eventually produces financial distress.

In addition an interpretative framework is
needed to assess the problems of crisis management
discussed in this chapter in order to go beyond a
mere description of events.

Theoretical work on such problems seems

curiously inadequate if one reflects on the fact
that financial crises and systemwide bankruptcy have
been a recurring feature of capitalist development
for centuries (Kindleberger 1978a). Economic theory
has largely ignored these problems in the past and
only recently contributions have appeared which try
to tackle the topic. Some of this literature will be
discussed in chapter 9. In the next chapter we will
present a conceptual framework elaborated by
H.Minsky (1975, 1982a) and we will extend it to an
international system. Such a framework should by no
means be considered as a fully workable model.
Rather it should be viewed as a first step towards a
better understanding of international financial
instability.

NOTES

1. For an assessment of the East European debt
crisis see Chapman 1984.
2. See World Financial Markets, October 1979.
3. See World Financial Markets, October 1979.
4. See World Financial Markets, November 1979.
5. The Fed was also concerned about the
exposure of banks with respect to American firms.
6. P. Montagnon, Us Ignored Mexican Warning,
Financial Times, July 25, 1984.
7. See H. O'Shaughnessy, Brazil Mexico Bloc
Debtor Plan, Financial Times, 23 June, 1984.
8. P. Montagnon, Argentina and Banks Reach Debt
Agreement, Financial Times, 30 June, 1984.
9. Pohel Gives Warning of Limit to Bonn Finance
for IMF, Financial Times, 20 October, 1983.
10. P. Montagnon, Brazil Battles for the Smaller
Banks, Financial Times, 24 October 1983.
11. P. Montagnon, Banks, Imf, Shotgun Marriage,
Financial Times, 6 October 1983.
12. See World Financial Markets, November 1982.
13. P. Montagnon, Mexico to Seek Loans on Free
Markets, Financial Times, 26 November 1984.
14. See World Financial Markets, November 1984.
15. A. Kaletzky, Debt Crisis: It Could Still End
with a Bang, Financial Times, 20 February 1985.
16. P. Blum, World Debt Forces Increases in
Countertrading, Financial Times, 21 September 1984.
17. Why American Banks are Getting Broker and
Broker, The Economist, 29 October 1983.
18. For an analysis of events which leads to
this situation see Moffit 1983.
19. Fed Pledge to Maintain Us Bank Stability,
Financial Times, 25 May 1984.

Chapter Seven

FINANCIAL INSTABILITY IN A CLOSED AND IN AN
INTERNATIONAL ECONOMY

This chapter provides a theoretical framework
for the discussion of financial instability. It is
based on a model developed by Hyman Minsky in a
number of articles and books (Minsky 1975, 1982a)
which describes the mechanisms governing the
accumulation process in a financially sophisticated
capitalistic system.
    Minsky has developed his model for a closed
economy, but the main features of the model can be
extended to the international economy. In doing so,
however, we will have to take into account the fact
that in an international economy the most important
actors involved are not only banks, financial
intermediaries, and firms but also national
governments and policy authorities as well as
international institutions.
    In the sections which follow, the financial
instability model in a closed economy will be
summarized and then reformulated for application to
the international economy. As we shall see, the weak
points of Minsky's framework, i.e. the turning
points of the financial instability cycle, will have
to be thoroughly reconsidered when we turn to the
international economy. This further development of
the model will be discussed in the following chapter.

Financial instability in a closed economy
    The financial instability model is centred on
the interaction between capitalistic firms and
financial intermediaries in the accumulation process
in a situation in which the finance needed for the
investment process is largely obtained through debt.

Financial Instability

Firms take investment decisions because they have expectations of positive future profits, they raise the funds needed for their investments through credit and, by so doing, they commit themselves to future cash outflows in order to service debt.

Loans are extended by banks who do so because they expect future money incomes (interests) which will allow them to repay their own debts, i.e. interest to depositors.

Minsky assumes a Kaleckian framework. In a closed economy, this means that gross profits are determined by the level of aggregate investments (plus government expenditure) (1) which, in turn, depend on expected returns. Given the level of expected profits the amount of investments is determined by the availability of finance.

The way in which investments are decided and financed determines the financial structure of the single units (banks and firms) and of the economic system as a whole. Minsky distinguishes among three different types of financial structures.

A hedge finance unit is defined as a situation in which anticipated gross profits are larger than future payment commitments to service debt for each of the time units in which the investment life span is divided (2).

A speculative finance unit is defined as a situation in which future gross profits are lower than payments due for some periods. Usually this condition holds only for the initial periods of the investment time span and not for anticipated gross profits of the periods which follow the first ones. In the early stages of the investment project the difference between inflows and outflows of cash might be covered by further debt which is raised only in order to service the one originally raised. Additional debt will be larger the larger the number of periods in which gross profits fall short of payment commitments and also larger the higher the interest rate on debt. The anticipated gross profits of the final stages of the investment project will therefore have to be higher in order to meet these commitments.

A ponzi finance unit is defined as a situation in which anticipated future profits are higher than future payment commitments only in the last few stages of the investment project. In order to be viable a ponzi finance structure will need very high gross returns in the final stages of the project, since for all previous periods new debt will have to

111

pe raised in order to service the initial debt
commitments.

A ponzi finance unit need not be considered as
an exceptional case. Minsky (1982a) reminds us that
all long term investment projects rest on ponzi
finance as their returns become positive only after
several years from the initial moment.

A crucial characteristic of a ponzi finance unit
is that it often runs into the danger of liquidity
crises and hence the probability of resorting to new
debt just to face liquidity problems is extremely
high. As a consequence ponzi units will be more
sensitive than speculative units to rises in
interest rates which increase debt service
commitments.

In any given moment the economy may be defined
relatively more or less fragile from a financial
point of view depending on the relative share of
hedge units with respect to speculative and ponzi
units. The larger the share of the latter the more
fragile is the financial structure of the economy.

A change in the financial structure of the
economy may be produced by a rise of the interest
rate. If the interest rate rises, payments
commitments generated by past debts are increased
for a given stream of anticipated gross profits.
Hence a hedge finance unit might become a
speculative unit and a speculative unit might
collapse into a ponzi finance structure.

The mechanism of increasing fragility

A system may be defined financially robust if
modest changes in cash flows and payment commitments
do not appreciably influence the ability of units to
fulfill payment commitments.

A system is, instead, structurally fragile when
modest changes of the interest rate do significantly
affect ability to service debts and hence even small
perturbations in financial relations may lead to
widespread distress and bankruptcy.

The financial instability hypothesis holds that
financial fragility increases as the result of an
endogenous process generated by the same forces
which govern the accumulation mechanism. This
process operates as follows.

A fall in aggregate profits worsens the
financial positions of units given the level of
interest rates (and hence of outstanding payment
commitments). As a consequence hedge finance units

will turn into speculative units while original
speculative units will become ponzi units. As
aggregate profits depend on the level of aggregate
investments (Kalecki 1934) a slowdown in the
accumulation process increases the fragility of the
system as a whole.

A rise in the interest rate increases the
fragility of the system as well given the level of
aggregate investments and profits.

In both cases the cash flows of the investing
units deteriorate and new debts must be raised just
to meet previous commitments. If financial positions
deteriorate both the interest rate and the level of
profits move so as to depress the inflow of funds
even further. The interest rate rises because the
creditworthiness (3) of investing units is
negatively affected. A higher interest rate will
depress investments. The fall in aggregate
investments will lead to a fall in aggregate
profits.

This mechanism explains how financial
difficulties which may arise in a part of the
economy will eventually spread out over the whole
system. If credit conditions are tightened because
the creditworthiness of a number of firms
deteriorates even the previously sound units will be
hurt (4).

This mechanisms rests on a Keynes-Kalecki
investment function. Investments are positively
related to expected profits and negatively related
to interest rates. Investments are jointly
determined, therefore, by the interaction of the
business firms and the banking system.

Banks play an active role in the determination
of financial fragility. They too are investing units
and have an interest in promoting investments by
firms which they consider profitable since they have
to lend in order to earn the profits needed to meet
payments obligations to depositors. Banks,
therefore, might be tempted to force accumulation
decisions by providing better loan conditions to
firms in order to increase profitable investments.
As a consequence speculative and ponzi positions
might arise as a response by business firms to bank
encouragement to invest.

Easier financial conditions produce higher
overall investments and profits which validate
initial financing decisions as cash flows increase.
Higher profits lead to higher expected profits and
investments which further enhance the process.

Financial Instability

Higher investments expand the time horizon of the economy since, if finance is readily available, longer term investment opportunities become viable. This, however, increases the fragility of the system since long term investments typically assume ponzi finance structures.

One of the crucial elements here is the link between current and expected variables. Higher current profits validate financial commitments and generate expectations that the situation will go on indefinitely.

The cumulative process might be further enhanced by the presence of what Minsky calls "big government", i.e. large public expenditure which produces the same positive effect on overall profits as aggregate investments.

Turning points

This process, however, cannot go on indefinitely (5). The cumulative process we have just outlined has two dimensions. A quantitative one which relates to the expansion of investment and a qualitative one which relates to the increase in financial fragility as the percentage of hedge finance units with respect to speculative and ponzi units decreases. In other words, a situation of initial financial tranquillity cannot remain stable but naturally evolves into fragility and collapse.

The instability hypothesis helps explain the so-called "paradox of sound finance" (see Davidson 1978). If all investing units wish to assume hedge positions the amount of aggregate investment will be short of the amount needed to produce enough profits to encourage new investment and allow an expansionary movement of the economy. In order to keep their financial structure sound units (at least some of them) must assume speculative positions as this will encourage investments and generate higher profits.

Interaction of quantitative and qualitative elements suggests that financial instability is not just a cyclical movement of the economy. Rather it is something more complex which resembles a cumulative process in which turning points (i.e. the crucial components of cyclical mechanisms) should be considered from both a qualitative and a quantitative viewpoint.

The financial instability hypothesis discussed by Minsky holds that turning points are completely endogenous to the process.

The upper turning point is produced as follows. Growing investment increases the pressure on financial markets for funds and this eventually produces an increase in the level of interest rates. Given the level of expected and current profits this deteriorates the financial position of firms in two ways. Current cash flows are curtailed both because gross current profits produce lower net profits as debt service increases and because current profits fall with the fall in investments which results from the rise in interest rates. Previously profitable business activities become unprofitable and bankruptcies may arise. The state of overall business confidence deteriorates and aggregate investment falls. A downward cumulative process starts off (Fisher 1933, Minsky 1982b) and financial panic may spread throughout the economy.

In debt deflation a qualitative change also takes place. Increasing pessimism about investment opportunities and profits reverses the lengthening of the time horizon process which, as we have seen, is a characteristic of the boom.

An investment boom produces financial distress and (eventually) debt deflation. This, however, may be explained as an endogenous process if particular assumptions are made concerning the behaviour of monetary authorities (Minsky 1980). The pressure that growing investment exerts on financial markets leads to tighter credit conditions if the central bank does not accommodate the higher demand for funds. If this is the case then the expansionary (and inflationary) process may go on indefinitely.

But this of course is not the case. Monetary authorities will intervene taking into account both the degree of financial fragility of the system and the inflationary pressures which the expansionary mechanism produces. If they wish to sustain the expansionary wave they might tolerate -at least to a certain degree- inflationary pressures which may be considered in this framework as a antidote to the financial distress of firms.

We may reconsider the demand and supply of inflation approach (Gordon 1975) in this framework. Ignoring for the moment other sources of demand for higher prices let us concentrate on the behaviour of firms.

If firms turn into financial problems they will demand higher prices in order to increase (or merely defend) their cash flows in order to meet debt service commitments. The monetary authorities may be sensitive to such a problem and thus accomodate higher prices to avoid upsetting the financial equilibria of firms.Both demand for and supply of inflation are thus increased as a consequence of the increase in financial fragility. In this respect growing inflation is just another aspect of increased financial difficulties.

Accommodation of inflation, however, may run up against other obstacles and it is reasonable to assume that monetary authorities, sooner or later, will stop accommodating expansion and inflation. This will lead to the upper turning point.

The lower turning point may be considered as an endogenous phenomenon if we assume that, at some point, monetary authorities will ease the monetary squeeze and give priority to the prevention of financial distress and bankruptcies (6).

The lower turning point will be produced by a reflationary policy (big government) which will increase aggregate profits and lower interest rates. Both events will improve the general investment climate and a new expansionary phase will be ready to start.

Financial instability in an international economy

We will now extend the mechanism described in the previous paragraph to the international economy. It is important to stress that an international economy is different from an open economy since it considers the interaction of a number of national economies while the latter simply involves the influences of the international system on a single national economy.

In an international economy the actors are national policy authorities, private banks operating in the international financial markets, as well as international institutions.

We will not focus on the behaviour of firms carrying on investment as in the closed economy case but rather on national governments pursuing development policies. By so doing the single countries will run into balance of payments problems and they will therefore seek to obtain loans to meet payment commitments.

In an international economy the ultimate source of finance is represented by exports. Net exports assume the role played by profits in the closed economy case. Insofar as the growth process produces negative net exports international credit will be demanded by developing countries.

A country will -in general- be willing to pursue a development process if today's negative net exports will be financed by positive net exports tomorrow. In this respect a country will assume a hedge finance position only if it expects to have positive net exports for each period so as to service outstanding debt in each period ahead. However in the first stages of a development process the country is more likely to assume a speculative (or even ponzi) position as repayments of debt will be covered by profits only in some periods in the future.

Positive gross exports will be needed immediately in order to pay interest on debt; however, positive net exports may be necessary only in some future periods if we assume that repayment of principal may begin only a few periods ahead (7).

If a development mechanism is successful and well monitored loans will be transformed into profitable activities (investments) which will generate enough profits (net exports) to repay initial debt. As a consequence we will observe an evolution of the external position of the country which is similar to that predicted by the balance of payments stages hypothesis. An initial current deficit will be financed by net capital inflows which will later be repaid by positive net exports. In other words, in the inital phase the country will be a net receiver of both goods and finance and will be a net supplier of goods and finance in the final stages.In terms of Minsky's classification this means that the developing country is a speculative finance unit.

A ponzi finance position may arise if current exports are so low that the country has to raise new debt just to meet payment of interest on outstanding debt thus increasing its debt burden.

We must now concentrate on the determination of two variables: exports and interest rates since imports will be a positive function of the growth rate of the economy. We will also assume for the sake of simplicity that exchange rates are fixed and that terms of trade do not vary (8).

Given the terms of trade, exports depend on world demand and on domestic capacity (domestic investment) while payment commitments depend -for a given outstanding debt- on the level of the interest rate.

Financial Instability

This produces a major difference with respect to the closed economy case. We must introduce three actors right from the start. In addition to (developing) countries and banks we must include the centre economy (the US) since, contrary to the closed economy case, exogenous (world) demand plays a crucial role.

This is not necessary in the closed economy case as the level of aggregate demand is determined in its crucial component (investments) by the behaviour of firms themselves (whose role is played by countries in this case). Not to make this assumption implies making another unrealistic point, namely that the developing countries as a group determine the level of world demand (9).

To put it differently, in a closed economy private investment plays the role of the autonomous source of effective demand. In an international economy such a role can be played only by the centre economy. The validity of this assumption rests, however, on the type of the prevailing international organization. The assumption is stronger if an hegemonic structure is in force (10).

In order to describe the buildup of financial fragility in an international economy, however, we will assume for the moment that the level of autonomous world demand is given. We will relax this assumption later and we will make this variable an endogenous one in the next chapter as this is crucial in the discussion of the turning points of the mechanism.

For a given level of world demand and of the world interest rate each developing country will set a rate of growth of investment. This will produce an excess of investments over savings and hence an excess of imports over exports.

Since demand for exports is given the rate of growth of exports will increase with domestic accumulation which relaxes supply constraints. Excess investment will repay itself if it produces enough excess exports in the future so as to repay the debt accumulated in the initial stages of the process.

If the country is initially successful in its export growth process it will be easier for it to find international credit as its creditworthiness will increase. Credit availability will enhance the country's investment opportunities and its export capacity. As long as favourable external conditions hold a virtuous circle of investment-exports

118

-creditworthiness-investment is at work.
This situation may change the attitude of banks and countries in the sense of increasing the euphoria of both. The success of the growth process will encourage countries to borrow more (11) and banks to lend more.

An additional and crucial condition must be added here. The amount of regulation present in the credit markets must be low enough to allow private banks to assume higher risks than in the closed economy case. This is certainly the case of Eurodollar markets (Guttentag and Herring 1983) and it reflects the fact that national monetary authorities are not in a position to enforce regulation rules on the international activity of private banks. Nor may they wish to do so if partial deregulation is a necessary condition for the international expansion of the national banking industry and if this represents one of the goals of international economic policy itself.

In the expansionary phase both borrowers and lenders will assume speculative (and possibly ponzi) finance positions. Countries, as we have seen, will borrow to finance trade deficits, while banks will de facto finance medium and long term investment processes while having to face short term deposit servicing on the liability side.

In an international economy, as we have seen, a hedge position implies that the country will display positive profits, that is, net exports larger than debt service commitments for all periods ahead. This amounts to saying that the country is a succesful neomercantilist.

A speculative position involves positive net exports larger than debt service commitments only from a given period onwards. A ponzi position involves positive net exports larger than debt service commitments only in the final periods of the development process.

The build up of international financial fragility
The shift towards increased financial fragility in an international economy depends on the interaction of the behaviour of borrowing countries, private banks and leader countries insofar as they determine the level of world demand, interest rates and exchange rates.

In the closed economy the link between single operators and system behaviour is much more

straightforward. The level of aggregate investments
derives as the sum of individual investment
decisions and this produces a macroeconomic feed
back on individual firms. The level of macroeconomic
activity is extremely important in determining the
state of expectations of single operators (both
banks and firms). In a boom microeconomic euphoria
arises because operators assume that this state of
affairs will last long enough to allow for financial
commitments to be respected.

In an international system this is even more
important. Banks will lend more and countries will
borrow more the higher the degree of international
financial stability and growth and hence the higher
future exports and (hence) profits.

The level of macroeconomic activity influences
the microeconomic one because it provides
information on which to base expectations. In this
respect a favourable macroeconomic environment
represents a public good for single agents (Head
1962, Kindleberger 1981, Wallace 1983).

In an international economy the level of world
demand, which determines the quality and quantity of
the public good involved is determined by the policy
followed by a small number of countries and cannot
be derived from the behaviour of the borrowing
countries. This implies that the buildup of
financial fragility will vary according to the state
of international economic relations which
determines, as we have seen in chapter 2, the supply
of public goods.

In an hegemonic fixed rate case systemic effects
are relatively simple. As long as the hegemon is
able and willing to actively play the role of
residual country the public good of international
stability will be supplied and the neomercantilism
of other countries will not produce excessive
systemic tensions. In addition, fixed exchange rates
will reduce the overall risk of international
lending (Guttentag and Herring 1983).

In an oligopolistic framework instability will
be much greater as the supply of public goods will
be much more problematic. The level of world demand
and world interest rates will be determined by
conflicts among oligopolists along the lines
described in chapters 2 and 3. In addition, exchange
rates will display a much higher level of
instability and this will significantly affect the
buildup of financial fragility as overall lending
risk will increase (Guttentag and Herring 1983).

Financial Instability

Let us now discuss how the process of financial fragility develops into a situation of financial crisis (upper turning point) and how and when a lower turning point (recovery) develops.

As we have seen above, the variable which feeds the growth-cum-debt process is the expansion of current and expected net exports in excess of payments commitments. When export expansion slows down (voluntary) lending will be progressively curtailed. This will put a constraint on the accumulation process of developing countries which will cut export capacity and, consequently, a downward cumulative process will start off.

The deterioration of the growth-cum-debt process will alter the behaviour of both borrowers and lenders. Investment opportunities in the developing countries will not be regarded as interesting even by domestic investors. As a consequence massive capital flights will take place. Banks, in turn, will react to the deterioration of creditworthiness by increasing the price for credit. Both elements will further deteriorate the financial position of borrowers who, on the other hand, will demand more funds. The share of ponzi finance positions in the international economy will dramatically increase. Banks will provide funds mostly through "involuntary lending". At this stage, however, the system is caught in a full-fledged financial crisis whose resolution will be discussed in the following chapter.

The lower turning point will instead materialize with the appearance of positive net exports and when financial conditions allow the voluntary debt mechanism to start again.

In the closed economy case the turning points are determined endogenously but assumptions about the behaviour of policy authorities have to be included. In the international economy case additional assumptions have to be introduced into the picture.

From a systemic point of view the deceleration of export growth as well as its pick-up after a recession crucially depend on the deterioration of the international macroeconomic environment.

As we have already mentioned the level of world demand, which determines exports, as well as the level of world interest rates, depend on the behaviour of the leaders of the system. Their behaviour also determines exchange rate patterns which feed back on the process.

121

Financial Instability

While the buildup of financial fragility -i.e. the increase and qualitative deterioration in the debt burden of borrowers- is mainly the result of the interaction of the behaviour of banks and countries (given the state of international banking regulation) the determination of turning points, both upper and lower, largely depends on the policy changes of the leaders of the system.

We could retain the hypothesis of fully endogenous turning points (with endogenous policy authorities) in the closed case because the implicit assumption there was that monetary policy reacted to pressures from the financial markets both in the upper and in the lower turning points. This assumption does not hold so strictly in the international case.

As we have seen in chapter 4, in oligopolistic interdependence the monetary and fiscal policies of the oligopoly leaders (and of the United States in particular) react to a number of variables and pressures. These include not only pressures caused by the international financial instability mechanism, and in particular by the necessity to provide lender of last resort intervention (lower turning point), but also pressures arising from the full spectrum of politico-economic interactions discussed above.

Other specific features have to be added in the international economy case. As in the closed economy case politico-economic interactions will determine the turning points of the international financial cycle as conflict resolutions. The actors involved in the international scene, however, are largely different from those operating in the closed case. In addition, even when they are the same as in the closed case (like banks) they face different constraints and environments. Some of them are also completely new as they include agents such as the International Monetary Fund. In some cases their behavioural patterns may be more complex since when sovereign states are involved their economic policy choices are taken in response to a wider range of constraints and pressures. This is straightforward for the leader of the system, the United States, but also holds for borrowing countries as long as they can exert political pressure on the other actors.

In addition, when we turn to the international economy case, group behaviour assumes different characteristics than in the closed economy case. Hence conflict analysis interacts with collective action problems. These issues will be discussed in chapter 8. The appendix to this chapter presents a simple diagrammatic exposition of the economics of the international financial instability mechanism.

NOTES

1. We wish to stress that Kalecki (1934) has clearly shown that this is to be considered a causal relation and not an identity. Several critics of Minsky's model fail to understand this point.

2. Non financial costs are not considered in this framework.

3. Country risk will be discussed more extensively in chapter 9.

4. The mechanics of financial crisis is one of the most neglected aspects in economic analysis. For an historical as well as economic treatement see Kindleberger 1978a.

5. Minsky analysis of the cumulative process is largely based on Keynes 1931 and Fisher 1933. For an analysis of institutional differences see Minsky 1982b.

6. Lower turning points were completely endogenous in the past when no official intervention was available. See Kindleberger 1978a.

7. There is a link here with results reached by the growth-cum-debt literature which will be discussed in chapter 9.

8. A simple analysis of terms of trade determination in a financially complex environment is discussed in chapter 10 and in the appendix to the chapter.

9. Even if the role of developing countries in sustaining world demand has not been irrelevant in some periods it is hardly conceivable that they might take on the role of "engine of growth" of the world economy.

10. Big government is not a necessary condition for the mechanics of Minsky's model. Its role may well be taken up by private investments and net exports.

11. Developing countries may well decide to use external funds to finance consumption expenditure rather that capital accumulation. For an analysis of this point see Kindleberger 1978b.

Financial Instability

APPENDIX

Borrower lender interaction in international markets
      What follows is a simple graphical exposition of
borrower-lender interaction in international markets
Its purpose is to show how financial instability may
develop.
      In fig A.7.1 the BB schedule is a transformation
curve of credit (C) into exports (X). It represents
the ability of the borrowing country to use funds
obtained in the credit market into exports by
increasing its productive capacity. The BB schedule
may be considered as a "production function" in
which credit is the input of the export producing
sector.
      The LL schedule represents a credit supply curve
of the banking system. Credit awarded is a positive
function of exports as increasing exports mean
higher creditworthiness. If we assume that credit
rationing conditions prevail the amount of credit
will be supply determined, in the sense that the
borrower will accept all the loans the banks will
decide to award.

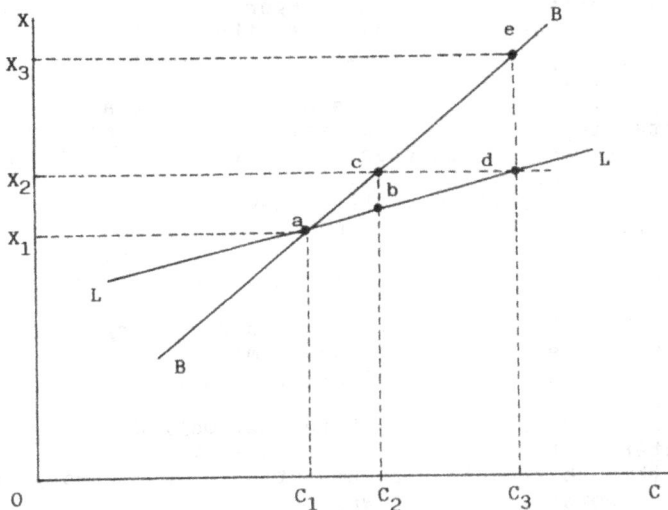

Fig.A.7.1.

124

Financial Instability

It is easy to see that the equilibrium described
in fig. A.7.1. is unstable. If, starting from the
equilibrium point a where OC1 credit is awarded,
banks decide to increase their advances to the
country (e.g. because sovereign lending has become
relatively more attractive) they will shift to point
b and the new amount of credit will be OC2. This
will allow the borrower to shift to point c on its
BB schedule thus increasing exports from OX1 to OX2.
Higher exports will induce banks to award a higher
amount of credit OC3 corresponding to point d on
their LL schedule and so on.
    The unstable motion away from point a clearly
depends on the relative slope of the two schedules.
It is easy to see that were the slopes of BB and LL
inverted the behaviour of the two agents would have
produced a stable motion towards point a. The slopes
in the figure reflect behavioural assumptions which
are in line with the financial instability
hypothesis discussed in this chapter. The marginal
propensity to lend with respect to exports
(creditworthiness) of banks is proportionally
greater than the ability of borrowers to transform
credit into exports. In other words we are assuming
that banks will be affected by "lending euphoria" in
sovereign lending.
    Of course this unstable movement will not go on
indefinitely. As the theory of financial instability
predicts financial distress will eventually
materialize and the upper turning point will come
about.
    The same graphical representation may be used to
show the effects of changes in the international
environment. We may assume that the position of the
BB curve in the diagram depends, ceteris paribus on
the level of world demand. A higher world demand
will shift the BB schedule to the left and
viceversa. The assumption here is that exports
depend on both domestic ability to increase
productive capacity through credit (supply
conditions) and on external (demand) conditions. For
a given amount of credit (and hence productive
capacity) exports will be higher the higher is world
demand.
    If higher world demand is associated with easier
monetary conditions in the international economy
banks will be willing to lend more for a given
creditworthiness assessment of borrowers and the LL
schedule will shift to the right. The opposite will
result in the case of tighter monetary conditions.

Financial Instability

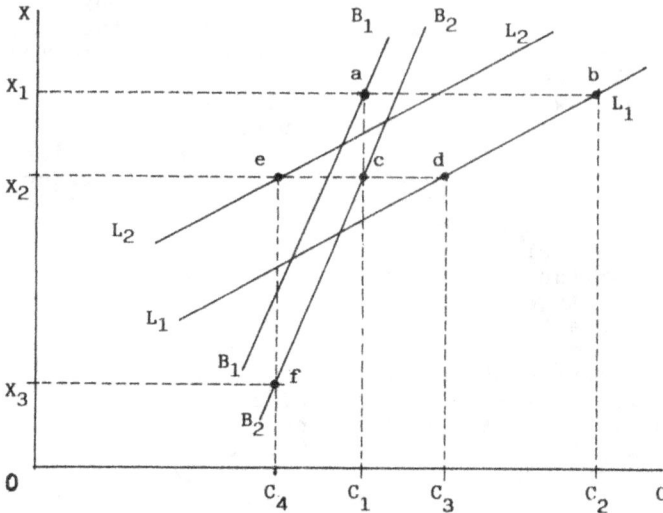

Fig.A.7.2.

Starting from point a in fig A.7.2 initial credit allocation OC1 will allow the borrower to export OX1 for a given state of world demand (B1B1 schedule). If general conditions do not change banks will react to OX1 by granting OC2 by moving to point b on their L1L1 schedule. Let us now suppose that general conditions take on a highly restrictive course. The drop in world demand will shift the borrowers export schedule into (e.g.) B2B2. The amount of credit OC1 will produce an amount of exports OX2. If banks were unaffected by the change in international conditions they would react to OX2 by granting OC3 credit (point d on their L1L1 schedule). However if we assume that tighter international economic conditions affect bank behaviour as well the credit supply schedule will shift (e.g.) into L2L2. Consequently for a given amount of exports OX2 banks will grant OC4 credit by moving to point e. This will allow borrowers to export OX3 (point f on the B2B2 schedule). The interaction will thus produce an explosive motion away from the initial equilibrium and the process will produce a debt deflation.

126

Chapter Eight

TURNING POINTS AND COLLECTIVE ACTION

In the international environment the main
determinant of both the upper and lower turning
points is the policy of the centre economy of the
system: the United States. However, the policy
choices of the US are implemented as a response to
the conflicts which arise with other actors in the
international system and, in addition, the
bargaining power which these actors display
vis-à-vis the United States varies over the
financial cycle. In other words the buildup of
financial fragility influences the outcome of
conflicts which arise between the US and the other
actors of the financial scene. In this respect the
turning points of the financial cycle may be
considered as fully endogenous outcomes.

The two dimensions of a financial crisis
    The upper turning point makes most of the
outstanding debt unserviceable even if it was easily
serviceable before the turning point was reached. In
Minsky's terminology the share of ponzi finance in
the system increases significantly. The upper
turning point materializes as a consequence of a
tightening of the monetary policy of the centre
economy.
    A tightening of US monetary policy produces
several effects which worsen the financial positions
of borrowing countries. It raises interest rates on
debt, and it raises the dollar value of debt. This
means that more goods have to be exported by
borrowers in order to fulfill payments commitments
for unit of debt. In addition the overall level (or
rate of growth) of exports falls as the level of
world demand is curtailed by the monetary squeeze.

Turning Points and Collective Action

In a word, indebted units must increase their
financial outflows in a situation in which profits
are severely curtailed.

When the shift in US monetary policy takes place
the indebted units may be said to enter a situation
of bankruptcy. However, as has been recently noted
(Aivazian and Callen 1983), a bankruptcy involves
two different although related aspects. An indebted
unit is in a situation of technical insolvency when
it materially lacks the finance needed to meet
payments commitments. Technical insolvency however
will transform itself into effective insolvency only
after the creditors decide to suspend financial
support, i.e. when creditors decide to deny debt
rescheduling. Whether or not technical insolvency
will turn into effective insolvency represents a
typical outcome of conflict resolution. A conflict
arises between debtors and creditors on the amount
and quality of further financial support (if any).
The upper turning point may be said to have fully
developed only after technical insolvency has turned
into effective insolvency.

In a international environment the conflict
which arises for the solution of problems posed by
technical insolvency involves a large number of
actors, and in addition it involves issue linkages
among different areas as the actors involved include
sovereign states.

The actors involved will be examined below and
their behavioural models will be briefly sketched.
In the second part of the chapter their interaction
will be discussed so as to provide a conceptual
framework for the determination of turning points.
The actors involved are: private banks, borrowing
countries, and international organizations. The
position and behavioural model of the most important
actor, the United States, has already been discussed
in chapter 4.

Private banks

Banks operate in groups in the international
credit markets, (Lipson 1981) hence their behaviour
should be analyzed according to collective action
paradigms. There are good economic reasons for
taking up such a perspective. As we have already
mentioned credit is a two-dimensional good,
identified by its quantity and its quality. The
quality of credit depends on the quality of the
borrower, its creditworthiness. This in turn is, by

definition, something which may not be assessed with certainty. In other words credit is a good which intrinsically involves ignorance at least to some degree.

Whenever credit must be granted a problem of confidence arises. Confidence is a public good (Hirsch 1977) and hence the problem of its supply arises. Collective behaviour in the banking community is a necessary condition for the supply of such a public good. Banks act as a group because this is the most effective way to build confidence and implement banking policies. Confidence is also a very fragile good which may break down much more easily than it is built up. Again the logic of collective action helps to explain this point (Olson 1965, 1982). As long as the group is made up of a small number of units the production of such a collective good is more efficient. Bankers may get to know each other better and thus make the exchange of information easier (Hirsch 1977). In addition this helps to produce the most effective type of international credit: syndicated lending.

Syndicated credits are a typical example of how collective goods are produced by (relatively) small groups. Syndicated credits diversify risks among lenders when they face a single large borrower like a sovereign state (Lipson 1981).

The structure of syndicated lending favours the provision of collective goods. Leading banks set the terms of the loans while smaller banks simply provide part of the funds. In terms of collective action the leading banks bear a more than proportionate share of the cost of providing the collective good "confidence" as it is they who assess the creditworthiness of the potential borrower. Smaller banks, which quite often do not have the expertise to assess country creditworthiness, rely on the indications of the larger banks in deciding whether or not to participate in the loan. As we shall see below, this kind of structure inherently involves a big free riding problem which tends to explode when financial distress breaks out.

Larger banks are willing to bear a more than proportionate share of the costs of supplying collective goods because they have an interest in the development of an international credit market. By providing these collective goods they expand and control the market.

There is however another element which

encourages larger banks to act as leaders in
syndicated lending. This is what might be termed
"implicit moral hazard". Larger banks know that in
case of distress they can count on lender of last
resort support from the central banks of their home
countries much more than smaller banks which are
less likely to be protected by monetary authorities
(Hirsch 1977, Guttentag and Herring 1983). This
element de facto decreases the costs of supplying
the collective good of confidence for the larger
banks and hence increases their propensity to act as
leaders of syndicated loans.

The structure of group behaviour we have
described is put under pressure when difficulties
arise, i.e. when rescheduling and bankruptcy threats
become widespread. However, free riding problems
also arise in boom periods (i.e. when financial
fragility builds up). In the expansionary phase,
smaller banks wish to increase their market share
and hence they offer easier conditions to borrowers
in order to increase demand for their loans
(Llewellyn 1982). This deteriorates the overall
quality of international lending as it increases
fragility (ponzi finance is encouraged). The result
is the production of a public bad which will turn
out to be extremely dangerous when the overall
situation turns from expansion to crisis.

The financial fragility mechanism implies that
the behaviour of the agents involved undergoes a
qualitative change during the different phases of
the mechanism. The propensity to lend freely during
expansion turns into a propensity to deny debt
rescheduling in periods of distress (Strange 1979a).
As a consequence collective action is much more
difficult to organize in the latter case when it
would be much more valuable to the banks themselves.
This difficulty is, on the other hand, tied to the
two-dimensional nature of credit. Since loans to
different borrowers have to be considered as
different goods and since borrowers are political as
well as economic agents, it is quite difficult to
agree once and for all on the rules of conduct in
carrying out debt negotiations. In such a situation
the only possible rule is discretionality.

Although no definite rules of conduct can be
laid out it is possible to offer a description of
how decision patterns differ if we split the banks
into two groups: leading banks and smaller banks.

Large and small banks

The behavioural patterns worth analyzing are those which obtain after the upper turning point of the financial cycle has been reached. That is, after the shift in policy of the dominant economy has produced a widespread situation of technical insolvency. The behaviour of banks will determine to what extent technical insolvency will turn into effective insolvency given the interaction with the other actors involved.

Small banks play the role of free riders in this collective action situation. When the crisis breaks out they try to get out of bad loans with as much money as possible and as fast as possible. Their free riding behaviour produces a public bad since it worsens the position of the debtor and hence increases the costs to those banks that wish to keep on lending in order to avoid ultimate bankruptcy. Small banks therefore not only exploit the public good supplied by the leaders of the credit syndicate but in addition they worsen the overall situation.

Larger banks have a much different perspective. When the crisis breaks out they have an interest in keeping the debtor afloat as long as possible. They will try to continue to finance the debt or, at least, to keep options open in debt rescheduling negotiations. This interest stems essentially from four facts. In the first place, larger banks usually have a much greater amount of funds involved in loans to countries (1). When a technical insolvency emerges the creditor's interest in continuing to lend to the debtor rises with the amount of debt outstanding as the loss which the creditor would suffer as a consequence of effective bankruptcy rises proportionately.

In the second place, leaders of credit syndicates have an interest in maintaining the public good of "confidence" at a minimum level, i.e. at that level below which the credit market would cease to exist.

In the third place, larger banks tend to act as a group inside the larger group which includes all banks. If a small bank goes bankrupt this will hardly affect the stability of the credit system as a whole. Instead, if a large banks goes bankrupt, the whole system might break down (Kindleberger 1978a, Kindleberger and Laffargue 1982). The chances of large banks surviving when a general crisis breaks out largely depend on collective support from other large banks. In this respect the large banks

Turning Points and Collective Action

act in a "regime of oligopolistic interdependence"
characterized by a high degree of cooperation, i.e.
by a supply of public goods. Our discussion of the
two-dimensional nature of credit should have made it
clear that only cooperation allows the market for
loans to operate smoothly.

In the fourth place, large banks have an
interest in collective action because they wish to
deter collective action on the part of the
borrowers, i.e. they wish to avoid the formation of
a debtors' cartel. This possibility will be
considered again later. Here it is sufficient to
note that this eventuality will be minimized as long
as negotiations between debtors and creditors are
kept open and this requires the will on the part of
the banks to keep on lending after the point of
technical insolvency has been reached.

In general it may be argued (Aronson 1979) that
large banks have a strong interest in international
cooperation. When conflict in the international
economy increases, financial and monetary
instability also increase and this decreases the
possibilty of sound international credit management.

In conclusion one might apply Hirschman's (1970)
"exit, voice and loyalty model" to the small vs
large banks relations. Small banks have a high
propensity to use the exit option when a crisis
breaks out, while larger banks will generally be
more loyal to their loan commitments and will
eventually raise their voice against both free
riding by small banks and, occasionally, by other
large banks which might be tempted to break the
rules of collective action.

Borrowers

Sovereign borrowers usually do not act as a
group. They might, however, be tempted to pursue
collective action by establishing a cartel when the
crisis mechanism increases their difficulties.   An
analysis of the behavioural pattern of borrowers has
been produced in the growth-cum-debt and in the
country-risk literature which will be discussed in
chapter 8. Here we will consider the options open to
the borrower once the technical crisis breaks out.
In such a situation the loan has obviously already
been granted and the real issue which the borrower
must face is the alternative between trying to
adjust in order to maximize debt servicing and
trying to increase its bargaining power in order to

132

obtain better conditions from the creditors.

The ultimate weapon in the hands of borrowers is unilateral repudiation of debt. This possibility, however, should be considered as remote since it would imply extremely heavy costs for the insolvent borrower not only in terms of denied future access to international credit markets but also to all other kinds of economic and trade relations with the banks' home countries which easily amounts to the whole group of western countries. Banks therefore run a low risk of running into effective repudiation

What a country is in a position to do, however, is to use its bargaining power in order to improve its credit terms and rescheduling conditions. The threat of repudiation of outstanding debt, or of part of it, may therefore be used as an instrument in order to hit a much more realistic target.

One should also add that (American Express Bank 1982) banks may be hurt differently according to the financial variable involved. As a consequence a borrower engaged in conflictual bargaining may choose the amount of financial injury it wishes (or is able) to inflict on the lender. A financial injury list might be exposed in terms of increasing damage produced to banks by the refusal of debtors to meet commitments as follows: loss of future due principal, loss of arrears of principal, loss of arrears of interests, loss of future due interests. Receipt of interest payments is critical for a bank as this will determine the degree of credit performance.

The problem then arises of trying to assess the bargaining power of the borrower in debt negotiations.

Eaton and Gersovitz (1981) have presented an analysis of the mechanics of international credit markets under the assumption that countries are rationed by banks in function of the probability that a country will repudiate its debt. The higher the probability the higher the amount of rationing, i.e. the lower the amount of credit granted.

It is possible to develop Eaton's and Gersovitz's model (1981) in order to establish links between the bargaining power of a country in the credit markets and its economic performance and structural characteristics. The idea is simple. The lower the costs to a country of being excluded from international credit, the higher is its bargaining power. The costs may be associated with a number of economic variables that will be listed below. We

will introduce some additional variables which take
account of political factors as well. The inclusion
of political elements is extremely important if one
wishes to distinguish (Lipson 1979) between the
capacity and the willingness of borrowers to engage
in a confrontation with banks.

If we assume systemic conditions as given (i.e.
the trend of world demand, the level of interest
rates and so on) the borrower's bargaining power
will be higher:

the lower the variability of export earnings.
Since a country faces a given inflow of imports for
a given rate of growth of output a high volatility
in export earnings will increase its need of
distress finance. This means, inter alia, that raw
materials exporting countries will have a much lower
bargaining power as their export revenue will be
greatly affected by exogenous volatility (2)

the lower the average propensity to import. This
determines not only the import coverage which is
needed for a given rate of growth of output but also
the vulnerability of the country to trade
retaliation by other countries

the lower the rate of growth of per capita
income which is financed by debt. This point may be
better understood if we recall the distinctions of
financial positions discussed in chapter 6. The
higher the proportion of speculative finance
investment in the country the higher is dependence
on future lending. In general (3) the higher the
financial fragility of the country the lower is its
bargaining power.

Scale variables such as population size will
increase the bargaining power of the debtor
especially if they are associated with a relatively
high level of per capita income as they are
indicators of politically and economically important
countries. From a strictly economic point of view a
large and relatively prosperous country constitutes
an important export market for the firms of
countries to which creditors belong as well. In this
case banks and firms might share a common interest
against the borrower and this will decrease its
bargaining power.

The degree of involvement of multinational
enterprises in the country will increase the
country's bargaining power also for the obvious
reason that the capital of foreign firms might be
frozen by the host government in retaliation against
suspension of bank lending.

134

The amount of official lending increases the bargaining power of the country for political and economic reasons.

Bargaining power obviously increases with the amount of debt outstanding.

Political variables include the kind of regime or, at least, the perception of the regime's friendliness in the opinion of the government of the country to which banks belong (4). Friendly regimes might have greater bargaining power than hostile ones. However this may produce ambiguities. Internally strong regimes might paradoxically have less bargaining power than weak ones as the fear of a regime change might induce the creditors' government to put pressure on creditors in order to avoid such an event. This might be desirable for banks as well since they do not know what kind of behaviour the new regime might adopt with respect to debt.

Conversely new regimes have a high bargaining power as they may refuse to consider commitments assumed by previous governments (5).

Political bargaining power may also be considered in terms of issue linkage (Tollison and Willet 1979) if a debtor nation is of political interest to the government of the country to which lenders belong, the borrowing country may wish to bargain for political aquiescence in exchange for financial relief (6). In other words the borrowing country will use its political bargaining power to improve its financial terms of trade. If such a situation materializes banks are, in some sense, sustained by their own government, who might also bear the costs of the financial arrangement in exchange for political support. Such a situation may, however, increase the financial risk involved as a problem of "political moral hazard" arises. If the borrower belongs to a political or military alliance, group behaviour complications might arise since preferential financial treatment might also be requested by other members of the alliance. If the lender government wishes to keep the alliance from weakening it must bear additional costs in terms of additional financial support. In other words, it must bear the costs of supplying a public good which are additional with respect to the traditional ones (Olson and Zeckhauser 1966) which derive from the establishment of a linkage between finance and politics.

The bargaining power of a country is also

affected by the general state of the internationl economy. During a deflation debt servicing costs usually increase while exports decrease, hence the propensity to repudiate debt increases. A deflation therefore has an ambiguous effect on the bargaining power of borrowing countries (Llewellyn 1982). This is increased as their propensity to repudiate debt increases but it is lowered as the default option is considered as unrealistic. However this ambiguity may be partially eliminated if we recall that banks are differently hurt by different types of payment suspension from borrowers. When a deflationary environment makes servicing conditions stricter a country may decide to increase the harm it inflicts on lenders by suspending repayment of principal and threatening to suspend repayment of interests (i.e. to declare a moratorium on debt).

A deflationary environment increases the propensity of borrowing countries to act as a group, i.e. to form a debtors' cartel. This is a major topic which can only be treated superficially here. Economic theory of cartels suggests a number of conditions that must be met for a cartel to be formed and to survive. The problem here is different as we must explain why the formation of such a cartel has met so many difficulties.

A typical collective action problem is involved. Since a cartel provides a collective good to its members (increased bargaining power), the problem of who will supply it arises. The problem will be solved if one of the borrowers acts as an "hegemon" by supplying this public good (i.e. assuming a collective action leadership in bargaining with banks). The costs of supplying the public good lie in the fact that the banks will try to undermine this leadership by offering better credit and repayment conditions to other members of the group thus creating free riding incentives.

It will be in a country's interest to act as the leader of a cartel if that country has an overwhelming interest in the formation of such a cartel. This may be the case if a particular country's outstanding debt is overwhelmingly larger that that of other borrowers. In this case its propensity to repudiate will be higher and hence its interest in supplying such a public good will also be higher. Experience of these last few years suggests that this kind of incentive distribution is not present in an amount large enough to allow for cartel formation. What is present is an incentive to what might be termed "linked behaviour" rather than straightforward collective action. During negotiations, which are conducted using a case by case approach, single countries might hold back their own requests in order to await for results in other country cases and then apply the conditions obtained from other countries as a starting base.

The free rider problem in international debt represents the strongest disincentive to the formation of a debtors' cartel. This may appear more clearly if we consider what the target of such a cartel would be. It is unlikely that a cartel would pursue effective global debt repudiation. Rather one would expect that cartel members would seek better conditions in debt rescheduling negotiations. However such a target is unlikely to form a strong base for cartel formation once debt negotiations are already under way. Debt rescheduling negotiations cannot be carried on indefinitely as the flow of funds must continue in both directions if the international credit mechanism is to be kept alive. Lenders must continue to obtain new funds just to run their economies while banks must receive interest payments in order to avoid debt cancellation and the risk of financial collapse.

This means that it is in the interest of both banks and borrowers to maximize the speed at which negotiations are carried out in order to avoid the mounting of financial instability. Since banks already act as a group (i.e. they act as a group even when financial conditions are in "equilibrium") it will be easier for them to prevent the formation of a debtors' cartel by encouraging free riding attitudes, i.e. by proposing easier conditions to single borrowers. In other words the very factors which strengthen collective behaviour among banks weaken incentives for collective behaviour among borrowers.

The IMF

Many students of international finance claim that the International Monetary Fund acts (or should act) (7) as the lender of last resort of the international financial system. We have discussed in chapter 4 why this is not the case. There is no single LLR in the international system as this function may be undertaken only with respect to transnational banks, i.e .banks belonging to national financial systems. As we have already seen

(Bagehot 1873, Guttentag and Herring 1983) the
traditional LLR function is to rescue single banks
or intermediaries in order to prevent financial
distress from spreading throughout the system and
degenerating into a full-fledged financial crisis.
In this respect the body which may most closely
approximate this function in the international
system is the Federal Reserve since the US banking
system represents the most important segment of
international credit markets.

The role the IMF has carried out in these last
few years in debt crisis management is different. It
adds up to providing "new creditworthiness" to
indebted countries in exchange for stabilization
programmes. Restoration of creditworthiness is a
necessary (although not always a sufficient)
condition for obtaining new credit from the private
banks in situations of distress. We must also recall
that the stabilization programmes imposed by the IMF
involve forms of political bargaining with the
debtor's government. Political involvement and
decision-making is, in general, outside the role of
an LLR.

The IMF is not even, as some argue, a Central
Bank (Scaperlanda 1978) as it does not control the
supply of world money and it does not control
monetary policy worldwide (8).It may at most be
considered as an official intermediary between
debtors and creditors as it organizes bargaining
between them.

What the IMF really does is to provide a very
precious collective action leadership as it
organizes groups of banks in collective bargaining
with borrowing countries. It provides a collective
good as it develops a function of group leadership.
It provides a collective good as (Lipson 1981) it
provides information to banks involved in
rescheduling (9). Information given to banks is the
seal of creditworthiness (Cohen 1982) and it is the
signal that banks can, once the stabilization
programme has been implemented, start lending again.
In other words, the IMF solves the "Bagehot problem"
(Hirsch 1977) as it bears the cost of deciding if
the lending climate is again safe enough. Only in
this respect can it be said that the IMF carries out
a Central Bank function.

Since creditworthiness requires the supply of a
public good a free rider problem on the part of the
banks is involved. As long as the stabilization
programme is perceived as successful by banks they

will try to lend at higher interest rates justifying
them with the higher risk involved once single banks
have regained freedom of action. This deteriorates
the quality of the public good supplied by the IMF
since higher interest rates mean higher risks of
insolvency and hence the creditworthiness seal
imposed by the IMF stabilization programmes may be
outdated.

The collective leadership function carried out
by the IMF is not without costs. In order to
appreciate this more fully one the objective
function of the IMF itself should be more explicitly
defined.

The IMF is an international organization which
operates as a club (Fratianni and Pattison 1982).
The goal of such an institution is to maximize its
standing in front of club members, i.e. the member
countries which include both borrowers and lenders.
In addition the IMF relies on member quotas to
operate successfully and it is also relatively
vulnerable to funding procedures (Lipson 1981,
Dreyer and Schotter 1980). The IMF is therefore
"naturally oriented" to act as an intermediary since
it relies on the support of both sides of the
international financial market in order to maximize
its utility. This means that, on the one hand,
stabilization programmes must be severe enough to
represent a seal of creditworthiness perceived as
"hard" enough by lenders. On the other hand, they
must be implemented by debtors in order to be
accepted as creditworthiness information, hence they
must be "soft" enough to be politically and
economically acceptable to borrowers.

The debtor country obviously has an interest in
accepting the stabilization programme as long as it
wishes to continue to receive funds from the banks.
If the debtor perceives the stabilization programme
as too hard this might increase its propensity to
repudiate debt. If the banks perceive the programme
as too soft they will increase their propensity to
free ride, i.e. to get as much money as they can and
run out of the deal to the extent that they no
longer consider the borrower creditworthy. In both
cases the IMF will lose support, i.e. it will fail
in its role as an intermediary and so it will
minimize its utility. IMF operations are also very
sensitive to the phase of the financial cycle.
During the boom years its power had been largely
diminished by the fact that countries did not resort
to IMF finance in order to avoid stabilization

programmes, while private banks did not care about
looking for IMF seal of creditworthiness as they
were operating in an euphoria situation and they did
not wish the Fund to impose (eventually) regulation
on their lending practices.

The way in which the "Bagehot problem",
consequently, is solved varies over the financial
cycle. In the boom phase banks and borrowers solve
it by themselves since the general expansionary
conditions produce a generalized perception of
creditworthiness. Things change drastically during
the crisis when the quality of credit is disrupted
and only collective leadership can solve the Bagehot
problem. In other words the different solution of
the Bagehot problem over the cycle means that
different macroeconomic environments alter the
quality of microeconomic behaviour which is
reflected in a different ability (and willingness)
of agents to produce collective goods.

Turning points as conflict resolutions

The upper turning point is the result of a
change in the policy of the dominant nation. An
endogenous explanation of such a turning point
requires the discussion of the operation of the
whole international political economic system. The
description of such a global model is beyond the
scope of this book. We have tried to assess in
chapter 4 the behaviour of the United States from an
international political economy point of view. In
chapter 10 we will provide a schematic
representation of the relevant interconnections
which should be included in a global
politico-economic model. One point, however, may be
made clear. The upper turning point is endogenous
not to the (international) financial system but to
the international politico-economic system.

The change in the course of the economic policy
of the United States at the end of the previous
decade may be considered, as we have seen in
chapters 5 and 6, as the factor which has led to the
upper turning point of the international financial
cycle. This dramatic change can be explained by
factors which do not directly concern the
relationships between US policy and the
international debt mechanism. Explanatory causes may
be found in the politico-economic motivations
discussed in chapter 4: the desire of the United
States to stop inflation and to put the dollar and

the American banking industry back at the top of the international financial system; in a word to regain as much as possible the power which had been eroding over the previous decade. In this respect the upper turning point may be seen as a US response to oligopolistic conflicts.

International financial mechanisms on the contrary may explain much more effectively why a lower turning point takes place. A lower turning point implies both that monetary conditions are eased and that LLR intervention takes place and that world demand expands so that units may increase realized profits. The crucial point is whether pressures arising within the financial system may lead to such a lower turning point; i.e. produce a significative change in US economic policy.

Interactions between US policy and the international debt mechanism take place at different levels. We may identify three levels:

a) The US may intervene directly or indirectly on rescheduling and refinancing agreements between the borrowers and the banks alongside the IMF, or in direct support of some particular borrowers if political and or economic motivations suggest it (As in the case of Mexico).

b) The Fed may intervene as LLR in support of US banks exposed towards indebted countries.

c) The US administration may shift its stance on policy issues allowing for higher growth and or easier monetary policies.

Only cases b) and c) may be defined as policies leading to a true turning point in the model of the international financial cycle described in chapter 7. Both must accrue in order for a full turning point to develop, i.e. a point from which the financial mechanism produces a new expansionary wave. In order for this to take place two fundamental conditions must be met. In the first place "long-term creditworthiness" must be restored (Keynes 1931, Kalecki 1931). Short term creditworthiness, such as that provided by IMF intervention, is not enough since the lenders must revise their expectations about the future profitability of lending and not just about the ability and willingness of borrowers to repay outstanding debt.

In the second place, the general evolution of the economy must be characterized by a high (and growing) level of expected profits for indebted units, that is, a high and growing level of exports

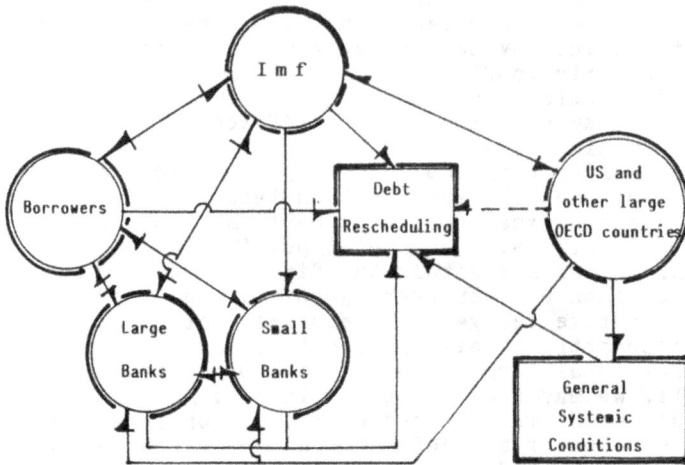

Fig. 8.1   Actors' Interaction in Debt Rescheduling

for borrowing countries.

The problem under discussion thus comes down to the following issue: to what extent will the outcome of level a) negotiations produce enough pressure on the US authorities to induce them to take steps b) and c) as well?

The outcome of level a) negotiations depends on the interaction of the choices of the three actors we have considered in the previous paragraphs: the debtors, the banks and the IMF. (see fig 8.1). In particular the outcome of the conflict between debtors and creditors largely depends on the ability of the IMF to find an effective solution to the problem for which it is institutionally equipped: the production of short term creditworthiness. The more solid the short term solution produced by this intermediation process the lower are the dangers of a non-cooperative solution arising. In this latter case the lower turning point may need to wait for a full-fledged debt-deflation process to develop before the authorities (the US authorities but also the other lender countries involved) decide to

implement levels b) and c) as only at that stage
pressures from the international financial system
might be strong enough to induce a shift in the
course of monetary and fiscal policy.

The success of the IMF as a negotiator is
crucially dependent on the support it receives from
the financially powerful members and from the US in
the first place. If the US is willing to provide the
IMF with enough funds, its ability to impose
adjustment conditions will be higher. In this
respect the willingness of the US to support the
solution of the crisis at level a) may be considered
as the price which has to be paid in order to avoid
heavier involvement later at levels b) and c).

If IMF action proves effective it may be
possible to find a "short term internal solution" to
the debt crisis. This form of limited cooperation
(Lipson 1981) does not in itself represent a final
solution to the problem but it may be sufficient to
buy time in the hope that the general economic
conditions will soon improve. From the US point of
view this implies that if level a) is successful
then the debt problem will not represent, in itself,
a strong pressure for a change in general policy. As
a result, the lower turning point of the cycle is
exogenous as shifts in general economic conditions
will take place as a consequence of pressures from
other sources operating on US policy.

A strong IMF bargaining position may be not
sufficient to restore even limited space for crisis
management, however, if generally adverse economic
conditions persist. If this is the case, the
propensities of the parties involved in debt
rescheduling negotiations to reach an agreement may
decrease. Borrowers will increase their propensity
to repudiate debt while banks will be faced with an
adverse situation as the propensity of smaller banks
to increase free riding behaviour will decrease the
group loyalty of lenders.

Both these pressures will eventually mount on US
policymakers as borrowers will increase political
pressure for financial support and reflation and
banks will increase demand for LLR intervention and
easier monetary conditions. These pressures for a
change in policy will add to pressures coming from
the other industrialized countries for easier
monetary and economic conditions. In other words,
oligopolistic conflicts within the North will add
their pressure to debt conflicts in North-South
relations.

Turning Points and Collective Action

The involvement of non-American Western banks in debt rescheduling negotiations is another factor which could give rise to conflict within the North. In this case the US might try to discriminate between support to US banks and support to non-US banks while political elements may also be involved (10).

To sum up, we have tried to show why endogenous explanation of the turning points requires the full statement of the policy behaviour. This implies that turning points may be considered as endogenous only if one considers the international system from a global perspective.

We have tried to assess the behavioural mechanisms of the actors involved and some of the interactions which may arise in the management of the debt crisis. This still leaves us far from having developed a full-fledged model of the management of the international financial crisis. One final point should however be emphasized. Students of international debt problems have recently suggested (Sachs 1982, Simonsen 1984) that game theory techniques should be applied to the discussion of this problem. As a matter of fact the interactions between players which take place in crisis management correspond to a typical game situation. Existing game theory models applied to debt problems, however, suffer from two major shortcomings.

In the first place, they usually take into consideration only two actors (borrowers and lenders) and ignore (also due to the exponentially rising formal complexity which n-persons game situations involve) the roles of the other actors who, as we have seen, are crucial to an understanding of the problem.

In the second place, they accept the view that only two extreme situations may arise, either full cooperation or absence of cooperation (prisoner's dilemma). Here again limitations arise due to the present state of development of formal game theory. In this case, however, the cost of sacrificing realism for formal rigour seems to be unbearably high. Intermediate cases may be considered and, in fact, real world situations usually fall into this area. The point we wish to make in this respect is that, as has been recently pointed out (Keohane 1984, Runge 1984), the amount of limited cooperation which is established is positively associated with the amount of information that each actor has on the

propensity to cooperate of the remaining players. In
other words, the system is characterized by a degree
of uncertainty (in Keynes' sense, Keynes 1936) in
each agent's expectations concerning the behaviour
of the others. Consequently actors must form
expectations on which to decide the amount of
cooperation (supply of public goods) they are
willing to provide.

The crucial point is that the information
available increases with the number and quality of
institutions present in the system. This amounts to
saying that the propensity to cooperate positively
depends on the quality of the existing regimes.
Whether or not the financial crisis will ultimately
be resolved, with the determination of a
full-fledged upper turning point, depends on whether
or not the conflicts going on in the international
system over the establishment of monetary and
financial agreements can be resolved, i.e. on the
possibility of reaching a state of cooperative
equilibrium in oligopolistic interdependence. Or, to
put it differently, the problem is whether the
existing institutions (public goods) are sufficient
to increase the propensity of actors to cooperate,
that is, to increase the supply of public goods
themselves.   In
this respect the solution of the problems posed by
international financial instability is ultimately
the solution of international cooperation tout
court. This point will be discussed in the final
chapter of this book.

NOTES

1. See evidence discussed in chapter 5.
2. See appendix to chapter 10.
3. Eaton and Gersovits 1981 do not discuss this
point.
4. This implies introducing an additional actor
into play: the governement to which banks belong.
5. A typical case is the change of attitude of
Argentina's government after the return to democracy
following the defeat in the Falkland war.
6. The interaction between political and
financial factors in country risk determination is
briefly analyzed in the appendix to chapter 9.
7. The extreme liberal position (Vaubel 1983)
holds that the IMF might seriously worsen the
operation of the international financial system if

it increases the moral hazard of private banks.
    8. Given the irrelevance of SDR in
international liquidity.
    9. An attempt undertaken by private banks to
organize rescue operations without the support of
the IMF failed in the case of Peru's debt. See
Aronson 1979.
    10. As in the Polish case. See Moffit 1983.

APPENDIX

Turning points in the financial cycle

    In this appendix we present a graphical
exposition of the financial cycle and of the
interaction of quality and quantity of credit in the
determination of turning points. As we have seen in
chapter 7 and in the appendix to the chapter, the
interaction of lenders and borrowers produces an
increase in the amount of debt in the expansionary
phase which takes the form of a cumulative process
away from equilibrium. This process however does not
go on indefinitely. An upper turning point will
materialize as a consequence of changes in the
international system which will eventually produce
changes in the behaviour of both lenders and
borrowers. Such a change in behaviour is (also) a
consequence of the bidimensional nature of credit.
As a matter of fact quality and quantity of credit
vary inversely over the cycle although not in a
mechanical way. The full operation of the financial
cycle (i.e. the determination of turning points)
requires that both quality and quantity of credit
reverse their direction.
    Quantity (C) and quality (R) of credit are
reported on the vertical axis of fig. A.8.1. Quality
of credit (borrower's creditworthiness) decreases
when the amount of credit increases in the boom
phase as financial fragility increases according to
the mechanisms described in the previous chapter and
appendix. This implies that, in the boom phase, C
acts as the explanatory variable of R. The quality
of credit starts to deteriorate with the approach of
the upper turning point (crisis) and it eventually
collapses (R moves from a to b). The discontinuous
behaviour of R may be explained by the fact that
lenders do not change substantially their
creditworthiness assessment until the situation
approaches the crisis point. Credit continues to

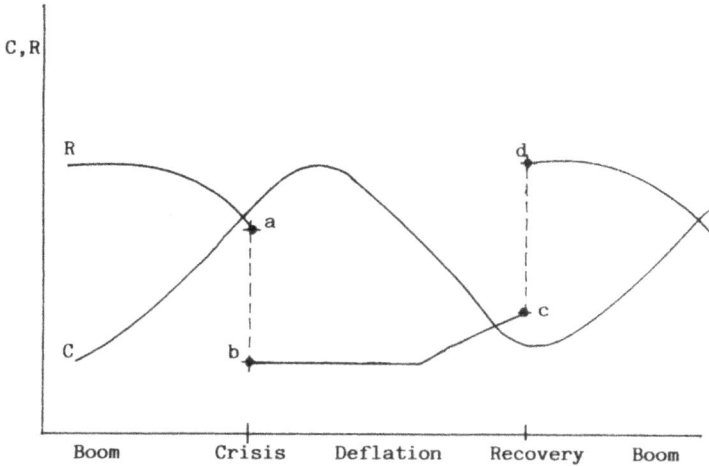

C,R

R

d

a

c

C

b

Boom   Crisis   Deflation   Recovery   Boom

Fig. A.8.1.

grow for a while after the crisis as a consequence
of forced lending. Banks will continue to lend even
if quality of credit has sharply deteriorated in
order to avoid that technical bankruptcy, which
occurs at point a, is transformed into effective
bankruptcy.

The amount of credit will then slowly decrease
in the deflation phase as a consequence of the
withdrawal of banks from the market. Quality of
credit will remain constantly low as long as this
withdrawal proceeds. It should be noted that the
amount of credit deterioration (the distance between
points a and b) crucially depends on the
effectivness of the rescue plan and on the ability
of lenders of last resort in providing the public
good of creditworthiness. The greater the efficacy
of intervention the lower the fall in the value of
R. In the deflation phase the causal link between C
and R is inverted. The low value of R now determines
the fall of lending as banks have changed their
perception of borrowers creditworthiness.

As the amount of loans decreases and the

adjustment programs of borrowers enter into effect
the quality of credit slowly starts to pick up
again. However the slight improvement in R is, in
itself, not sufficient to produce a full recovery.
In order for this to materialize a strong
improvement in the quality of credit is needed. This
explains why the quantity of credit continues to
decrease even if R starts to grow at the end of the
recovery phase. The recovery fully takes place as R
jumps from c to d. This is the result of a radical
change in profitability conditions resulting from a
substantial increase in the level of effective
demand which arises from a major shift in the policy
of the leader country of the international economy.
At this point expectations of growing profitability
encourage banks to return to lending (i.e. the
market is characterized by a new wave of
"euphoria"). At this stage a new boom phase may
start.

To sum up. The way in which quality and quantity
of credit interact varies in the different phases of
the cycle. C determines the behaviour of R in the
boom (R deteriorates) while it is determined by R in
the deflation (C decreases). Both turning points
however must be explained by the introduction of
major shifts in the international environment and in
the policy of the leader countries. In addition
while the upper turning point (crisis) is jointly
determined by the change in the environment and by
the perception of lenders of the value of R, the
lower turning point (recovery) requires the full
intervention of lender of last resort and effective
demand conditions to materialize.

Chapter Nine

GROWTH, DEBT AND COUNTRY RISK

In this chapter we will use some of the results
so far reached in the description of the
international debt process in order to review the
literature on country risk analysis. We will also
discuss the links between country risk analysis and
the growth-cum-debt literature.

Over the last ten years country risk analysis
has been rapidly expanding at both the technical and
the academic level (1). Although several different
techniques and approaches have been followed, the
majority of country risk analyses share a common
characteristic. They aim at providing a number of
"leading indicators" which make it possible to
assess the ability of a country to earn enough
foreign currency to service debt. In some cases the
probability of default or rescheduling of a
sovereign borrower is assessed.

As several studies have pointed out (Saunders
1983, Saini and Bates 1984) country risk assessment
carried out using traditional techniques has not
proved of much help in providing early warning. The
depth and difficulty of the international debt
crisis is there to confirm it. It is therefore
necessary to understand why these approaches have
performed so poorly.

A first general answer is that these approaches
are seldom based on a satisfactory assessment of the
international debt mechanism. In what follows we
shall reconsider country risk analysis in the light
of our previous assessment.

Country risk and market behaviour
A first element to consider is international
credit rationing. As we have seen above, not all

149

countries have been admitted to international credit
markets. Many high risk (and low income) countries
have been excluded as their creditworthiness has not
been considered satisfactory by private banks.
    Credit rationing implies that the supply curve
for credit has to be specified taking account of
risk factors in order to decide the quantity of
credit that may be supplied to a risky borrower. In
the case of international credit markets the supply
curve does not exist for a number of potential
borrowers. To put it differently, the credit
rationing mechanism works on a two-step basis. In
the first place, lenders decide which borrowers to
admit to the market; in the second place, they
decide the quantity of loans to allocate to each of
them.
    The problem, therefore, is to understand why a
supply curve for some countries is formed in the
first place. Keeping in mind the financial mechanism
discussed in chapter 7 this means that these
countries have not been able to produce a rate of
growth of net exports high enough to attract banking
investment.
    Once this first selection has been made credit
rationing analysis may be applied to those countries
which are admitted to the market. Since sovereign
countries are involved, traditional financial
considerations are not sufficent. As a matter of
fact it has been suggested that (Agmon and Dietrich
1983) once credit relations are established country
risk analysis ceases to be an economic problem and
becomes mainly a political one since intercountry
relations are involved. We shall return to this
point later. What interests us here is the
distinction between ability and willingness to repay
debt. If country risk assessment is to provide a
guide to credit rationing it must distinguish
between these two aspects which entail respectively
a financial and a political problem.
    A second element is collective behaviour. As we
have seen in the previous chapter, a collective
action (Bagehot) problem arises if the
bidimensionality of credit is taken into account.
Quality definition cannot be considered only as a
single country problem but must be assessed in a
collective action framework including both borrowers
and lenders.
    On the one hand, a country will display
different risk levels according to whether it
operates in a group or by itself.

150

Growth Debt and Country Risk

On the other hand, the very fact that banks act
collectively means that the country risk involved is
not independent from the behaviour of the banks
themselves, which, in turn varies according to the
degree of collective action involved. A country's
sovereign risk will vary depending on whether the
lender acts on its own (as a free rider) or as a
member of a group.

A third element comes from banking theory. Once
a country is admitted to the market a sort of
customer relationship is established. The
establishment of customer relationships is essential
to the operation of credit markets.

Customer relationship (Wood 1975) develops when
borrowers are depositors as well (i.e. they lend to
the banks). This is a positive fact for the bank in
various respects. In the first place, it provides
the bank with a sort of permanent source of funds
through deposits. In the second place, it allows the
bank to acquire a better knowledge of the client
thus reducing lending risk.

Customer relationship builds up with the
financial instability process. Increasing
willingness of the banks to lend to expanding
countries in the boom phase derives (also) from the
fact that banks become increasingly convinced that
their clients are creditworthy (Guttentag and
Herring 1984). In the boom phase, on the other hand,
developing countries tend to "overborrow" with
respect to their current financing requirements and
to redeposit their excess funds in the same lending
banks.

The borrower-lender interaction which develops
as a consequence of this "dynamic" customer
relationship provides an explanation of the flaws
which are traditionally ascribed to creditworthiness
indicators.

Let us consider as an example the critique of
the most traditional debt indicator: the debt
service ratio. As is well known, a low ratio is
generally considered a sign of good creditworthiness
if it is assumed that the country in question will
have to devote a relatively small part of its export
earnings to debt service. On the other hand,
however, a low ratio may be the result of previously
low creditworthiness which has produced a low amount
of lending.

These ratios are determined by the interaction
between supply and demand of credit. Hence, if a
bank were to take its lending decisions on the basis

151

of this indicator it would be basing its decisions not just on the behaviour of the borrowing country but also on the behaviour of the banking system as a whole.

A fourth element is the presence of moral hazard in the behaviour of banks which may result from the interaction of borrowers with institutions and or friendly governments of lending countries.

What this means is that we must also consider the political aspects of country risk, which will be discussed below.

A final consideration may be drawn from this section. Country risk analysis should not be analyzed in terms of traditional financial risk assessment. What lenders are really facing should instead be termed "uncertainty", in the Keynesian (1936) sense of the word. When sovereign lending is involved banks are facing an event (rescheduling or default) which is not associated with a probability distribution (Davidson 1982).

It has been argued (Goodman 1981) that country risk analysis may be carried out in terms of traditional risk diversification once it is made clear that country risk is made up of two components: diversifiable and non-diversifiable risk.

Diversifiable risk is associated with country specific characteristics and it represents country risk in a strict sense. Non-diversifiable risk is associated with general economic conditions. It is an implicit assumption of this proposed classification that only diversifiable risk should guide a bank's decisions about credit allocations. In other words, country risk is what remains of a country's creditworthiness once systemic risk has been taken account of.

The above discussion allows us to question the logical plausibility of such a distinction. In the first place, one would have to accept the hypothesis that systemic risk and country specific risks are unrelated; in other words, that the policies pursued by borrowers -which are one of the major determinants of a country's debt servicing capacity- are independent of general systemic conditions. This is not acceptable if one recalls the discussion carried out in chapter 8, which showed that the propensity to repudiate debt is in fact closely related to general systemic conditions.

In the second place, this approach neglects the collective behaviour which may be pursued by borrowers, and which is partly a function of general systemic conditions.

In the third place, systemic conditions themselves may to some extent be affected by the behaviour of borrowers if one accepts the view that a) general conditions are determined by the policies of oligopoly leaders, and b) that these policies are also a function of the general financial conditions in the international markets and hence of borrowers-lenders relations.

This point is all the more pertinent if we recall the distinction, introduced above (Aivazian and Callen 1983), between technical insolvency and effective bankruptcy, the latter being determined by the lender's decision to stop financing the borrower. Consequently any financial transaction involves a double risk. A technical insolvency risk and a strategic risk, which is the risk taken by the lender -if he decides to continue financing the insolvent borrower in order to postpone bankruptcy and increase future returns- that the conflict which arises with the borrower (and with other lenders as well) may turn out unfavourable to him.

Technical insolvency and effective bankruptcy are interdependent. Technical insolvency arises if a borrower fails to implement adjustment policies so as to restore debt servicing capacity. The propensity to adjust, however, is also dependent on the ability to exploit the willingness of the lender to postpone effective bankruptcy.

A final point has to be stressed as far as this question is concerned. As we have seen in chapter 7 when discussing the mechanics of the financial instability hypothesis, systemic conditions alter the quality and the response of the single agents in the different phases of the financial cycle. Consequently the propensity to implement adjustment policies (or to repudiate debt) will vary over the cycle. In other words, the microeconomics of country risk (both in its "technical" and in its "strategic" component) is not independent from the macroeconomics of country risk (and the converse is also true).

Analysis of borrower-lender interaction is, however, starting to develop. Jeffrey Sachs (1982, 1984) has produced a theoretical analysis of the borrower-lender relationship on lines which follow closely those investigated by Eaton and Gersovitz (1981). Sachs assumes that credit rationing on the international markets is determined by the

153

propensity to repudiate debt by borrowers which, in
turn, depends on the efficacy of retaliatory
measures by the banks. He discusses this hypothesis
in cooperative and non-cooperative (prisoner's
dilemma) settings, both with and without certainty.

Sachs assumes that the ability to repay debt is
positively correlated with the rate of growth of
capital stock of the borrowing economy since this
increases the supply potential of the country and
hence its net exports. In addition the implicit
assumption is made that world demand and price
conditions (pertaining to terms of trade and
interest rates) are given so that exports depend
only on the country's productive capacity. Banks
view investment plans favourably since this raises
debt servicing capacity. As a consequence the
borrower faces an intertemporal trade-off between
consumption and investment when using credit
resources.

In a non-cooperative setting actors follow a
prisoner's dilemma model which may lead to default.
In this case the total credit supplied is inferior
and the borrower's welfare is lower than in the no
default case.

A cooperative setting is established when rules
of the game are set down in the sense that borrowers
agree with banks on the implementation of an
investment plan which raises the country's capital
stock and credit is awarded prior to the
implementation of such a plan. In the cooperative
case total credit is higher thus increasing overall
welfare.

Results change when uncertainty about the future
is introduced. In this case banks may find
themselves trapped in bad debt (which may lead to
default) even if rules are agreed upon and this
implies that some of the risk is borne by banks (who
charge higher interest rates).

Sachs' approach is interesting in many ways as
it provides a tentative answer to some of the
problems discussed above, such as the need to
consider borrower-lender interaction, the role of
agreements as well as the distinction (which Sachs
does not take up explicitly) between economic and
strategic risk.

His work implicitly assumes "country specific
risk" but not "systemic risk". However, what Sachs
considers as uncertainty may be in fact be
considered as systemic risk since the investment
plans undertaken by the borrower are made under the

assumption of a given international environment
(world demand, terms of trade, interest rates). Once
we recognize that systemic risk and country specific
risks are at least partially connected then there is
room for reducing uncertainty by trying to model the
interaction between the behaviour of single agents
and the evolution of the international economy.

Country risk and political risk

It has been suggested (Agmon and Dietrich 1983)
that the international credit mechanism is radically
different from the one affecting domestic credit
market on the following assumptions. The debt
relationship between countries and international
banks has assumed the form of a permanent relation
since it is not realistic to assume that outstanding
debt will be repaid in the near future. Hence what
keeps such a relation alive (and, it should be
added, keeps the international financial system from
collapsing) is the maintenance of a debt service
flow in exchange for new loans which are in part
necessary to service previous commitments. In
Minsky's terminology this implies assuming that the
international debt mechanism can survive only if
speculative and ponzi finance positions dominate the
market.

The country risk issue is thus transformed into
a conflict between borrowers and lenders over the
intertemporal distribution of resources. Borrowers
will be able to tax lenders, i.e. to avoid repayment
of debt service in part or totally, much in the same
way that a government is able to tax citizens in
order to repay debt obligations which it has raised.
The real issue associated with country risk
assessment then is the analysis of the intertemporal
conflict which arises between lenders and borrowers.

Agmon and Dietrich use this approach to suggest
that such a conflict, and hence country risk
analysis, is mainly a political question about which
traditional economic analysis has little to say.

Agmon and Dietrich indicate a fruitful line of
research. We accept their point that country risk
analysis may be viewed as a conflict over the
distribution of resources and we also agree on the
political implications. The approach developed in
this book suggests, however, that systemic
interactions between political and economic factors
(i.e. the political economy of debt) must be
considered as a more fruitful starting point.

155

Growth Debt and Country Risk

   As we have repeatedly admitted, international
debt relations involve both political and economic
factors. The analytical problem here is to establish
logically convincing links between political and
economic factors in decision-making. We may suggest
a possible starting point in what follows.
   This starting point derives from issue linkage
analysis (Tollison and Willet 1979). International
debt negotiations may be considered as one of the
several bargaining grounds in which borrowing and
lending countries are involved. This implies that
debt relations involve the governments of both
borrowing and lending countries and international
institutions as well as private banks.
   If negotiations on debt are carried forward
along with negotiations on other kinds of
international relations (e.g. defense), then the
possibility of a political exchange arises.
   The borrowing country may wish to exchange
political support (or military support) for more
financial assistance. The lending country might find
it politically profitable to provide (for example)
less military assistance and more financial support.
The amount of financial support which the borrower
will receive is consequently not merely a function
of its bargaining power vis-à-vis the lender but
also of its ability to establish issue linkages
which will lead to mutually advantageous political
exchanges.
   The establishment of a political exchange which
increases the availability of funds to the borrower,
however, may increase the financial instability of
the system. This is intuitive if we accept the
hypothesis that the possibility of increasing the
transfer of funds is higher during the expansionary
phase of the financial cycle. If this is so the new
funds will increase the fragility of the system in
two respects.
   In the first place, the borrower will have more
funds available and hence will move further away
from the initial equilibrium position for reasons
pertaining to the mechanics of "pure" financial
interrelations (2). Secondly, if a borrower is
successful in establishing issue linkages it will
exploit the benefits of a political moral hazard in
that the banks' propensity to lend will increase as
a result of their perception that the country's
creditworthiness has increased by virtue of the
lender country's intention to support the borrower
for political reasons.

Growth Debt and Country Risk

Liquidity and solvency risk

It has been noted (Kharas 1984) that country risk and creditworthinesss are long run concepts. This sounds convincing if we recall that debt has been used by borrowers to finance their development programs and not only (or mostly) payments imbalances. Hence country risk analysis should really be considered part of the economics of growth and debt.

The literature on growth and debt is based on the pioneering contribution of Avramovic (1964) on the conditions which must be fulfilled for the stability of a debt-financed growth process. The Avramovic problem may be stated as follows. In the first stage of its development process a country will run into a resource gap, i.e. an excess of investment over savings (and a corresponding trade balance deficit) which will have to be financed internationally. The growth-cum-debt process will be "well behaved" if the country is able to produce enough resources to fill the gap and at the same time repay the debt it has accumulated.

A well behaved growth-cum-debt mechanism produces the well known (Avramovic 1964, Simonsen 1984) debt cycle which includes three distinct phases (see fig 9.1).

In the first phase the excess of investment over saving will produce an accumulation of net debt. In the second phase the excess of investment over saving will come down to zero but debt servicing will continue to rise as a consequence of past accumulation of debt on which interest has to be paid. In the third phase the country will have to produce an excess of savings over investments in order to allow for the decumulation of debt.

Literature on growth and debt has defined the conditions which must be met so that foreign indebtedness does not produce a vicious spiral of growing indebtedness. These well known conditions require that the rate of growth of output of the borrowing country be equal to the rate of interest to be paid on debt. If this condition holds then the output debt ratio will not decrease. An alternative way (Simonsen 1984) to express this condition is that the rate of growth of exports has to be equal to the rate of interest. Both conditions amount to saying that the country must be able to produce resources at the same speed at which resources must be transferred to the lenders in order to service debt.

Growth Debt and Country Risk

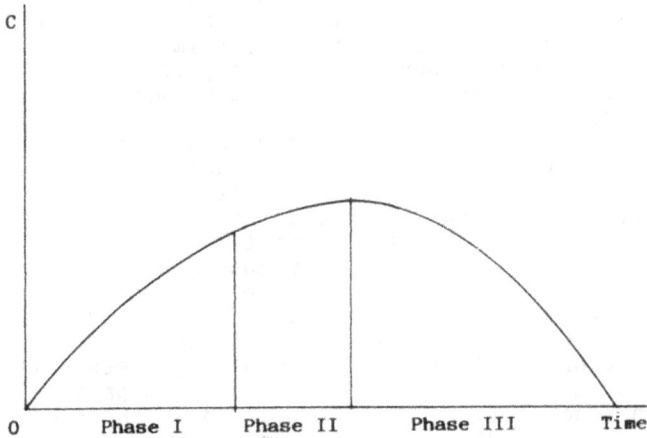

Fig.9.1   The Phases of the Debt Cycle

The beauty of the Avramovic condition lies in
its simplicity; its major defect lies in the fact
that it rests on a number of oversimplifying
assumptions which cast doubt on its utility as a
guide for creditworthiness analysis.

The assumptions are: a) that the growth of
exports (which represent the source of foreign
currency needed to service debt) depends on the
growth of output (3); this amounts to saying that a
country will be able to sell abroad all of its
production and that no demand constraints will be
operating; b) that the amount of credit that a
country will need given its internal development
process will be obtained in full on the
international markets; in other words, that the
amount of credit will be demand determined and no
credit rationing will be in force; c) that relevant
variables such as the interest rate, the terms of
trade, the exchange rate, and the rate of growth of
world demand are given exogenously; d) that the
economy is well behaved in the sense that relevant
parameters such as its propensity to invest, save

158

and export do not vary over the cycle.

Many of the above limitations have however been overcome in more recent contributions. Solomon (1977) has modified the Avramovic model by allowing for a change in the propensity to save, in the capital output ratio and in the rate of growth of capacity.

If appropriate domestic policies can alter these relevant parameters then the growth-cum-debt process may be steered towards an equilibrium path.

Spaventa (1983) has introduced into the Avramovic-Solomon framework an export function which depends on the (exogenous) rate of growth of world demand. He also notes how the rate of growth of world demand is inversely correlated to the international rate of interest. As a consequence an international depression accompanied by a monetary restraint (i.e. the situation prevailing in the first part of this decade) will hurt an indebted country twice, by increasing the burden of debt and by worsening its export performance.

The Avramovic approach has been used to derive creditworthiness indicators from long run aspects of the indebted economy. In this case the limitations under point c) above (i.e. that credit is demand determined) is overcome since the implicit assumption is that the amount of credit awarded will be a function of the country's creditworthiness.

Feder (1980) has produced an analysis of the probability of default of a number of countries deriving standard creditworthiness indicators (debt service ratio, reserves imports ratio, etc.) from the Avramovic-Solomon model. Katz (1982) has introduced a partially endogenous determination of the interest rate (the spread over Libor for the country involved) by assuming that country risk, and hence the interest rate, increases with the amount of debt outstanding. The implicit assumption in this case seems to be that of the principle of increasing risk (Kalecki 1937).

In a more recent contribution Kharas (1984) has derived formally and tested the determination of credit obtained in international markets. The crucial condition (in the theoretical model only, however) is that the stock of fixed capital in the indebted economy does not fall below an endogenously determined critical value. If this condition is met then the country will be in a position to use the funds obtained so as to produce enough resources as to repay the debt.

Growth Debt and Country Risk

The fact that the country faces a private
international credit market is analyzed as a policy
problem in a contribution by Feder and Just (1977) .
The authors discuss the determination of an optimal
policy plan that has to be implemented by a country
wishing to maintain access to the international
credit markets. Access crucially depends on
creditworthiness and thus on two indicators
(debt export ratio and reserves over imports). The
policy must be designed so as to allow for an
acceptable behaviour of the variables entering the
two indicators. This implies that not all the
resources the country is able to raise will be
directed to the maximization of the rate of growth.
A part of them will be allocated to the production
of that good (creditworthiness) which is a necessary
input for the production of credit.

Well behaved models and systemic risk

The literature on growth and debt is rapidly
progressing and will no doubt produce new insights
on the problem. At this stage we can identify two
major limitations in the approach that has been
followed so far.

In the first place, the hypothesis that
borrowers and lenders follow well behaved rules of
the game seems unwarranted. Some of the studies we
have mentioned (Sachs 1982, 1984; Katz 1984;
Simonsen 1984) explicitly discuss the interaction
between sovereign borrowers and international credit
markets. They investigate the conditions at which
this interaction produces a stable dynamic behaviour
of the model, i.e. they try to establish the
conditions at which the debt relationship will
eventually die away as the entire amount of debt
will be repaid. This is the idea behind the debt
cycle investigated by the growth-cum-debt models and
it is also the problem considered by those models in
which the borrower's behaviour is explicitly
considered.

The financial fragility hypothesis we have
discussed in chapter 7 maintains that the
interaction between a profit maximizing banking
system and a profit or growth maximizing borrower
(be it a firm or a sovereign borrower) produces a
cumulative process which transforms tranquillity
into financial distress. The endogenous capacity of
financially sophisticated systems to produce
financial distress and breakdown is the very essence

of the financial fragility hypothesis. What prevents
this mechanism from leading to a full-fledged
financial crisis is the intervention of a lender of
last resort and, eventually of a source of
autonomous effective demand such as government
expenditure. In other words, the interaction between
borrowers and lenders, if not assisted by some
institutional intervention would fatally push the
system into financial disaster. This is a well known
result of the literature on financial crisis dating
at least as far back as Bagehot (1873) and on which
Minsky's theory heavily draws. It is therefore
surprising that models describing such an
interaction simply rule out this aspect.

It must be stressed that the possibility of
financial distress in such a scenario should not be
considered as a "case of instability", i.e. as a
case in which the values of the relevant parameters
produce unstable eigenvalues. If this were the case
then a traditional growth-cum-debt and
borrower-lender interaction would be well suited to
analyze such a situation.

A financial crisis may well be considered the
result of an explosive dynamic behaviour. But this
is not the crucial point. The financial instability
hypothesis holds that such a dynamic behaviour
depends on endogenous change of those parameters
which determine the dynamic path of the system. This
endogenous change is the result of the interaction
between macro and micro behaviour. As we have seen
above the propensity of banks to lend and the
propensity of borrowers to absorb new funds varies
over the cycle. Both increase when growth is
expanding and both fall during recessions producing,
respectively, manias and euphoria and panic.

Propensities to borrow and lend are
(necessarily) treated as fixed parameters in the
growth-cum-debt models. This does not mean that such
models are of little use. They are certainly a
valuable tool in attempting to identify the
necessary conditions that should be met in order to
avoid a cumulative financial distress scenario. They
produce little insight, however, when they are used
to describe the process of the accumulation of debt
and the distress which follows as they take place in
the real economy.

One of the reasons for this state of the theory
lies in the fact that the outside world, the
international environment in which the
growth-cum-debt process develops, is generally

assumed to be given and unchanging.

This brings us to the second point. How can systemic variables such as world demand and world interest rates be considered in such an analysis in a satisfactory way?

Stability conditions usually associated with these models actually amount to answering the following question. Given the rate of growth of world demand, international terms of trade and interest rates, how should an indebted economy adapt itself to these outside conditions in order to complete its debt cycle?

The problem with this kind of approach is that the domestic economy may well pass from a stable into an unstable situation because the external conditions have changed and not because the borrower is pursuing the "wrong" policies.

Consider the fundamental stability condition of the Avramovic-Solomon approach. If a country manages to achieve a rate of growth of output (exports) equal to, or even higher than, the interest rate on its debt it will bring its debt onto a steady or even declining path and its debt cycle will eventually come to a close (Simonsen 1984). This well behaved path will, however, rapidly be turned into a disaster scenario if the interest rate increases and the rate of growth of world demand falls for reasons that are completely outside the borrowing country's control. As long as these models assume such strategically important variables as exogenous their insight on this kind of problems is bound to remain limited.

To proceed further, however, is not an easy task.

In chapter 7 we have sketched a description of the financial instability hypothesis in an international economy. In chapter 8 we have pointed out how the turning points of such a mechanism crucially depend on the behaviour of the leading country of the international system. What we really need is to produce a global approach in which growth-cum-debt mechanisms are integrated with the behaviour of the system as a whole.

Economic theorists are usually skeptical about such a program as the only systemic model they can think of is a perfectly competitive general equilibrium one in which no place for institutions, national governments and, of course, financial instability is to be found. Economic theory has however produced a few attempts to build "global

Growth Debt and Country Risk

models" in which the interaction between different
actors of the international economy is explicitly
considered. The next chapter is devoted to a brief
examination of some of these attempts.

NOTES

1. For extensive surveys see Saunders 1983, and
Saini and Bates 1984.
2. See the appendix to chapter 7 and the
appendix to this chapter.
3. This explains why the rate of growth of
output and the rate of growth of exports may be
considered as interchangeable variables.

APPENDIX

Issue linkage and financial instability
    The unstable cumulative process of borrower
lender interaction discussed in appendix A.7 may be
started off by adjustment in the political relations
between the borrower and a politically and
financially stronger country which also acts as a
lender. We may assume that the existence of such a
relation is a necessary condition for the access to
international financial markets as it provides
"political creditworthiness" to the borrower.
However equilibrium in the political market may
entail disequilibrium in the financial market.
    A political market model is presented in fig
A.9.1 . The box diagram confronts the indifference
curves of two countries, the borrower and the
lender. Borrower's utility (which is measured from
OB origin) increases if both political and financial
support received from the lender increase. Lender's
utility (which is measured from OL origin) increases
if financial support and political support it gives
to the borrower decrease. (Note that while financial
support and political support are considered as
benefits for the borrower, and hence its utility
increases when they increase, they are considered as
costs to the lender and so its utility decreases
when they increase. Both the amount of financial and
political support should be read starting from the
OB origin).
    Suppose that the initial condition is at point a
where C1 financial support and P1 political support
are granted to the borrower. It is easy to see that

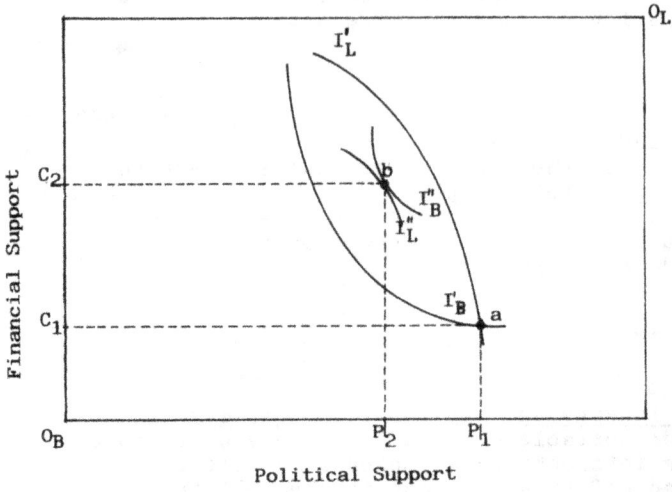

Fig.A.9.1.

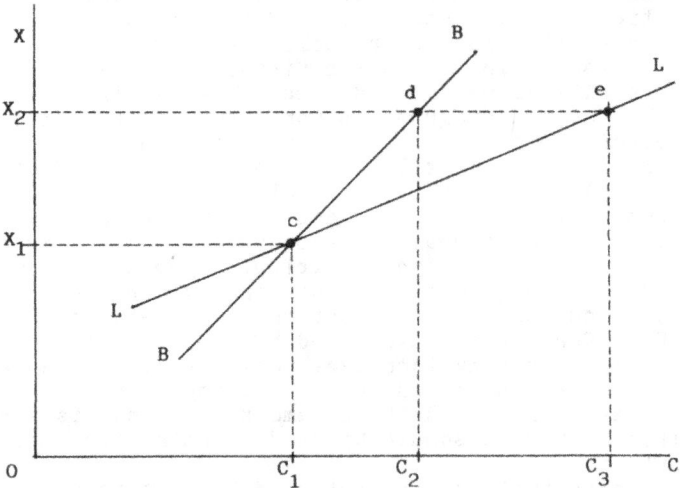

Fig.A.9.2.

both countries will increase their utility by moving to point b in which the borrower receives more financial support (C2>C1) but less political support (P2<P1). In this respect point b is an equilibrium point for the political market.

Let us now turn to the financial market presented in fig. A.9.2. and represented by the BB and LL schedules discussed in appendix A.7. This implies introducing a third agent in the picture, i.e. the private banking system. If we assume that this market was in equilibrium at the beginning of the process then the amount of finance C1 of fig. A.9.1. produces an amount X1 of exports given the BB schedule (point c). The increase of funds from C1 to C2 allows the borrower to produce an amount X2 of exports (point d). At this stage the private banking system (which is here considered as an additional lender with respect to the official lender represented in fig. A.9.1) will react by granting C3 loans (point e) and a cumulative process will start.

This simple example shows the effects of the interaction of political and economic conditions in financial relations. It also suggests that while political exchange might be viewed as a way to improve the political creditworthiness of the borrower the effects of an improved political equilibrium may be the destabilization of financial relations. We stress, once again, that this results derives from the assumption of "lender euphoria" embedded in the LL schedule. As a matter of fact if equilibrium in the political market improves the lender's perception of the borrower's creditworthiness the euphoria of the banks might increase even further. This would produce a flatter LL schedule (the marginal propensity to lend would increase) and the process of financial instability would be enhanced.

Chapter Ten

THE GLOBAL POLITICAL ECONOMY OF INTERNATIONAL
RELATIONS

The brief survey we have carried out in the
previous chapter has led us to the conclusion that
the investigation of the problems posed by
international financial instability badly needs the
development of global models. A global approach, on
the other hand, presents other shortcomings with
respect to single country models, the most obvious
being the loss of information (which can be very
high) implied in the aggregation needed to treat the
international system as a whole.

Global frameworks, however, exist and in some
cases they are based on economic models. In this
chapter we will present a short summary of some
alternative views on global modelling. We will first
describe what may be considered the "traditional
view" of global economic relations in the post-war
period. Subsequently we will consider how different
theoretical approaches analyze the post-hegemonic
system.

None of the models considered includes political
economy aspects. We will discuss the implications of
such an omission both in the traditional view and in
the subsequent models. The last section of the
chapter includes what we have called "an agenda for
research". In this section the fundamental relations
of the political economy of an international system
are singled out.

The traditional view: an exposition and some
comments

We will now discuss what may be considered as
the "traditional view" of international economic
(North-South) relations in the Bretton Woods system.

166

It is a very stylized model which builds on both neoclassical and Keynesian literature. It is expounded here simply to provide a support for further discussion of later models (1). Its role is propedeutic also as far as the problems discussed in the previous chapter are concerned as it neglects international private indebtedness, it assumes fixed exchange rates and the absence of substantial politico-economic conflicts in North-South relations.

It will be easy to see how the working of such a model crucially depends on the assumptions made regarding the institutional setting which supposedly regulates international relations. In particular its plausibility heavily depends on the fulfillment of the hegemonic stability conditions discussed in chapter 2.

The world is made up of two regions. The North produces a manufactured good whose price is "cost determined" by a mark-up mechanism. The South produces a primary commodity whose price varies according to excess demand in the international market. The demand for primary commodities depends on the production of manufactured goods and the supply of commodities varies with the national product of the South. As a consequence the price of the commodity will increase whenever the rate of growth of the North exceeds the rate of growth of the South.

The price of the manufactured good will rise as a consequence of pressures which may be both internal and external to the northern region. The former may result from internal wage push (which, in turn, may be linked to the level of activity), while the latter may derive from the rise of the price of primary commodities which the North imports from the South.

As the exchange rate between the two regions is assumed to be fixed, the terms of trade will vary in favour of the South whenever its rate of growth falls below the rate of growth of the North, as this increases the excess demand for primary commodities and vice versa (Findlay 1980, Grilli and Yang 1981). The assumption of fixed exchange rates may be justified on the following grounds. The exchange rate is obviously fixed within the Northern region as we are assuming that the Bretton Woods arrangements hold. We may also assume for simplicity that the South will peg its currency to the North on account of strong currency option considerations

(Moon 1982).
The crucial variables are the rate of growth of output of the two regions. The rate of growth of the South will be directly related to its balance of payments (Thirlwall 1979, Thirlwall and Hussain 1982). This rests on the idea that the South must acquire foreign currency in order to pay for imports of the manufactured good which is essential to its growth process. The amount of foreign currency will depend positively on the volume of exports (which depends on the demand generated by the North) and on the terms of trade (which are determined by growth differentials), on the amount of capital flows which are either official aid flows or (net) direct investments. The South will use currency to pay for imports (which depend positively on its rate of growth) (2).
In this model the growth rate of the South is completely endogenous and it depends on two variables: the terms of trade and the rate of growth of the North. Actually the terms of trade too depend on the behaviour of the rate of growth of the North which takes on the role of crucial variable par excellence. No wonder this variable is usually left unexplained in the literature on global North-South interdependence.
To try to find an endogenous explanation to this variable would require a discussion of the (unsatisfactory) state in which growth theory is (Findlay 1985). We may however recall our discussion of the characteristics of the hegemonic system which may be considered as the necessary conditions for a "policy induced" growth cycle mechanism.
If hegemonic stability prevails then the North as a whole will not incur balance of payments constraints on growth. Hence we may assume that cyclical growth mechanisms depend on the behaviour of government expenditure (3) which, in turn, will follow some kind of political business cycle.
The above assumptions will produce a cyclical growth motion depending essentially on the politico-economic as well as the institutional conditions prevailing in the northern region. The growth process will, in turn, produce cyclical movements in all the other variables including the terms of trade. A diagrammatic representation of the operation of the model is offered in fig 10.1
The "traditional model" stylized above relies heavily on politico-economic assumptions in order to be operative. Several other political economy

168

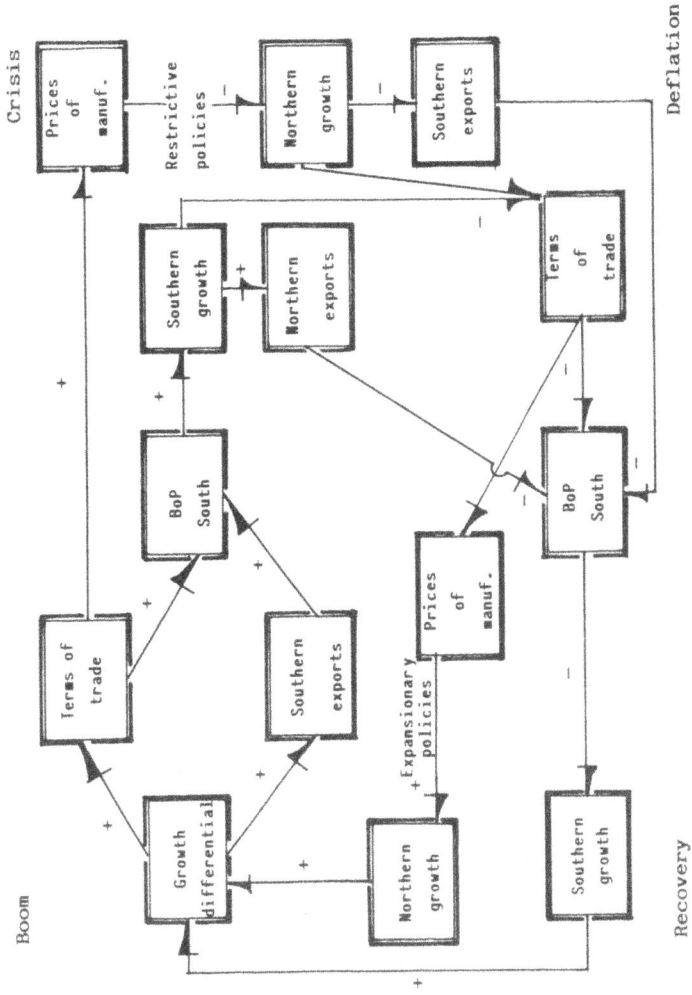

Fig. 10.1   North South Interaction : The Traditional View.

implications might be singled out both at the
domestic and at the international level. We shall
now briefly discuss them.

In the first place, if we consider the
international system as a whole the traditional view
that foreign trade is the "engine of growth" of the

169

world economy is no longer sustainable. From a
systemic perspective not all national economies can
pursue export-led growth simultaneously if the
conditions for hegemonic stability discussed in
    chapter 2 do not hold. This also implies that
one should investigate whether the US economy may be
considered the true engine of growth of the system.
We are not in a position to provide evidence on or
discuss this point here. We may simply point out
that if the conditions for hegemonic stability hold
then the rate of growth of the North as a whole may
be said to depend on: 1) the ability of Europe and
Japan to exploit neomercantilistic opportunities by
pursuing export-led growth, 2) the ability and
willingness of US authorities to implement an
expansionary policy, 3) the efficacy of US
policy-induced growth to produce spillover effects
on the rest of the system, 4) the existence of an
international political business cycle.
    Points 1) and 2) represent the conditions of
mutual convenience of, respectively, Europe-Japan
and the US to participate in the hegemonic system.
They are therefore fulfilled by definition. Point 3)
would require a lengthy discussion of an abundant
literature which we will not pursue here. We may
recall as an example, a recent investigation
(Felmingham 1984) that supports the view that US
monetary policy does have an effect on the rate of
growth and employment of the rest of the western
economies.
    The problem then arises of how US monetary
policy behaves. If we assume that this depends at
least partially on political considerations (Laney
and Willet 1983, Beck 1984) then we may accept the
view that the traditional model discussed in the
previous paragraph heavily depends on
politico-economic developments in the United States.
    Point 4) is much more controversial. Tufte's
(1978) original hypothesis of an international
political business cycle has been challenged
(Thompson and Zuk 1983) on the grounds of new
evidence. In our opinion Tufte's hypothesis deserves
some deeper consideration. We may just recall that
if conditions 1) and 2) hold then single
industrialized countries have enough economic leeway
to exploit domestic political cycles as the
international expansion eases the balance of
payments constraint which would pose a limit to the
pursuit of expansionary policies in preelection
periods. In this respect we must look for the

170

international political conditions which are
necessary for the exploitation of domestic political
cycles.

In conclusion, a general criticism of the
traditional view is that it ignores political
economy aspects which are central to its operational
applicability. This point should not be
overemphasized, however. The traditional model is a
"pure" economic model and it suffers from the
shortcomings which are common to all economic growth
models. The points discussed above suggest that the
traditional view should be integrated in a full
politico-economic framework to overcome its defects.

The point under discussion is different. How is
the traditional model to be transformed in order to
take account of the transformations in the
international system after the collapse of the
hegemonic regime?

Economists seem particularly resistent to global
analysis (4) which is, on the contrary, relevant for
our analysis. Few exceptions exist. We will now
discuss some of those that include North-South
financial relations or are relevant for an
understanding of the problem.

The post Bretton Woods world: alternative views
World inflation. Systemic approaches to
post-hegemonic international relations have
initially focused on the problem of world inflation.
Walter Salant (1977) has proposed a supranational
approach to the analysis of world inflation
suggesting that the international economy should not
be considered as the mere aggregation of national
economies and markets. If inflation is correctly to
be considered a global phenomenon qualitative
modifications should be introduced into the
traditional model. Two points seem particularly
relevant in this respect.

In the first place, the international economy is
made up of "segments" which cannot be said to belong
to any national economy in particular; the most
obvious example being the Eurodollar market.
Secondly, Salant suggests that the prices of
internationally traded goods are set in world
markets on which no single national economy may be
said to exert a monopolistic power.

Although Salant introduces some interesting
points into the traditional view, his approach risks
throwing at least part of the baby out with the

water. The role of national policies is still
crucial in a context of international
interdependence in defining global phenomena. The
reintroduction of national policies into a
supranational model is still not enough, however, if
one does not distinguish between different countries
of different size and role in the international
system.

The global monetarism approach (Genberg and
Swoboda 1977) to international inflation suggests
that the monetary policy pursued by the centre
economy is crucial in determining world money supply
and hence inflation. Global monetarism, however, may
be criticized using the same arguments which apply
to closed economy monetarism. No reasonable
political economy explanation is provided of the
reasons why the monetary policy of the centre
economy becomes too inflationary at some point. No
focus is devoted to the consideration of factors
affecting the demand for inflation which the money
supply should accommodate (Gordon 1975, 1977). As
far as the real side of the economy is concerned, it
is assumed that it operates according to general
equilibrium and perfect flexibility mechanisms. It
is not surprising that global monetarism loses much
of its heuristic potential once it tries to explain
world inflation after the collapse of the fixed
exchange rate system.

A demand and supply of inflation approach is
followed by Biasco (1979) who discusses the
interaction between the "great world inflation" of
the seventies and the breakdown of monetary cohesion
between industrialized countries. In Biasco's
analysis inflationary pressures were contained
within industrialized countries as long as
"inflation shy" countries such as Germany were able
and willing to prevent "inflation prone" economies
such as Great Britain, France and Italy to pursue
inflationary policies. The former countries did not
provide the latter with the supply of inflation (and
devaluation) which they demanded.

A general anti-inflationary defense was possible
as long as the fixed rate Bretton Woods system was
in operation. When the hegemonic arrangements could
no longer be sustained flexible exchange rates were
the only possible solution to mounting inflationary
pressures.

Biasco's analysis provides interesting insights
on international inflation from a systemic
perspective. What is relevant here is the conflict

which arises between national policy goals
(expressed in terms of inflation and relative
competitiveness) and systemic constraints.

Biasco's economic analysis of inflation could
easily be intergrated with Keohane's (1979, 1982)
political analysis of global inflation. Keohane
suggests that international inflation should be
analyzed in terms of a conflict over power
distribution in the international system. He shows
how different internationl (exchange rate) regimes
are differently conducive to power conflicts which
may produce inflationary tendencies.

One point is particularly relevant to our
discussion. Inflationary conflicts increase when
power distribution shifts away from a previous
setting which provided relative stability as long as
it lasted. Keohane cites the increase of oil prices
as a consequence of the increased market power of
OPEC countries and the subsequent dollar inflation
as the response of the IEA countries (but especially
of the United States) to such a shift in power
distribution. This point is an application of the
(revised) theory of hegemonic stability to inflation
(Keohane 1984) and it shares many aspects with the
analysis of oligopolistic interdependence and
inflationary conflicts we have discussed in chapter
3.

Models of global inflation are promising,
especially if they integrate political end economic
aspects, much in the spirit of the political
analysis of domestic inflation on which literature
has been mounting over the past few years. Inflation
is a crucial element of the global political economy
of debt insofar as it is related to exchange rate
and terms of trade changes. We must, however,
consider also other kinds of models.

The Keynesian view. William Cline has produced a
number of interesting analyses on the international
debt problem. He has recently presented (1983)
results of a simulation study in which he considers
the possibilities of indebted countries to meet
their payments commitments. His simulation model may
be taken as an example of the traditional "Keynesian
view". This view may be considered an extension of
the traditional model discussed in the first part of
this chapter. It consists in adding to the global
model variables such as flexible exchange rates, the
international interest rate, the price of oil. The
possibility of indebted countries to meet their
commitments depends on alternative values assigned

to international and domestic variables. Single
indebted countries are considered. Their rate of
growth depends on domestic economic policies and on
exchange rate policy. A higher rate of growth of the
OECD economies (considered as a whole) will improve
the borrowers' balance of payments prospects as a
consequence of improvements in both the volume and
value (terms of trade) of exports much in accordance
with the traditional view dicussed above.

The most relevant result of this exercise is the
traditional Keynesian tenet that global growth will
alleviate debt problems more than any other single
policy measure. Its major shortcoming lies in the
fact that OECD growth is considered as exogenous
while no role is allowed for intra-OECD policy
problems.

Neoclassical transition theory. Contrary to the
Keynesian approach, the neoclassical transition view
(Beenstock 1983) considers the debt problem which
mounted in the 1970s as the result of a transition
between two different equilibrium situations. In
this respect this view may be termed generally
optimistic as it considers the present problems
manageable by world market forces.

Transition theory may be summed up as consisting
in the following six stages. 1) In the second half
of the 1960s a number of LDCs started an intensive
industrialization growth process centred on the
manufacturing sector and on more open and free
market oriented economic policies which turned out
to be successful in those countries which were later
to be known as newly industrialized countries
(NICs). 2) The widespread industrialization process
produced an excess supply of manufactured goods
which led to a fall in their prices relative to the
prices of raw materials. This change in relative
prices produced deindustrialization effects in the
developed countries. 3) Deindustrialization led to a
fall in the relative share of profits with respect
to wages in industrialized countries. As a
consequence the market power of wages (union
militancy) increased. 4) This induced adjustment
within sectors and nations which was not
frictionless. 5) The industrialization process in
the LDCs and the relative fall in the share of
profits in industrialized countries produced a
profit differential in favour of LDCs. As a
consequence international capital was attracted to
LDCs which ran capital account surpluses to which
corresponded current account deficits. In this

respect the debt problem is an equilibrium and not a disequilibrium phenomenon as it reflects changing investment opportunities. 6) Transition theory predicts that once adjustment frictions have been overcome, the debt problem will solve itself as the LDCs will witness a fall in relative profitability and hence capital will flow back towards developed countries.

Transition theory is based on a general equilibrium framework. Its explanation of the debt problem of the 1970s, therefore, cannot include discussion of crucial variables such as the level and rate of growth of world demand, the problem of financial instability, the determination of exchange rate changes. It is not surprising that it conveys a fundamentally optimistic view of the debt crisis.

A Keynes-Kalecki approach. Darity and Fitzgerald (1984) have produced a theoretical model of the world economy based on Keynesian-Kaleckian lines. The model was built to offer a systemic view of the growth-cum-debt problem and it provides an endogenous determination of crucial variables such as world demand and interest rates.

The model takes into consideration two economic areas: the industrialized Centre and the developing Periphery. An international credit market allocates financial resources between the two areas. The Centre is in a privileged position as it can obtain all the credit it wishes at the existing terms while the Periphery will obtain credit only once the Centre's demand has been fulfilled.

The growth process in the Centre is led, in a Kaleckian fashion, by the autonomous demand for investments whose aggregate amount also determines the overall profits which accrue to the capitalists of the Centre. Higher profits provide more finance and hence lower the demand for loans by the Centre for a given amount of investment demand.

The expansion of investment in the Centre sustains expansion in the Periphery as exports of the latter, and hence profits, are enhanced. This may, however, have ambiguous effects on the amount of credit that the Periphery is able to obtain since this depends on the amount of internal financing that is available to Centre firms and on the elasticity of demand for loans with respect to credit market conditions. The best possible situation for the Periphery is when high investment in the Centre is accompanied by a high propensity to save on the part of the capitalists as this decreases their demand for loans; consequently international banks are willing to lend more to the Periphery. Alternatively, the Periphery will build up a large amount of debt when the Centre is in a recession and its demand for credit is low.

The model does not reach any definite results as these depend crucially on the values of the parameters involved. The authors claim that the model will produce a cyclical growth mechanism depending on the cyclical swings in investment in the Centre which is the true "engine of growth" of the system. Investments, in turn, depend on the expectations of profits that business firms hold. In a traditional Keynesian fashion profit expectations (animal spirits) are left exogenous.

The model provides some interesting insights and presents certain similarities with the financial instability hypothesis discussed in this book. It also contains a number of unsatisfactory points, however. Here, we will mention just two. In the first place, exogenous profit (growth) expectations imply that most or all political economy (regime) influences on the propensity to expand are neglected. Secondly, the Keynes-Kalecki approach followed by the authors is not pushed far enough, and hence fails to recognize that the credit based growth mechanism they describe will eventually lead to financial distress and generalized bankruptcy if no institutional supports (such as LLR and big government) come into play. In other words, although the model's aim is to depict the world economy we are presently operating in, it neglects the fundamental institutional aspects that allow this system to operate.

A Marxist view. We will finally discuss a Marxist interpretation of the debt crisis which provides a systemic view. The author (Lipietz 1984) belongs to the so-called "ecole de regulation" which has recently been producing a new view of the present capitalistic crisis.

According to Lipietz the debt crisis arises from the interaction of "peripheral Fordism" and "central monetarism". Peripheral Fordism consists in the transfer of Fordist industrial relations from the centre (industrialized) economies to a small number of developing countries. Fordism is intended as the combination of intensive capital accumulation, which leads to high productivity gains, and high wages, which allow for a growing domestic demand. Wages, however, cannot rise beyond certain limits as this

will conflict with the productivity gains. Part of
the domestic production in LDCs will have to be
exported. Exports are also necessary to earn the
finance needed to repay imports of capital goods
which are necessary for the accumulation process.

Credit is granted to peripheral Fordism
economies on the expectation that high productivity
growth will lead to high exports and hence debt
servicing capacity. The absence of regulation in
international financial markets facilitates the
process of credit allocation and eventually leads to
the build up of financial fragility.

In sum, this global mechanism rests on three
conditions: a) the Fordist mechanism is transferred
from the centre to the periphery; b) the centre
provides a Keynesian demand pull for the periphery's
exports; c) the international credit markets provide
the finance for the accumulation process in the
periphery. The last two conditions are removed once
the centre economies change their economic policies
from generalized Keynesism to central monetarism,
i.e. the adoption of tight monetary policies in the
UK and in the US.

The crucial point in this view is that the
policy change in the Centre, and the consequences it
produces on the international credit mechanism,
should be considered as changes in the "regulating
mechanisms" of the world economy and not just
cyclical phenomena. In other words, the financial
crisis is the result of a fundamental institutional
change which depends on a change in policy views in
the centre economies.

Central monetarism is adopted in the centre
economies in order to push back the claims of both
centre unions and devoloping countries. Central
monetarism cannot be pursued indefinitely, however,
as widespread bankruptcies of Western banks
constitute a threat to the soundness of the central
economic system. As a consequence LLR operations
will be needed and the monetary squeeze will be, at
least partially, arrested.

This neomarxist view presents many similarities
with the financial instability model discussed in
this book. It partially shares the central role of
monetary policy of western countries in determining
the overall feasibility of the indebted growth
mechanism. It gives much space to institutions and
structural aspects. We feel, however, that the
economic model developed is somewhat unsatisfactory
as it fails to explain the mounting of debt. In

addition, as is the case with other Marxist analyses, it neglects balance of payments links within the different regions of the world economy. It explains changes in the international regime assuming that no policy conflicts take place within the Centre economy, thus confirming the Marxist propensity to oversimplify policy conflicts.

An agenda for research

The above models provide different views of the global functioning of the world economy. We do not intend to criticize them globally nor do we claim that our proposed interpretation is superior to them. Our intent is simply to suggest how pure economic interpretations may be integrated in a political economy framework. In what follows we will provide some suggestions for such an integration whose full set up is beyond the scope of this book.

In the first place, political and economic interactions should not be confined to political business cycle considerations. We have already criticized the traditional political business cycle approach from an economic point of view in chapter 4. We have also mentioned that Tufte's (1978) hypothesis of an international political business cycle needs some further clarification at both the theoretical and the empirical levels (Thompson and Zuk 1983).

In the second place, political business cycle considerations should be integrated with what we have asserted to be the industrial states' leading principle of action in international economic policy: neomercantilism. Unfortunately very little theoretical work (and almost no empirical investigations) has been produced on the consequences of the political business cycle in an open economy. From a theoretical point of view we may note that international payments constraints may represent a limitation to the full exploitation of the political manipulation of the business cycle. In the pre-election expansionary phase a trade deficit is likely to arise, consequently the restriction which takes place in the post-election phase is aimed not only at curbing inflation but also at restoring the trade surplus which the previous expansion had probably eroded.

A major implication of the introduction of open economy considerations into a political business cycle is that such a policy will be influenced by the prevailing international monetary regime. We have discussed in chapters 2 and 3 the interaction between neomercantilism and international payments regimes. The introduction of political business cycle considerations into that framework may be carried out by taking into account Willet's and Mullen's (1982) point that a crawling peg (or possibly other kinds of managed flexibility) encourages the exploitation of the unemployment-inflation trade-off which is implicit in the political business cycle model. Since currency devaluation gives a negative impression of the administration that resorts to it, it should as a rule be implemented after the elections. By so doing, the current account deterioration which has (probably) resulted from the pre-election expansion will be partly reabsorbed. This is also consistent with the attempt to pursue neomercantilistic policy with greater vigour after the election tournament (5).

This leads us to another point. Political manipulation of the economy should not be considered only in terms of political control over fiscal and monetary policy. Industrial relations management should also be included if we admit that under conditions of collective bargaining the rate of inflation also depends on the degree of compliance of trade unions to general macroeconomic constraints. (Gylfason and Lyndbeck 1982)

We do not wish to push this argument too far. We simply recall that once all political economy interactions within a single economy are taken into account the "pure" political business cycle hypothesis does not seem to provide a large enough framework to deal satisfactorily with the problem. A fruitful line of research might be to take up once again the supply and demand approach to inflation proposed by Gordon (1975) and extend it to the whole range of macroeconomic management.

In considering the international economy, however, the interactions of economics and politics are rather different. Just to give an example, if manipulation of the domestic economy is designed to maximize the chances of re-election (possibly under some ideological constraint; see Frey 1978), the manipulation of the international economy is aimed at something else, like the maximization of power. Once again the state of international regimes will influence the type of political economic conflict. We have already discussed the characteristics of the oligopolistic system and we will not repeat the arguments here. We may simply add that the level and performance of the relevant economic variables, such as world demand, terms of trade and exchange rates, will be strongly affected by the state of international relations and the degree of conflict prevailing.

One obvious example is that in oligopoly the role of the residual country is not automatically solved and, as we have seen in chapter 3, this depresses, ceteris paribus, the rate of growth of world demand. Another consequence is that, under oligopoly, exchange rate flexibility will be much more pronounced and hence financial instability will be enhanced.

One general conclusion of our investigation is that political manipulation of the economy cannot be limited to cyclical fine tuning. Indeed, the political economy of international financial instability explains not just a cyclical movement but rather a qualitative transformation of the international financial system which will eventually produce financial distress and crisis. The explosive or self-regulating nature of the system will depend, as we have seen in chapter 7, on the interaction of economic forces and institutional factors. Adjustment mechanisms do not involve only economic variables as a "pure" economic interpretation would hold. Rather adjustment mechanisms are provided by the interaction of economic variables and institutions. Insofar as adjustment is also the result of policy changes its success will depend on the degree of cooperation or conflict which, in turn, is also a function of the institutional structure of the system (Keohane 1984). In this respect international oligopoly presents a high degree of instability since its institutional and economic structure have been changing over time producing changes in the adjustment mechanisms as well.

The rest of this chapter is devoted to the exposition of a very simple conceptual framework in which we try to clarify the fundamental links of the political economy of international financial instabilty in international oligopoly. The conceptual framework is described by laying out a small number of equations whose only purpose is to identify variables and parameters which could represent the base for the development of testable hypotheses. In so doing we will build on existing

contributions of global economic models some of
which we have been recalled in the previous section.
The theoretical economic basis is the traditional
view discussed in the first part of the chapter,
enriched to take into account the modifications of
the international financial system in oligopolistic
conditions.

Our map of the world is made up of two regions.
The South, which is made up of a single country, (6)
and the North, which is divided into the United
States and the rest of the industrialized countries.
We assume that there is only one international
currency, the dollar, in which both trade and
financial flows are denominated. In addition we
assume that the rest of the world (the South and the
other industrialized countries) share a common
currency different from the dollar (or that they
keep fixed exchange rates among their currencies).

Capital letters identify variables while small
letters identify parameters. The equations should be
considered only as indications of causal
relationships as no functional form research is
attempted, nor is it strictly necessary at this
stage.

Equation (1) states that the level of output of
the South (Y_s) is a positive function of the balance
of payments of the South expressed in dollars, where
P_s is the price of the good exported by the South
(which is assumed to be a primary commodity) X_s is
its quantity, R is the exchange rate (defined as
number of units of South's currency for one dollar),
P_n is the price of the manufactured good which the
South imports from the North, X_n is its quantity, K
is the net flow of autonomous capital movements
comprehensive of both direct investments and aid
flows, I is the interest rate, C is the stock of
credit outstanding, DC is the flow of new credit.
The four latter variables are all defined in dollars.

$$(1) \quad Y_s = Y_s(P_s X_s \, R - P_n M_n + K + DC - IC)$$

Equation (1) states that the level of output of
the South is a positive function of the amount of
finance it is able to obtain in the international
market. The approach we follow aims at pointing out
the political economy links and constraints which
determine such a flow. This also means that the
framework presented here omits many economic
components. The discussion of politico-economic

elements starts with equation (2)

$$(2) \quad Xs=Xs(aYn,bYs); \quad a,b>0.$$

Equation (2) states that the exports of the South are a positive function of the level of income of the North Yn, and a positive function of the level of (income) in the South, Ys. The first effect takes account of the role of international demand on the expansion of Southern exports, the second effect considers that exports are limited by supply factors in the South. While the economic rationale for these effects is straightforward its political economy element deserves some clarification. Southern exports will react to world demand, given the degree of protection in the Northern economy; in this respect a reflects the outcome of the "supply and demand" of protection in the North (7). Southern exports will react to Southern domestic growth given the amount of resources that will be devoted to the exporting sector; as a consequence b reflects the outcome of the politico-economy conflicts going on in the South for the allocation of resources (8).

The next equation is straightforward.

$$(3) \quad Ms=Ms(a'Ys); \quad a'>0.$$

It says that the quantity of imports from the North is positively correlated with the output of the South. The political element a' is analogous to a in equation (2). It depends on the degree of protection in the South (9).

The next equation is more complex. It determines the price of the primary good exported by the South Ps.

$$(4) \quad Ps=Ps(c(Yn-Ys), dI,eR,fPn); \quad c,e,f>0 , \quad d<0.$$

Equation (4) reflects the fact that the price of primary goods in international markets depends on two distinct groups of factors (Grilli, Yang 1981). These two groups of factors descend from the two roles which primary commodities play in the world market. The first one is the traditional consumption production role. Since the price of primary commodities reacts positively to excess demand, Ps rises whenever demand from the North is larger than supply from the South. The parameter c reflects the degree of market power which the South as a producer has in the international market. It

could therefore include political elements
determining cartel formation. The second group of
factors reflects the speculative role of primary
goods in a financially complex system. In periods of
high financial instability primary commmodities are
demanded for their store of value role. As a
consequence demand for (and hence the price of)
primary goods will rise whenever the value of the
dollar, which may be considered the most relevant
store of value asset, falls (i.e. R rises). Primary
commodities will be demanded for speculative reasons
whenever inflation in the North increases. The
political element in e reflects the amount of
confidence the international market has in the value
of the dollar (which has wide political economy
aspects as we have seen at length in previous
chapters). The political element in f reflects the
credibility of anti-inflationary policies in the
North. Finally demand for primary commodities for
speculative purposes will be negatively correlated
to the amount of tightness in international
financial markets which is here represented by the
level of the interest rate I. The political element
d represents the degree of confidence and propensity
to lend of international credit markets. As we have
seen in chapter 7 this is heavily influenced by the
overall degree of confidence which prevails
throughout the international system. The appendix to
this chapter contains a simple graphical exposition
of the determination of Ps.

Let us continue to discuss this aspect by
considering the determination of the amount of
credit flows DC that the banks grant to the South.
The implicit assumption here is that credit
rationing prevails and hence that banks determine
the amount of credit extended to the South.

(5) $DC = DC(gI, hYs, 1PsXs\ C)$; $g < 0$, $h, 1 > 0$.

The amount of credit will be inversely related
to the degree of tightness of monetary policy in the
centre economy (which in turn affects the degree of
tightness in international credit markets). The
political element g associated with the
representative interest rate reflects the degree of
control US monetary authorities exert over
international banks and hence the conflicts we have
recalled in chapter 4.

The next two factors reflect creditworthiness
assessment. The South's creditworthiness is

positively related to the level of output and to the
ratio of the value of exports to outstanding debt.
The economic meaning of these representative
indicators is straightforward. The political element
embedded in parameters h and l is also obvious.
Political elements of country risk have been
discussed in the previous chapter and shall not be
taken up again here. What is relevant to note,
however, is the interdependence which arises between
direct and indirect political elements of country
risk.

The following equation is very simple. It states
that the amount of autonomous capital flows directed
to the South K, including both aid flows and direct
investments, are a positive function of the rate of
growth of output in the North. Political econometry
analysis of official aid flows (e.g. Beenstock 1980)
has shown that such a positive correlation exists
but that political influences will also play a
strong role in determining such a relationship. As
far as direct investments are concerned, we may say
that the parameter z includes political risk
considerations in the determination of these
investment decisions. The positive relation with the
level of output of the host country has several
theoretical justifications which are well known in
the literature on aggregate direct investments.

(6) $K=K(zYn)$; $z>0$.

The following equation determines the price
level of the manufactured good produced in the
North. As a consequence we may consider its
determinants the same as those affecting the rate of
inflation in the region. The equation follows the
supply and demand of inflation model introduced by·
Gordon (1975). Hence both monetary and non-monetary
elements are included in the equation.

(7) $Pn=Pn(mPs,pT,qYn,oI)$; $m,p,q>0$, $o<0$.

The first element takes account of the amount of
inflation imported from the South; the political
parameter m takes account of the degree of
protection and hence of the tariff structure which
the North has erected. The second variable T and its
associated parameter p represent the "social
pressure" element in the determination of inflation.
This is a long debated topic in the political
economy of inflation and need not be recalled here

(Hirsch and Goldthorpe 1978). Finally we may allow for a short run element in the determination of inflation represented by the level of output Yn. Here again the political element q may be said to represent the short run political economy determinants of inflation, including political cycle effects. The supply of monetary accommodation to inflation is here represented by the level of the interest rate I. A monetary squeeze will increase the interest rate and therefore the supply of inflation will be decreased.

The next two equations should be considered together. They explain the determination of the level of output if the North as a region and the level of output in the United States which is a part of the North.

(8) $Yn=Yn(rYusa, tYs); r,t>0.$

Equation (8) states that the expansion of the North is a positive function of the expansion in the US and in part a positive function of the expansion of the South. The meaning of the political parameter r should be clear to the reader by now. It reflects the effects of the oligopolistic interdependence and conflicts we have discussed in the previous chapters. It also implies that the rest of the northern economies cannot, by themselves, act as the engines of growth of the whole region. It may also be representative of international political business cycle effects if these exist.

The second element reflects the positive effect which the demand of manufactured goods from the South exerts on the output of the North. The political element embodied in t reflects the degree of protection the South erects against northern exports.

The following equation is in a sense the crucial element in our stylized framework.

(9) $Yusa=Yusa(I(uPn,vYn,wPsXs\ C),G); u,w>0, v<0.$

This equation states that the output of the US grows with monetary expansion (inversely) represented by the level of the interest rate, and with government expenditure G. Monetary policy, in turn, is a function of a number of variables which have been discussed in chapter 4. We will simply recall them here. Political business cycle elements are reflected in the parameters u and v and are

associated with inflation and output. We have
included inflation and output of the whole northern
region in order to take account of international
political business cycle considerations and of the
propensity of the US to act as an hegemon by
providing the public good of expansion whenever the
region is in recession. The third element included
as an argument of US monetary policy is the debt
service ratio (which appears also in eq (5)) and may
be considered an indicator of the degree of
financial fragility of the banking system which is
here assumed to depend only on international lending
activities. Monetary policy will expand whenever US
monetary authorities act as the lender of last
resort of the international system.

The expansion of the US economy is also a
positive function of the amount of US public
expenditure. The political element included in this
variable is obvious and need not be discussed
further here. For simplicity's sake we have assumed
G to be an exogenous variable (10).

The final equation determines the behaviour of
the exchange rate of the dollar vis-à-vis the
currency of the rest of the world. We have discussed
in chapter 3 the state of the theory of the
determination of exchange rates. We have seen how
the state of the theory is unsatisfactory. We do not
intend to propose an alternative approach here. The
final equation of our framework simply states that
the exchange rate of the dollar R is a function of
the difference between Yusa and Yn, and of the
degree of monetary tightness in the centre economy,
represented by the level of I.

(10) $R = R(y(Yusa-Yn), I); y < 0.$

The parameter y may be either positive or
negative, this means that the dollar will
respectively depreciate or appreciate if Yusa is
greater than Yn. The sign of the effects depends on
two sets of elements. The first is the behaviour of
US monetary policy as reflected in the level of I.
If the US expands more than the rest of the region
this will produce an appreciation of the dollar if
US monetary policy is tight and vice versa. The
political element contained in y reflects the degree
of confidence the rest of the world has in US policy
and in the behaviour of the US economy in general.
In this case too the determinants of such a factor
have been widely discussed in this book.

186

Global Political Economy

This completes the description of our "agenda for research". We wish to stress once again that no claim is made of having produced a politico-economic model of global financial instability but only an attempt to suggest new lines of research. One point should be made clear, however, about this issue. The understanding of global politico-economic problems requires that a systemic view is adopted. This means that issue links and policy interdependence should be considered more relevant than the single parameters involved.

NOTES

1. For a post-keynesian approach see Kaldor 1976; for a neoclassical approach see Findlay 1980.
2. Interest payments are neglected.
3. This is a crucial point which should require further discussion. We may reasonably assume, however, that exports cannot play the role of engine of growth for the North as a whole.
4. Which is to be considered as qualitatively different from multi country models.
5. Examples are the French and German realignements within the EMS after the 1983 elections.
6. The OPEC countries are not considered for simplicity.
7. See Frey 1984a for a survey of the political economy of protection.
8. Feder and Just 1979 discuss this problem from an economic point of view.
9. None of these two goods are considered to be price elastic.
10. Endogenous treatment of the determinants of G would require discussion of domestic (welfare) and foreign (defense) policy.

APPENDIX

Real and financial determinants of the price of primary commodities.

The "agenda for research" sketched in this chapter assumes that the South is a primary commodity producer and exporter. Consequently its balance of payments will be largely affected by the evolution of the price of the commodity. In a situation of oligopolistic interdependence the excess demand, and hence the price, of commodities is affected by both real and financial factors. We present here a graphical exposition of the interaction of these two effects.

On the vertical axis of fig A.10.1 the change in the production of manufactured goods (DYM) indicates that the demand of commodities is a direct function of the expansion of the production of the North. The quantity of primary commodities is indicated on the horizontal axis of the right hand quadrant.

The left hand quadrant indicates the positive relation between the growth of demand and the growth in the price of the commodity (DPA). This may be either positive or negative depending on the sign of the excess demand. The D' schedule is the demand function for primary commodities and the S' schedule is the supply of commodities (which does not depend on DYM) when financial effects are not taken into account. Their intersection yelds a value of DYM equal to OA'. This is an equilibrium situation in the market for primary commodities as the resulting change in prices is zero. This may be read in the left hand quadrant on the upward sloping schedule E'.

Let us now consider the influence of financial factors by considering an expansion in international liquidity. This will produce a twofold effect. In the first place the supply of primary commodities will decrease into S'' as the South will have easier access to international borrowing and hence it will be in the position to cut the supply of primary commodities for liquidity reasons. Demand of primary commodities will instead rise into D'' as easier financial conditions will make it profitable to increase speculative demand for commodities. In addition we may assume that the expansion in international liquidity might encourage portfolio diversification which will enhance the store of value role of commodities. Consequently the point at

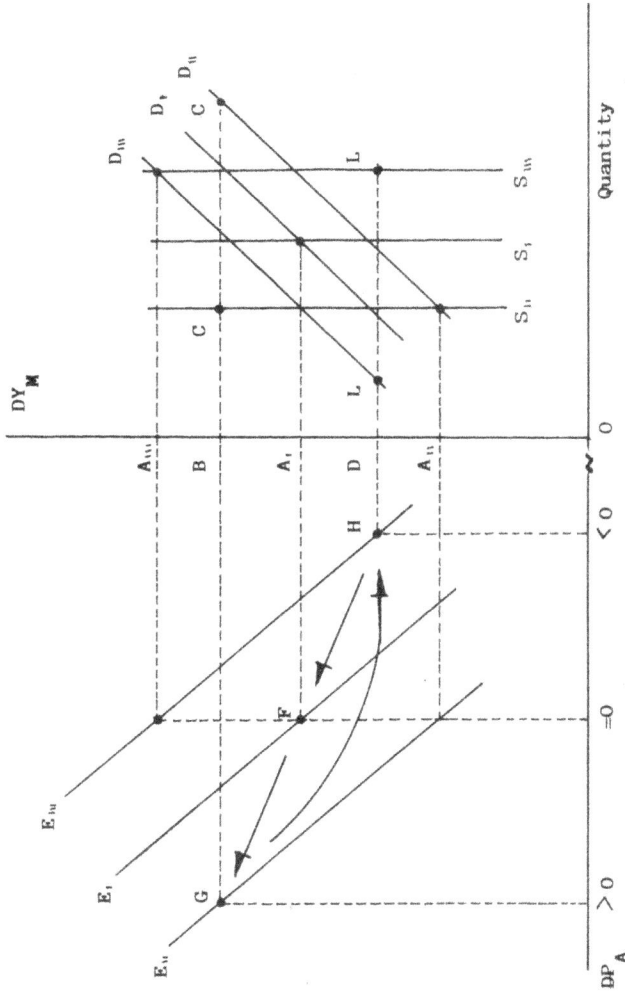

Fig.A.10.1   Real and Financial Factors in Primary Commodities Markets.

which supply and demand are in equilibrium, that is
when the change of prices is zero, corresponds to a
lower change in production in the North (OA''),
while the value of DYM which yielded a zero value of

189

DPA in the previous situation (OA') would now yield
an increase of the price of commodities. The shift
in the supply and demand schedules in the right hand
quadrant produces a shift in the schedule in the
left hand quadrant into position E".
    An opposite situation will hold in the case of a
restriction in international financial conditions.
The supply schedule will shift into O''' as the
South will increase its distress sales in order to
increase export, receipts while demand will shrink
into D''' as speculative and diversification motives
will suggest to do so. Consequently the left hand
schedule will shift into position E''' which
reflects the fact that equilibrium in the commodity
market is reached at a higher value of DYM.
    The graphical device allows us to describe the
cyclical interaction of real and financial
determinants of the price of primary commodities.
Starting from equilibrium at point OA' (the D', S',
E', schedules hold) suppose that a monetary
expansion increases the growth of North's output to
OB (while the D'', S'', E'' schedules now hold). The
excess demand CC in the right hand quadrant produces
a value of DPA coresponding to point G on the E''
schedule.
    When the expansion turns into restriction D''',
S''', and E''' schedules hold while DYM falls to
(e.g.) OD. An excess supply of commodities equal to
LL appears which corresponds to point H on the E'''
schedule.
    The G and H points correspond to the turning
points in an international cycle as they are
generated by international financial conditions and
hence by shifts in the policy of the leader country.
It is easy to see that at the upper turning point G
the growth of output is high while inflation is
increasing and currency diversification is at a high
point. In addition the indebtness of the South has
also increased due to the relatively easy access to
finance which the D'', S'' condition entails. At
point H the opposite conditions hold and so a lower
turning point may materialize.
    In conclusion the cycle in the price of primary
commodities we have described may be considered as a
component of the debt cycle we have discussed in
chapters 7 and 8 and may be explained as the outcome
of the interaction of the same forces which
determine the financial instability process.

Chapter Eleven

AFTER OLIGOPOLY?

The main idea discussed in this book may be summarized as follows. International financial instability results from the fact that the interaction of oligopolistic conflicts and private financial markets provides the institutional environment for the mounting of financial fragility which results as an endogenous outcome of the behaviour of financially complex capitalistic systems.

Both oligopolistic conflicts and the disorderly expansion of private credit markets reflect the inadequacy of existing rules in the international system. It follows that the main normative prescription which may be derived from our analysis is that the control of international financial instability is linked to the development of new cooperative arrangements, new regimes, that will decrease the intolerable amount of conflicts present in the system.

This conclusion may well be considered not satisfactory. We have tried to show, however, that short run cures of the debt problems are liable to be worse that the disease if the global international environment does not improve substantially towards higher growth and stability.

This final chapter is devoted to a brief discussion of the prospects facing the two areas involved in international financial instability: oligopolistic conflicts among the major industrialized countries and the international credit markets.

The first issue area obviously involves the prospects of the international monetary system as a whole. Our discussion will deal with one crucial point in this issue: the possibility that the outcome of the conflicts presently going on in oligopolistic interdependence be a new form of United States hegemony.

The second issue area deals with the prospects of the international financing regime, starting from the premise that, for many years to come, the private international credit system will play a fundamental role in international financial intermediation. This premise implies that the forces tending to produce widespread financial fragility will continue to operate. Consequently a viable international financial system will need an adequate institutional environment in order to provide the two sets of conditions which are necessary for a financially complex system to operate with an acceptable degree of stability. The first set of conditions includes the presence of the two fundamental functions of an adequate source of effective demand and the presence of an efficient lender of last resort. The second set of conditions is the establishment of an adequate set of procedures to regulate the international activities of private banks.

Neither set of conditions will be met if an adequate amount of cooperation is not reached in the area of oligopolistic conflicts so that a more stable international environment is assured.

New hegemony or struggle for power ?

The favourable performance of the United States economy in the first part of the decade, and the dramatic rise in the value of the dollar could be considered as a sign that the international system is entering a new era of American hegemony. Such an impression might be further enhanced by the state of widespread frustration which has characterized all attempts by the other industrialized countries to resist the rise of the American currency in the international markets and to minimize the damage that this is producing on their economies.

The failure to reach agreements on the control of international monetary relations was a constant feature of the first half of the present decade and confirmed once again just how very difficult it is to implement cooperative policies in an oligopolistic environment (1). It is our opinion that the present state of international relations is still far away from a situation of new hegemony. We also think that the conditions for a return to a new

192

hegemonic structure of international relations in the near future are lacking.

A fruitful discussion of our statements may be carried out with the help of the theory of hegemonic stabililty taking into account the modifications recently suggested by Keohane (1984).

Hegemonic stability theory, in its traditional form, asserts that hegemonic systems will collapse as a consequence of a shift in the distribution of power against the hegemon. This will decrease the ability and willingness of the hegemon to supply the public goods required for the establishment and maintenance of an international regime.

Keohane's (1984) criticism of this version of the theory is based on two major points. In the first place, this theory accounts for only some of the major regime changes which have come about in the post-Bretton Woods period. While the collapse of the energy regime seems to be well explained by the theory, it is more difficult to say the same for changes in money and trade regimes. In the second place, the theory in its most widely accepted version is far too mechanistic in the sense that it neglects the role of policy choices in the production and management of international regimes. A corollary of this critique is that it is incorrect to view non-hegemonic regimes as associated with widespread conflicts and that it is necessary to recognize the fundamental role of institutions in providing information and hence increasing the propensity to cooperate among actors (Runge 1984).

We agree with Keohane's point and may assume a modified version of the theory in order to carry on our discussion. The modified version should retain the fundamental links between the behaviour of economic variables, the shift in the distrubution of power and the supply of public goods. These links have to be integrated in a more policy oriented framework. Policy choices may heavily alter the causal relations implied in the original version of the theory by enhancing or weakening the original effect. In addition we should recall that a major feedback exists between changes in the institutional environment (supply of public goods) and the behaviour of the economic variables. A diagrammatic representation of the theory is included in fig. 11.1.

In order to assume that the structure of oligopolistic interdependence is turning into a new hegemonic structure the causal relationships implied

After Oligopoly?

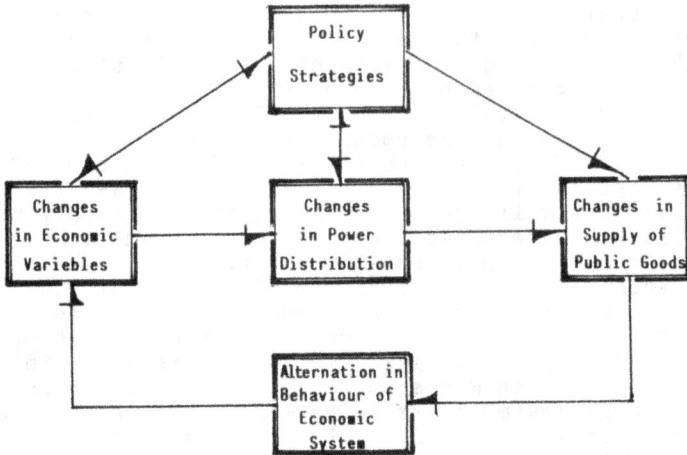

Policy Strategies

Changes in Economic Variebles

Changes in Power Distribution

Changes in Supply of Public Goods

Alternation in Behaviour of Economic System

Fig. 11.1 The (Modified) Theory of Hegemonic Stability

in the theory of hegemonic stability should work backwards. This should hold both for the "necessary" condition, the shift in the distribution of power, and the "sufficient" conditions, the willingness and ability of the leading country to use that power to supply the public goods. Let us start with the first point.

The first problem to be discussed is the definition of power. Several suggestions have recently been advanced to deal with this problem.

Keohane (1984) defines the four conditions which, in his view, the hegemonic economy must meet in order to fulfill its role in the international economy. The hegemon must exert control over: 1) raw materials, 2) capital, 3) markets, and 4) must hold a competitive advantage in the production of highly valued goods. Strange (1982) suggested a definition of financial power directly associated with the role of the currency as an international vehicle of exchange as well as with the capacity of a country to act as a financial centre of the international system. According to this approach the power of a country derives from the necessity that others have to obtain credit from it. Lake (1984) provides an interpretation of the transformations of the international system based on long run productivity changes. His definition emphasizes real aspects of economic power while Strange's approach centres on financial aspects. Keohane's approach is more comprehensive but it does not provide a full defintion of the links between the elements of what could be called a "power vector".

A related point has recently been raised by Padoa-Schioppa and Papadia (1984). They discuss a classification of national currencies which are ranked according to their relative quality. The quality of a currency, in turn, is directly related to its purchasing power stability (i.e. inversely correlated to the rate of inflation). The determination of the relative quality of a currency is discussed in an oligopolistic setting in which central banks are considered as the oligopolistic firms which produce the quality and quantity of the currency. Each central bank is faced with a trade-off between short term and long term strategies. Quality is achieved only if a long term strategy is pursued.

The approach followed by Padoa-Schioppa and Papadia rests on Hayek's (1976) ideas on currency competition. In an international setting deterioration of a currency (inflation) leads to devaluation. Inflation, in turn, depends only on monetary policy. Free market forces will punish central banks who choose short term strategies which let inflation depreciate their currencies. Low quality currencies will be substituted with high quality ones.

The Padoa-Schioppa and Papadia argument contains useful suggestions for the understanding of international monetary conflicts. What is to be rejected, however, is the Hayek approach they follow. As we have seen in chapter 2, the international position of a currency (and hence of the issuing country) ultimately depends on the country's creditworthiness. The quality of a currency is not dependent only on its capacity to minimize transaction costs as Hayek holds but, more importantly, on its capacity to denominate international credit. Credit, as we have seen, is a two dimensional good but the quality of credit must be distinguished from the quality of money. The approach we have followed in chapter 2 (Minsky 1979) maintains that the quality of a currency as a credit denominator depends on the ability of the issuing country to make profits, i.e. to run a current account surplus.

This "creditworthiness" approach to international currencies presents one major advantage with respect to the Hayek approach. It allows us to consider simultaneously real and financial elements as determinants of the quality of a currency. In this respect this approach could reconcile Lake's (1984) suggestion to base the international position of a country on its productivity performance with financial elements suggested by Minsky's approach.

We may now sum up our brief dicussion of financial power.

The financial power of a country is an increasing function of three variables: 1) the extension of the use of the national currency in the international system (quantity); 2) the quality of the currency; 3) the flexibility of the country to adjust to changes in the external environment. The meaning and role of quantity is straightforward. It is useful to note that the extension of the use of a currency in the international system is directly associated with the international extension of its banking industry. In this respect state power is directly associated with the power of its private financial system.

Quality has been discussed above. Let us repeat that quality, in turn, is a multi-dimensional variable if we follow the creditworthiness approach. Insofar as this is dependent on the ability of an economy to make profits in the international system, financial power also depends on real (productivity) elements.

The ability of a country to make adjustments determines the time dimension of power. The higher the adjustment flexibility the less the country's power is dependent on short term or contingent elements. This may also be stated differently. The power of a country will be directly correlated, in the long run, to its ability to give up short term goals for long term ones.

The ability and willingness of a country to make adjustments, in turn, depends on its ability to impose on other countries the costs of such an adjustment if this is needed.

One important clarification is necessary here. The use of this ability involves a consumption of

After Oligopoly?

power (Keohane 1978, 1982). Consequently one should
not confuse the margins for adjustment that a
country has (which increase its power) with the use
of such margins. To be powerful means that one can
dispose of one's power, i.e. one can consume some of
it.

The structure of the balance of payments of a
country provides a useful synthetic description of a
country's financial power as it provides an
immediate description of a country's relative
profitability (trade balance) in relation to its
financial payments commitments (capital movements)
vis-à-vis the rest of the world. In this respect,
the discussion of the conditions for the stabilty of
the hegemonic system carried out in chapter 2 may
easily be reformulated in terms of power analysis
(and we might therefore talk of seigniorage power).
Analogously Minsky's approach to international
financial relations may provide a useful base for
the discussion of international financial power.

US financial power and the dollar

We may now address the problem raised at the
beginning of the chapter, that is, whether the
United States has increased its international power
to the point where it is in a position to reassume a
hegemonic role if it wishes to do so. We recall that
our discussion is limited to the analysis of
financial power. In this respect the problem is not
whether a full Bretton Woods-type system can be
reestablished but, more modestly, whether a
US-centred financial hegemony can be reestablished.

It is tempting to consider the dramatic rise in
the value of the dollar as a sign that American
financial power is again tremendously large. We
suggest that such a temptation should be resisted.

The behaviour of the dollar on international
markets cannot be explained by traditional exchange
rate theories. We have discussed in chapter 3 why
traditonal theories are unsatisfactory and we have
suggested that a more useful approach to exchange
rate determination requires that the analysis of the
entire national economic system be taken into
account. It is a widely held view that the value of
the dollar is far out of "equilibrium". This however
requires a definition of an equilibrium exchange
rate and hence an exchange rate theory.
Paradoxically the dollar may be considered at the
same time over and undervalued. From a trade point

of view the dollar may be considered "overvalued" (Williamson 1983) insofar as it depresses the competitiveness of US industry . However the dollar may be "in equilibrium" (or even "undervalued") if we accept the view that its dramatic rise reflects the excess demand for dollar denominated assets in the international system.

A simpler approach suggests that the dollar is the residual variable on which the behaviour of the US economy vis-à-vis other countries is discharged. In other words the movement of the dollar reflects the fact that the United States does not face an external constraint to the pursuit of its policies. This, however, is only a short term answer which does not allow an assessment of the problem of the United States's power position.

The dollar's strength must be assessed from a long run and systemic point of view, i.e. assessing whether the strength of the dollar reflects an increase in American financial power. Of the three components of financial power discussed above the most crucial appear to be the last two: the creditworthiness of the United States and its ability to make substantial (long term) adjustments. These two elements must be considered together. If one looks at the issue of creditworthiness one should conclude that the demand for dollar assets reflects the fact that international investors consider the United States as the most creditworthy economy in the world. This however could be only a short run phenomenon and in this respect it may reflect the fact that the United States is consuming its power rather than accumulating it. The inflow of capital to the United States could be considered an indication of long run creditworthiness and thus a clear indication of power accumulation if this may be considered as an irreversible phenomenon in the short and medium run. Unfortunately it is not possible to assess with certainty this crucial point, which would require a full investigation of the evolution and the modification of the real and financial accumulation process in the United States in the last few years.

A few insights may be obtained, however, by the consideration of the changes in the international investment position of the United States. At the end of 1983 (see tab 11.1) the net international investment position of the United States had declined with respect to the previous year being slightly above 100,000 million dollars. This is the

After Oligopoly?

Table 11.1. International investment position of the
United States Year-end values 1980-83 (billions of
US$)

	1980	1981	1982	1983
Net international investment position	106.1	143.0	149.6	105.9
US assets abroad	606.9	719.6	838.1	887.5
of which				
Direct investments	215.3	228.3	221.5	226.1
Claims by US banks	203.9	293.5	404.6	429.9
Foreign assets in the United States	500.7	576.5	688.6	781.5
of which				
Direct investments	82.9	106.2	121.9	133.5
Liabilities by US banks	121.1	165.4	231.3	280.4

Source: Survey of Current Business.

result of the following elements. The first is the
slowdown in the accumulation of private US assets
abroad, which has only slightly increased since
1982, producing a substantial decrease in its rate
of expansion. The most important slowdown is the one
relative to the expansion of US claims reported by
US banks which reflects the breakout of the debt
crisis while since 1980 the rate of expansion of US
direct investments abroad has practically stagnated.
    Two elements deserve consideration on the
liability side. The first is the substantial
increase in US liabilities reported by US banks

which accounts for about half of the increase in
foreign assets in the United States. The second is
that the increase in foreign direct investment in
the United States has not shown substantial
deviations from the trend of the previous years.

This evidence suggests that the dramatic
increase in demand for dollar denominated assets is
largely a phenomenon related to the shifts in the
flows intermediated by the US banking system which
is the joint consequence of the international debt
crisis and of the shift in US policies after 1979.
In a word, this shift may be considered as the
international financial system's reaction to the
consequences of the "upper turning point" of the
international financial cycle.

An examination of the United States stock
position suggests that it has considerably
strengthened its position as world banker. However,
in order to assess the banker's creditworthiness,
this analysis must be completed with an examination
of flow behaviour.

The current account of the United States has
followed an increasingly negative trend in the past
few years (see tab 11.2). In fact, the estimated
trade deficit for 1984 will, by itself, increase US
liabilities vis-à-vis the rest of the world so as to
make the US a net international debtor for the first
time since the beginning of the century.

The evolution of the balance of payments of the
United States suggests that, in the medium run, the
profitability of the American economy is
progressively declining.

In this respect the role of the United States as
a world banker cannot be considered as a clear sign
of increased financial power as the extrapolation of
the flow trends suggests that the profitability and
hence the creditworthiness of the US economy (as
reflected in the current account's behaviour) is
rapidly declining.

Let us now discuss the third element which
determines the amount of financial power: the
ability to adjust. As we have said, this in turn is
a function of the ability to discharge abroad
internal disequilibrium.

In this respect the behaviour of the dollar
seems to suggest that the
other countries, and the other oligopolists in
particular have de facto accepted (if not gladly)
that the American economy would shift the burden of
adjustment to the rest of the world. Consequently

After Oligopoly?

Table 11.2. Balance of Current Accounts of the
United States 1983-85 (billions of US$)

	1983	1984	1985 (*)
Exports	202.2	212.0	231.3
Imports	260.7	317.5	352.8
Trade balance	-60.6	-105.3	-121.5
Services and			
private transfers net	27.3	27.0	25.0
Public transfers net	-7.5	-8.0	-8.5
Balance of current			
accounts	-40.8	-86.3	-105.0

(*) forecasts

Source: OECD.

one would be tempted to conclude that US power in
the international oligopoly has increased. In this
case too, however, one should distinguish between
short and long term elements.

In the short run the expansionary effects of US
fiscal policy have supplied a public good to the
rest of the world. Other countries have reaped
neomercantilistic benefits from the growth of
American demand for their exports, boosted also by
the revaluation of the dollar. The countries which
have most benefited are Japan and Germany, i.e. the
most important non-US oligopoly leaders of the
international system. In this respect American
policy has succeeded in overcoming the resistance of
other oligopolists by exchanging more short run
power against neomercantilistic benefits.

This short term outcome of oligopolistic
conflicts cannot be considered as a return to
hegemony as it lacks the long run power accumulation
needed for the restoration of a such a structure. In
fact, the short run behaviour of US policy has to
some extent increased the long run power costs for

the US itself. This stems from the two facts that
the United States has become the world's largest
debtor and that expected trade flows point to a
decrease in long run creditworthiness.

The ability of the United States to adjust in
the long run rests on its ability to absorb the
"twin deficits" (Volcker 1984) of the budget deficit
and the trade deficit. The issue of the budget
deficit has complex systemic implications which
cannot be discussed here. We may simply note that
the evolution of the federal deficit reflects long
run strategic choices in domestic (welfare) and
foreign (defense) policy. More importantly the
absorption of the federal deficit involves
oligopolistic relations only marginally. The
situation is quite different for the trade deficit.

The absorption of the trade deficit depends
essentially on the evolution of two variables: the
exchange rate of the dollar and the rate of
expansion of the American economy with respect to
the other industrialized countries (2). However, a
fall in the dollar's value which restores US
competitiveness might turn out to be worse than the
disease insofar as it leads to higher monetary
instability and hence to a deterioration of the
United States's creditworthiness.

The dollar's trend might be reversed in -at
least- two ways: with an abrupt fall (the financial
collapse hypothesis) or through a "soft landing".

The first hypothesis seems, however, scarcely
realistic. A full-fledged financial crisis requires
that "technical insolvency" be followed by
"effective insolvency", i.e. that the borrower and
the lender "agree" to produce a disruption of the
financial relation in the sense that they refuse to
find a cooperative solution (3) to the crisis,
letting market forces go through the debt deflation
process which would follow. If this is the case,
then the resulting instability in international
relations would further decrease the supply of
public goods in the system. This solution would
confirm that both the United States and the
remaining countries are only in a position to deter
the definition of a general agreement but do not
have the power to unilaterally provide a public good
(financial stability).

The second hypothesis, which is obviously the
more preferable, requires however that a degree of
coordination also be reached on the macroeconomic
policies of the oligopolistic countries, i.e that

the adjustment of the American trade deficit be pursued both through a depreciation of the dollar and through greater expansion of the economies of the other oligopolists which would lead to higher US exports.

All this means that the present state of relations among the oligopolists is caught in a dilemma.

Industrialized countries other than the United States have an increasing interest in maintaining the stability of the dollar, i.e. American creditworthiness, for the mere fact that, by so doing, they defend their interests as creditors towards the big borrower. Insofar as American creditworthiness depends on a lower US trade deficit and hence higher US exports, they have an interest in expanding their economies in order to increase imports from the American economy. By so doing they would also stabilize the international economy as a whole thus providing public goods. However, this would run against their neomercantilistic goals. In other words, the problem of the US trade deficit represents the way in which the neomercantilism-public good trade-off appears itself in the present situation.

The very fact that such a dilemma presently exists implies that the main variable which determines American long run financial power, its creditworthiness, largely depends on the policy of other economies. This seems sufficient to reject the hypothesis that the distribution of (financial) power is such that the United States is in a position to unilaterally supply a public good, i.e. in a position to act as an hegemon.

One might be led to believe that this situation presents only short term difficulties on the basis of the following argument. The growing indebtedness of the American economy is the outcome of a major investment effort that the US economy is undertaking. Once the transformations in the American productive system have been completed the productivity of the American economy will have increased to such a degree that the internal dynamics of the American economic system will be in a position to produce the resources needed to repay the mounting debt. By that time the American economy will have fully reacquired the economic strength and power to act as a hegemon in the international system. In the terms of our discussion of the Bretton Woods system in chapter 2 this would amount

to saying that the American economy is presently in
the position of a "young" or "adult debtor" in the
balance of payments life cycle. Consequently the
future performance of the US economy is bound to
improve both its position and that of the whole
international system.

We are not in a position to discuss this
argument and we will just note that such a medium
and long term perspective is producing short term
costs to the international economy which may lead to
a disruption of the system itself so acute as to
prevent the full evolution of the the American
economy to the healthier stages of the balance of
payments life cycle. Such a possibility requires, to
be credible, that the other economies (mostly Europe
and Japan) accept to bear the costs of such a
transition by providing more expansion and giving up
their neomercantilistic strategies. Consequently the
dilemma discussed above emerges again.

The international financing regime

The difficulty in reaching a cooperative
solution among oligopolists is aggravated by the
fact that such conflicts are deeply entangled with
those deriving from the interrelations with the
private financial markets and with the fact that no
solution to the long run stability problems of the
international debt problem has yet been found.   As
we have seen, the most relevant factor pushing up
the value of the dollar in 1983-84 has come from a
dramatic shift in international credit flows.
International banks have reacted to the 1982 debt
crisis by decreasing their lending to LDC borrowers
and have increased their investments within the
United States also as a response to higher interest
rates and expanding investment opportunities within
the American economy. This process has been
partially enhanced by the implementation of
International Banking Facilities in New York at the
beginning of the decade (Hawley 1984). This process
may continue (although at a decreasing rate) as long
as the expansion of US demand and tight US monetary
policy provide favourable conditions for banking
operations in the United States relatively to other
bank lending operations in the Third World and also
in European countries which have followed a
(neomercantilistic) deflationary policy.

This means that as soon as private credit
markets begin to consider these economies attractive

again the flow of capital into the United States
might reverse its course thus weakening the dollar.
This does not mean that neither higher non-American
Western expansion nor restored LDC creditworthiness
are undesirable. Rather it means that the production
of international financial stability requires that
the issue of international capital regulation and
control be seriously considered as well and, with
it, that a new international monetary regime cannot
be established without the parallel edification of
an international financing regime (4).

Oligopolistic conflicts over power distribution
are present here too. As we have seen in chapter 4 a
conflictual relation exists between the private
banks and the monetary authorities over the amount
of regulation of banking activities. Private banks
tend to minimize their demand for government
intervention in the phase of expansion of lending
activities as regulations decrease profitable
activities, while they increase the demand for state
intervention (mostly in the form of lender of last
resort intervention) when financial distress arises.
Monetary authorities, on the other hand, wish to
increase the regulation of financial markets if this
is considered insufficient to prevent the mounting
of financial fragility which is endogenously
produced in private financial markets. However they
wish to encourage and sustain the expansion of the
national banking industry as this increases the
international financial power of the country.(Hawley
1984) In this respect the 1970s witnessed an
increase in American financial power as a
consequence of the expansion of the activity of
American-based international banks. This process
eventually led to conflicts with the monetary
authorities of other countries over the acquisition
of credit market shares (which in this respect may
be considered as conflicts over the distribution of
power).

In the 1970s oligopolistic conflicts over the
issue of international banking regulations were at
least as fierce as exchange rate and monetary
conflicts (Hawley 1984). Attempts to find an
agreement on regulation of euromarkets failed at the
beginning of the decade. Subsequently the United
States promoted the development of International
Banking Facilities in New York (5). It may be
misleading, however, to infer that the further
expansion of the American banking industry in the
international markets has unambiguously increased US

financial power. This expansion has increased the US economy's capability to attract financial flows, both American and foreign, from outside but it has also increased the necessity for the United States to monitor its creditworthiness vis-à-vis the rest of the world. In this respect the expansion of US financial markets has increased the dependence of the United States on oligopolistic cooperation as far as this is necessary to sustain dollar creditworthiness.

The potential vulnerability of US financial power has not decreased also if we consider the solution which has been reached for the international debt problem. The major borrowers have implemented adjustment programmes which have produced dramatic improvements in their current account performance (6). While this has made it possible to keep the credit relations alive and has avoided the danger of widespread bankruptcy it has by no means solved the structural problems of the international financing mechanism. The international financing regime has not been improved in the sense that its endogenous financial fragility mechanisms are still in operation. In fact it could be said that the mechanism has simply started to complete its lower turning point.

The debt crisis had produced a tremendous amount of proposals aimed at modifying the financing regime (Bergsten, Cline and Williamson 1985). The proposals differ in several technical aspects, but they share the common view that the restoration of long run financial stability requires a major modification in the relations between private and public operators and calls for greater involvement of official agencies, be they the existing ones, such as the World Bank, or newly created ones.

A power issue is involved here too. If we accept that one of the attributes of financial power is the determination of access to credit (Strange 1982) the establishment of a new financing regime requires that financial power be shifted in favour of institutions and thus subtracted from both private banks and national monetary authorities. On the other hand, institutions may receive new power if the oligopolistic countries reach an agreement on this issue. As the 1982-84 debt negotiations have shown the major opposition to this policy has come from the United States.

Recent dollar developments, however, might produce new pressure in this direction. As the

present policy of the United States requires greater
control over international credit flows, US
authorities might be tempted to encourage
modifications in the international financing regime
towards both greater regulation and deeper official
involvement. US dependence on private international
flows implies high vulnerability with respect to the
fact that funds might be diverted towards investment
outside the United States as soon as better
opportunities both in LDCs and in other
industrialized countries materialize. Increased
financial complexity and fragility are posing new
dilemmas to the United States authorities. On the
one hand they have an interest in restoring the
stability of the American-based banking system and
hence they are interested in restoring the
creditworthiness of LDC borrowing countries. On the
other hand they must compete with other borrowers
for funds in the international markets at a growing
pace. In this respect the immediate implication is
that the United States does not have an immediate
interest in restoring the long-run creditworthiness
of LDC borrowers insofar as this implies a
systematic outflow of funds. Nor do they have an
interest in establishing an international financing
regime over which they would not exert enough
control.

If this line of reasoning is correct it unveils
a nationalistic US interest which in a certain sense
goes beyond traditional neomercantilistic goals and
which implies a trade-off between short run and long
run policies. In the short run American policy
requires that international funds be absorbed by the
United States rather than by other economic systems.
In the long run the pursuit of financial power
requires that the United States promote the
international expansion of its banking system both
quantitatively and qualitatively (i.e. through
regulation). The presence of such a dilemma is
another indication that the present position of the
United States is not that of a (potential) hegemon.

After oligopoly ?
    The attempt to draw any reasonable conclusion to
the argument of this book is bound to fail because
of the very nature of the topics we have discussed
which are both far from having been exhaustively
analyzed and far from a final solution to the
problems involved.

After Oligopoly?

One lesson which may be drawn from our discussion is that the interaction of national economic policies and private international financial markets has led to an increase in neomercantilism. Non-US industrial countries have been pursuing neomercantilistic goals to such a degree that they are unable to reach forms of limited cooperation in regional arrangements. The present state of European relations, and the failure of the European Monetary System to produce qualitative improvements is one of the most striking examples. Initiatives such as the implementation of the role of the ECU (Triffin 1983) as an alternative to the dollar have not been implemented fundamentally because of German resistance to the transfer of national monetary power to a supranational authority.

International Monetary Fund adjustment programmes have requested that LDC borrowers maximize their trade surpluses in order to restore their long eroded creditworthiness. The cost of borrowers' neomercantilism has been a dramatic fall in per capita income and an explosion of inflation whose yearly rate has in some cases reached over 700 per cent. While in other cases (Argentina) has led to the adoption of last resort measures such as the change of the national currency and heavy cuts in government spending.

The maintenance of dollar creditworthiness requires that the United States reabsorb its soaring trade deficit so as to earn funds to service the mounting foreign debt.

It is obviously impossible that all these trade surpluses be attained simultaneously. As we have seen in chapters 2 and 3 widespread neomercantilism may be compatible with a situation of stability only if a regime which provides an ex ante solution to the problem of the residual country exists. If the potential for a hegemonic system exists this problem may be solved. If this is not the case, as in the present situation, neomercantilism inevitably leads to widespread conflicts.

The situation is made more untenable by the heritage of the financial instability mechanism which operated over the previous decade and which is still operating now. The main characteristic of the economic developments of the last fifteen years may be identified in the rapid and, in many respects, violent redistribution of financial wealth throughout the economic system. The increasing

flexibility of private international financial
markets has produced a cumulation of borrowing and
lending positions that have to be financed. In order
for these positions to be financed, and eventually
smoothed out, the international economic system has
to restore an overall rate of growth which is far
higher than the one now prevailing or to be expected
in the near future in the absence of major changes
in the operation of the world economy.

Higher growth is needed for both quantitative
and qualitative reasons. Higher growth means higher
exports and easier debt servicing. When growth is
insufficient debt relations cannot be maintained and
financial distress spreads throughout the system.
Higher growth, in addition, enhances the propensity
to cooperate of lenders and borrowers alike
(Simonsen 1984) since it improves the expectations
of both as to future debt servicing capacity. In
this respect a high and stable rate of growth is a
public good (Kindleberger 1981, Wallace 1983).

The propensity to cooperate also increases with
the amount of information that each actor has on the
behaviour of the others. Information in turn
increases with the amount of institutions and rules
present in the system (Keohane 1984, Runge 1984).
The restoration of stable growth and the
strengthening of an international system interact
with each other and both imply an increase in the
production of public goods in the world political
economy.

NOTES

1. Examples are the several attempts to
organize joint interventions in currency markets in
1983 and 1984 which failed mainly beacuse of the
lack of cooperation on the part of the United States
authorities.

2. For a given amount of protectionism in the
world economy. For alternative scenarios relative to
the international position of the US economy and of
the dollar see World Financial Markets, March April
1985.

3. The example to be recalled is, once again,
the failure to organize joint interventions in
currency markets. In this respect the decision taken
in September 1985 by the G-5 countries (France,
Germany, Japan, United States, and United Kingdom)
to intervene jointly in currency markets to push
down the dollar may represent a fundamental change

in the international scenario. Some commentators
have not hesitated to define it an "historical
event". See on this episode World Financial Markets
November 1985.
4. Another fundamental issue is the one related
to the trade regime which is under strain as a
consequence of protectionist pressures fed by the
overvaluation of the dollar.
5. See World Financial Markets, November 1981.
6. See chapter 6.

REFERENCES

Aglietta M. 1982, World Capitalism in the Eighties,
New Left Review, n.136 pp. 5-41

Aglietta M., A.Orlean and G.Oudiz 1981, Des
Adaptations Differenciées aux Constraintes
Internationales, Revue Economique, july
pp.660-712

Agmon T.and J. Dietrich 1983, International Lending
and Income Redistribution, Journal of Banking
and Finance vol.7 pp. 483-95

Aivazian V. and J. Callen 1983, Reorganization in
Bankruptcy and the Issue of Strategic Risk,
Journal of Banking and Finance, march pp.
119-33

Alessandrini P. 1974, Composizione delle Riserve e
Crisi del Sistema Monetario Internazionale,
Rivista Internazionale di Scienze Sociali,
may-june pp. 171-97

Aliber R. 1982, The Evolution of Currency Areas, in
R. Cooper, P. Kenen, J. de Macedo, J. van
Ypersele (eds.), The International Monetary
System under Flexible Exchange Rates: Global,
Regional and National, Ballinger Publishing
Company

American Express Bank 1982, Sovereign Debt
Rescheduling, Amex Bank Review Special Papers,
n.4

Aronson J. 1979, Debt and the Less Developed
Countries, Westview Press

Avramovic D. 1964, Economic Growth and External
Debt, The Johns Hopkins Press

Bagehot W. 1873, Lombard Street, Richard D. Irwin
Inc

Bank for International Settlements, 1983 Annual
Report

Basevi G. and M.Calzolari 1982, Multinational
Exchange Rate Determination: a Model for the
Analysis of the European Monetary System, in
J.Bilson, R.Marston (eds.) Exchange Rate Theory
and Practice, U. of Chicago Press

Beck N. 1984, Domestic Political Sources of American
Monetary Policy 1955-82, Journal of Politics,
pp.785-817

Beenstock M. 1980, Political Econometry of Official
Development Assistance, World Development, n.1
pp 137-44

Beenstock M. 1983, The World Economy in
Transition, George Allen and Unwin

References

Benassy J.P., F.Boyer and F.Gelpi 1977, Regulation
    des Economies Capitalistiques et Inflation,
    Cepremap working paper
Bergsten F, W. Cline, and J. Williamson 1985, Bank
    Lending to Developing Countries: the Policy
    Alternatives, Institiute for International
    Economics
Bergsten F., R. Kehoane and J. Nye 1975,
    International Economics and International Poli
    tics, in F. Bergsten and L. Krause (eds.) World
    Politics and International Economics, Brookings
    Institution
Biasco S. 1979, L'Inflazione nei Paesi Capitalistici
    Industrializzati, Feltrinelli
Biasco S. 1984, Coordinamento Spontaneo e Anarchia
    del Mercato nella Formazione della Domanda
    Mondiale, in P. Guerrieri, P.C. Padoan (eds.) Un
    Gioco Senza Regole: l'Economia Internazionale
    alla Ricerca di un Nuovo Assetto, Franco Angeli
Black S. 1983, The Use of Monetary Policy for
    Internal and External Balance in Ten Industrial
    Countries, in J. Frenkel (ed.) Exchange Rates
    and International Macroeconomics, University of
    Chicago Press
Boyer R. J. Mistral 1983, Accumulation, Inflation,
    Crise, Presse Universitaire de France, 2nd
    edition
Brown B. 1979, The Dollar Mark Axis. On Currency
    Power, Mc.Millan
Bryant R. 1980, Money and Monetary Policy in
    Interdependent Nations, Brookings Institution
Bryant R. 1982, Increasing Economic Interdependence
    and National Economic Policies: an American
    View, Lo Spettatore Internazionale, n.2
    pp.113-42
Burbidge J. 1978, Post-Keynesian Theory: the
    International Dimension, Challenge, May June
    pp.40-64
Buzan B. 1984, Economic Structure and International
    Security: the Limits of the Liberal Case,
    International Organization, n.4 pp. 597-624
Calleo D. 1981, Inflation and American Power,
    Foreign Affairs, Spring pp. 781-812
Cameron D. 1978, The Expansion of the Public
    Economy: a Comparative Analysis, American
    Political Science Review, December pp. 1243-61
Carron A. 1982, Financial Crises: Recent Experience
    in US and International Markets, Brookings
    Papers on Economic Activity, n.2 pp.395-418
Chapman S. 1984, The Foreign Debt of the Cmea

References

Nations: a Move Towards Adjustment?, Economic
Notes, n.2 pp. 51-73
Ciocca P. 1981, Disproportionalities, Allocative
Mechanisms and Stagflation, Journal of Post
Keynesian Economics, Winter pp. 231-9
Ciocca P. and O. Vito-Colonna 1978, La Politica
Economica della Germania Federale e i suoi
Riflessi Internazionali, in V. Valli (ed.)
L'Economia Tedesca, Etas Libri
Cline W. 1983, International Debt and the Stability
of the World Economy, Institute for
International Economics
Cohen B. 1977, Organizing the World's Money, Basic
Books
Cohen B. 1982, Balance of Payments Financing:
Evolution of a Regime, in Krasner 1983
D'Arista J. 1979, Private Overseas Lending: Too Far,
Too Fast?, in Aronson 1979
Darity W. and E. Fitzgerald 1984, A Keynes-Kalecki
Model of World Trade, Finance, and Economic
Growth, International Finance Discussion paper
n.238
Davidson P. 1978, Money and the Real World, Second
edition, Mcmillan
Davidson P. 1982, Rational Expectations: a
Fallacious Foundation for Studying Crucial
Decision Making Processes, Journal of Post
Keynesian Economics, Winter
De Cecco M. 1968, Il Sistema di Gold Standard
Internazionale dal 1944 al 1965: Note
Interpretative, in Saggi di Politica Monetaria,
Giuffre'
De Cecco M. 1974, New Dimensions for
International Lending, The World Today, n.9 pp.
388-93
De Cecco M. 1975, Money and Empire: The
International Gold Standard 1890-1914, Rowman
and Littlefield
De Cecco M. 1976, International Financial Markets
and US Domestic Policy since 1943, International
Affairs, July pp. 381-99
De Cecco M. 1979, Origins of the Post-war Payments
System, Cambridge Journal of Economics, n.3
pp.46-61
De Grauwe P. and M. Fratianni 1984, The Political
Economy of International Lending, International
Economics Research Paper n.42, Centrum voor
Economische Studien, Leuven
e Witte R. and J. Petras 1979, Political Economy
of International Debt: the Dynamics of Financial

References

Capital, in Aronson 1979

Diaz-Alejandro C. 1983, Some Aspects of the 1982-83 Brazilian Payments Crisis, Brookings Papers on Economic Activity, n.2 pp. 515-42

Diaz-Alejandro C. 1984, Latin American Debt: I Don't Think We Are in Kansas Anymore, Brookings Papers on Economic Activity, n.2 pp. 335-89

Dreyer J. and A. Schotter 1980, Power Relationships in the International Monetary Fund: the Consequences of Quota Changes, Review of Economics and Statistics pp. 97-106

Dufey G. and I. Giddy 1981, Innovations in the International Financial Markets, Journal of International Business Studies, Fall pp. 33-51

Eaton J. and M.Gersovitz 1981, Poor Country Borrowing in International Financial Markets and the Repudiation Issue. Princeton Studies in International Finance n.47

Emminger O. 1985, The International Debt Crisis and the Banks, Intereconomics, n.3 pp. 107-13.

Fair D.E. and R.Bertrand (eds.) 1983, International Lending in a Fragile World Economy, Martinus Nijhoff Publishers

Feder G. 1980, Economic Growth, Foreign Loans and Debt Servicing Capacity of Developing Countries, Journal of Development Studies n.3 pp. 352-68

Feder G. and R. Just 1979, Optimal International Borrowing, Capital Allocation and Creditworthiness Control, Kredit und Kapital n.2 pp. 207-20

Felmingham B.S. 1984, The Recovery of World Labor Markets and the US Monetary Stance: Rationale and Evidence, Kyklos, pp. 424-43

Fieleke N. 1977, The Growth of US Banking Abroad, an Analytical Survey, in Key Issues in International Banking, Federal Reserve Bank of Boston Conference Series

Fieleke N. 1983, Comment in D. Hodgman (ed.) The Political Economy of Monetary Policy: National and International Aspects, Federal Reserve Bank of Boston, Conference series

Findlay R. 1980, The Terms of Trade and Equilibrium Growth in the World Economy, American Economic Review, n.2 pp. 291-99

Findlay R. 1985, Growth and Development in Trade Models, on R.Jones, P.Kenen (eds.) Handbook in International Economics, Elsevier

Fisher I. 1933, The Debt-Deflation Theory of Great Depressions, Econometrica, n.2 pp. 337-50

Fisher S. and J.Frenkel, 1984, Economic Growth and

References

the Stages of the Balance of Payments: a
Theoretical Model, in G.Horwich, P.Samuelson
(eds.), Trade, Stability and Macroeconomics,
Academic Press

Fratianni M. and J. Pattison 1982, The Economics of
International Organizations, Kyklos n.2 pp.
244-62

Frey B 1978, Politico-Economic Models and Cycles,
Journal of Public Economics, n 2 pp. 203-20

Frey B. 1984a, The Public Choice View of
International Political Economy, International
Organization n.1 pp. 199-223

Frey B. 1984b, International Political Economics,
Basil Blackwell

Frey B. and F.Schneider 1982, International
Political Economy: an Emerging Field, Institute
for International Economic Studies, seminar
paper, n 227

Friedman M. 1959, A Program for Monetary Stability,
Fordham University Press

Gandolfo G. and P.C.Padoan 1984, A Disequilibrium
Model of Real and Financial Accumulation in an
Open Economy: Theory, Evidence and Policy
Simulations, Springer Verlag

Genberg H. and A. Swoboda 1977, Causes and Origins
of Current Worldwide Inflation, in E. Lundberg
(ed.) Inflation Theory and Anti-Inflation
Policy, Macmillan

Gilpin R. 1975, US Power and the Multinational
Corporation, Macmillan

Goodman L. 1981, Bank Lending to Non-Opec Ldc's, are
Risks Diversifiable?, Federal Reserve Bank of
Boston Quarterly Review n.2 pp. 10-21

Gordon R. 1975, The Demand for and the Supply of
Inflation, Journal of Law and Economics n.4 pp.
185-219

Gordon R. 1977, World Inflation and Monetary
Accomodation in Eight Countries, Brookings
Papers on Economic Activity, n.2 pp. 409-77

Gowa J. 1984, Hegemons, IOs, and Markets: the Case
of the Substitution Account, International
Organization, n.4 pp. 661-84

Grilli E. and M. Yang 1981, Real and Monetary
Determinants of Non-Oil Primary Commodities
Price Movements, paper presented at the
conference on Distribution, Effective Demand and
International Economic Development, Trieste 4-6
September

Guerrieri P and P.C. Padoan 1985, Neomercantilism
and International Economic Stability,

References

International Organization, forthcoming
Guttentag J. and R. Herring 1983, The Lender of Last
    Resort Function in an International Context,
    Princeton Essays in International Finance,
    n.151
Guttentag J. and R. Herring 1984, Strategic Planning
    by International Banks to Cope with Incertitude,
    paper presented at the conference on Strategic
    Planning in International Banking, Rome, may
Gylfason T. and A. Lindbeck 1982, The Macroeconomic
    Consequences of Endogenous Governments and
    Labour Unions, Institute for International
    Economics, Seminar paper n.232
Halevi N. 1971, An Empirical Test of the "Balance of
    Payments Stages" Hypothesis, Journal of
    International Economics, February pp. 103-17
Hamada K. 1976, A Strategic Analysis of Monetary
    Interdependence, Journal of Political Economy,
    pp. 688-95
Hamada K. 1977, On the Political Economy of Monetary
    Integration, in Aliber R. (ed.) The Political
    Economy of Monetary Reform, Macmillan
Hamada K. 1979, On the Coordination of Monetary
    Policies in a Monetary Union, paper presented at
    the Colloqium on New Economic Approaches to the
    Study of International Integration: Applications
    of Economic Analysis to Political
    Decision-Making, European University Institute,
    Florence May 31-June 2
Hart J. 1976, Three Approaches to the Measurement of
    Power in International Relations, International
    Organization, n.2 pp. 289-308
Hawley J. 1984, Protecting Capital from Itself: US
    Attempts to Regulate the Eurocurrency System,
    International Organization, n.1 pp. 131-65
Hawtrey R. 1928, Currency and Credit, Longmans,
    Green and Co.
Hayek F.von 1976, Denationalization of Money,
    Institute of Economic Affairs, London, Hobart
    Special Papers n.70
Head J.G. 1962, Public Goods and Public Policy,
    Public Finance n.3
Herring R. and R. Marston 1977, National Monetary
    Policies and International Financial Markets,
    North Holland
Hirsch F. 1977, The Bagehot Problem, The Manchester
    School, n.3 pp. 241-57
Hirsch F.e M.Doyle 1977, Politicization in the World
    Economy: Necessary Conditions for an
    International Economic Order, in F.Hirsch,

References

M.Doyle and E.Morse, Alternatives to Monetary
Disorder, McGraw-Hill
Hirsch F. and J. Goldthorpe (eds.) 1978, The
Political Economy of Inflation, Martin
Robertson
Hirschman A. 1970, Exit, Voice and Loyalty,
Cambridge University Press
Horne J. 1983, The Asset Market Model of the Balance
of Payments and the Exchange Rate: a Survey of
Empirical Evidence, Journal of International
Money and Finance, n.1 pp. 89-100
Johnson H. 1972, Political Economy Aspects of
International Monetary Reform, Journal of
International Economics, n.2 pp. 401-23
Kaldor N. 1976, Inflation and Recession in the World
Economy, Economic Journal, December pp. 703-14
Kalecki M. 1931, La Crisi Finanziaria Mondiale in M.
Storaci (ed.) 1983, La Crisi del '29,
Zanichelli
Kalecki M. 1934, On Foreign Trade and Domestic
Exports, reprinted in Selected Essays on the
Dynamics of the Capitalist Economy, 1971
Cambridge University Press
Kalecki M. 1937, The Principle of Increasing Risk,
Economica, November pp. 440-7
Katz L. 1982, The Cost of Borrowing, the Terms of
Trade and the Determination of External Debt,
Oxford Economic Papers, n.2 pp. 332-45
Katzenstein P. (ed.) 1978, Between Power and Plenty:
Foreign Economic Policy of Advanced Industrial
States, University of Wisconsin Press
Keohane R. 1978, American Policy and the Trade
Growth Struggle, International Security n.2 pp.
20-43
Keohane R. 1982, Hegemonic Leadership and U.S.
Foreign Economic Policy in the Long Decade of
the 1950's, in W.P.Avery, D.P. Rapkin (eds.)
America in the World Political Economy,
Longman
Keohane R. 1984, After Hegemony, Princeton
University Press
Keohane R. 1985, The International Politics of the
Great Inflation, in L. Lindberg and C. Maier
(eds.) The Politics of Inflation and Recession,
Brookings Institution
Kenen P. 1960, International Liquidity and the
Balance of Payments of a Reserve Currency
Country, Quarterly Journal of Economics,
November
Keynes J. 1931, The Consequences to the Banks of the

References

Collapse of Money Values, _The Collected Writings of JMK_, vol IX, pp 150-58, Cambridge University Press

Keynes J.M. 1936, _The General Theory of Employment, Interest, and Money_, Harcourt Brace

Kharas H. 1984, The Long-Run Creditworthiness of Developing Countries: Theory and Practice, _Quarterly Journal of Economics_, August pp. 415-38

Kindleberger C. 1970, _Power and Money_, Mit Press

Kindleberger C. 1978a, _Manias, Panics and Crashes_, Basic Books.

Kindleberger C. 1978b, Debt Situation of Developing Countries in Historical Perspective, in S.M. Goodman (ed.) _Financing and Risk in Developing Countries_, Praeger.

Kindleberger C. 1981, Dominance and Leadership in the International Economy: Exploitation, Public Goods and Free Rides, _International Studies Quarterly_, n.2 pp. 242-54

Kindleberger C. and F.Laffargue (eds.) 1982, _Financial Crises_, Cambridge University Press

Kouri P. 1983, Balance of Payments and the Foreign Exchange Market: a Dynamic Partial Equilibrium Model, in J.S. Bhandari and B.M.Putnam (eds.), _Economic Interdependence and Flexible Exchange Rates_, MIT Press.

Krasner S. 1977, US Commercial and Monetary Policy: Unravelling the Paradox of External Strength and Internal Weakness, _International Organization_, n.4 pp. 635-72

Krasner S. (ed.) 1983, _International Regimes_, Cornell University Press

Krause L. and W Salant (eds.) 1977, _Worldwide Inflation_, Brookings Institution

Kreinin M. 1979, _United States Foreign Economic Policy_, Institute for International Economic Studies seminar paper, n.124

Krugman P. 1980, Vehicle Currencies and the Structure of International Exchange, _Journal of Money Credit and Banking_, August pp 513-26

Krugman P. 1982, The International Role of the Dollar: Theory and Prospects, paper presented at the conference on _Exchange Rate Theory and Policy_, Bellagio, January 25-26

Lake D. 1984, Beneath the Commerce of Nations, _International Studies Quarterly_, n 1

Laney L. and T. Willet 1983, Presidential Politics, Budget Deficits and Monetary Policy in the United States 1960-76, _Public Choice_, n.1 pp.

References

53-69

Lipietz A. 1984, La Mondialization de la Crise Generale du Fordisme: 1967-1984, Cepremap paper n. 8413

Lipson C. 1979, The IMF, Commercial Banks, and Third World Debts, in Aronson 1979

Lipson C. 1981, The International Organization of Third World Debt, International Organization n.4 pp. 603-32

Llewellyn D. 1982, Avoiding an International Banking Crisis, National Westminster Bank Quarterly Review, August, pp. 28-39

Lombra R. and W. Witte (eds.) 1982, Political Economy of International and Domestic Monetary Relations, Iowa State University Press

Mattione R. 1985, Opec's Investment Strategies and the International financial System, Brookings Institution

McDonald D. 1982, Debt Capacity and Developing Country Borrowing: A Survey of the Literature, International Monetary Fund Staff Papers n.4 pp. 603-46

McKinnon R. 1982, Currency Substitution and Instability in the World Dollar Standard, American Economic Review, n.2 pp. 320-33

McMahon C. 1978, Is There an International Monetary System?, Bank of England Quarterly Bulletin, June.

Meese R.A. and K. Rogoff 1981, Empirical Exchange Rate Models of the Seventies: Are Any Fit to Survive?, International Finance Discussion Paper n.184, Federal Reserve Board

Meltzer A. 1967, Major Issues in the Regulation of Financial Institutions, Journal of Politcal Economy, supplement, August.pp. 482-501

Micossi S. and S. Saccomanni 1981, The Substitution Account, the Techniques, the Politics, Banca Nazionale del Lavoro Quarterly Review, June

Minsky H. 1979, Financial Interrelations, the Balance of Payments and the Crisis of the Dollar, in Aronson 1979

Minsky H. 1980, The Federal Reserve: Between a Rock and a Hard Place, Challenge, May-June, reprinted in Minsky 1982a

Minsky H. 1981, The United States Economy in the 1980's: the Financial Past and Present as a Guide to the Future, Giornale degli Economisti, n.5-6 pp. 301-17

Minsky H. 1982a, Inflation, Recession and Economic Policy, Wheatsheaf Books

References

Minsky H. 1982b, Debt-Deflation Theory in Today's
Institutional Environment, Banca Nazionale del
Lavoro Quarterly Review, September
Minsky H. 1984, Conflict and Interdependence in a
Multipolar World, paper presented at the
conference on Adjusting to Shocks, a North-South
Perspective, Milan, 21-24 november
Moffit M. 1983, The World's Money, Simon and
Schuster
Moon B. 1982, Exchange Rate System, Policy
Distortion and the Maintenance of Trade
Dependence, International Organization, n 3 pp.
715-40
Neumann M. 1984, Intervention in the Mark Dollar
Market: The Authorities' Reaction Function,
Journal of International Money and Finance n.3
pp. 223-39
O'Brien R. 1981, Private Bank Lending to Developing
Countries, World Bank Staff Working Paper,
n.482
Odell J. 1982, US International Monetary Policy:
Markets, Power, and Ideas as Sources of Change,
Princeton University Press
Oecd 1980, Access of Developing Countries to
International Financial Markets, Financial
Market Trends, February
Officer L and T. Willet 1969, Reserve Asset
Preferences and the Confidence Problem in the
Crisis Zone, Quarterly Journal of Economics,
November pp. 688-95
Olson M. 1965, The Logic of Collective Action,
Harvard University Press
Olson M. 1982, The Rise and Decline of Nations, Yale
University Press
Olson M.and R. Zeckhauser 1966, An Economic Theory
of Alliances, Review of Economics and
Statistics, august pp. 266-79
Onitsuka Y. 1974, International Capital Movements
and the Patterns of Economic Growth, American
Economic Review, n.2 pp. 24-36
Oudiz G. and J. Sachs 1984, Macroeconomic Policy
Coordination among the Industrial Countries,
Brookings Papers on Economic Activity n.1 pp.
1-75
Padoan P.C. 1980, Assessment of Country Risk on the
Euromarkets, Lo Spettatore Internazionale. n.2
pp. 93-110
Padoan P.C. 1985, The European Monetary System:
Pyramid or ECU?, The International Spectator,
n.1

References

Padoa-Schioppa T. 1981, <u>Problems of Interdependence in a Multipolar World</u>, Commission of the European Communities Economic Papers n.19

Padoa-Schioppa T. and F. Papadia 1984, Competing Currencies and Monetary Stability, in R. Masera and R. Triffin (eds.) <u>Europe's Money</u>, Clarendon Press

Parboni R. 1981, <u>The Dollar and its Rivals</u>, New Left Books

Revell J. 1981, The Complementary Nature of Competition and Regulation in the Financial Sector, in A. Verheirstraten (ed.) <u>Competition and Regulation in Financial Markets</u>, Macmillan

Robinson J. 1965, The New Mercantilism, reprinted in <u>Contributions to Modern Economics</u>, 1978, Blackwell

Runge C.F. 1984, Institutions and the Free Rider: The Assurance Problem in Collective Action, <u>Journal of Politics</u>, n.2 pp. 154-81

Sachs J. 1982, <u>Ldc Debt in the 1980's: Risk and Reforms</u>, National Bureau of Economic Research Working paper n.861

Sachs J. 1984, <u>Theoretical Issues in International Borrowing</u>, Princeton Studies in International Finance n.54

Saini K. and P. Bates 1984, A Survey of the Quantitative Approaches to Country Risk Analysis, <u>Journal of Banking and Finance</u>, vol.8 pp. 415-38

Salant W. 1977, A Supranational Approach to the Analysis of Worldwide Inflation, in Krause and Salant 1977

Sandler T. (ed.) 1980, <u>The Theory and Structure of International Political Economy</u>, Westview Press

Saunders A. 1983, <u>The Determinants of Country Risk: A Selective Survey of the Literature</u>, International Monetary Fund mimeo

Scaperlanda A. 1978, The IMF: an Emerging Central Bank?, <u>Kyklos</u> n.4 pp. 679-90

Schmitt H. 1979, Mercantilism: a Modern Argument, <u>The Manchester School</u>, June pp. 93-111

Shaffer J.R. and B.E. Loopesko 1983, Floating Exchange Rates after Ten Years, <u>Brookings Papers on Economic Activity</u> n.1 pp 1-70

Simonsen M. 1984, <u>The Developing Countries Debt Problem</u>, Foundation Getulio Vargas mimeo

Solomon R. 1977, A Perspective on the Debt of Developing Countries, <u>Brookings Papers on Economic Activity</u>, n.2 pp 479-501

Solomon R. 1982, The Elephant in the Boat ?: the

References

United States and the World Economy, _Foreign Affairs_, n.3 pp. 573-92

Spaventa L. 1983, Risk to the Stability of the International Financial System: Gloom without Drama, in Fair and Bertrand 1983

Spero J. 1980, _The Failure of the Franklin National Bank_, Council on Foreign Relations

Strange S. 1979a, Alliance Theories in an Authority Market Paradigm: The Case of EMS and Community Diplomacy in Market-Sharing. paper presented at The Colloquium on _New Economic Approaches to the Study of International Integration: Applications of Economic Analysis to Political Decision-Making_, European University Institute, Florence May 31-June 2

Strange S. 1979b, Debt and Default in the International Political Economy, in Aronson 1979

Strange S. 1982, Still an Extraordinary Power: America's Role in a Global Monetary System, in Lombra and Witte 1982

Swoboda A. 1983, Exchange Rate Regimes and European-US Policies Interdependence, _International Monetary Fund Staff Papers_ n.1 pp. 75-112

Thirlwall A. 1979, The Balance of Payments Constraint as an Explanation of International Growth Rate Differences, _Banca Nazionale del Lavoro Quarterly Review_, n.1 pp. 45-53

Thirlwall A. and M. Hussain 1982, The Balance of Payments Constraint, Capital Flows and Growth Rate Differences Between Developing Countries, _Oxford Economic Papers_, November pp. 498-509

Thompson W. and G. Zuk 1983, American Elections and the International Electoral-Economic Cycle: a Test of the Tufte Hypothesis, _American Journal of Political Science_, n.3 pp. 464-84

Thygesen N. 1979, _Exchange Rate Experiences and Policies of Small Countries: Some European Examples of the 1970's_, Princeton Essays in International Finance n.136

Tollison R. and T. Willet 1979, An Economic Theory of Mutually Advantageous Issue Linkages in International Negotiations, _International Organization_, n.4 pp. 425-49

Triffin R. 1960, _Gold and the Dollar Crisis_, Yale University Press

Triffin R. 1983, _The Future of The European Monetary System and of the ECU?_, paper presented at the annual conference of the Center for European

References

Policies Studies 23-26 November

Tsoukalis L. 1977, The Politics and Economics of European Monetary Integration, George Allen and Unwin

Tufte R. 1978, Political Control of the Economy Princeton University Press

Vaubel R. 1983, The Moral Hazard of IMF Lending, The World Economy, n.3 pp. 291-304

Vines D. 1980, Competitiveness, Technical Progress and the Balance of Trade Surplus, The Manchester School, December pp. 378-91

Volcker P. 1984, Facing up the Twin Deficits, Challenge, March-April

Wallace M. 1983, Economic Stabilization as a Public Good What Does it Mean?, Journal of Post Keynesian Economics, Winter pp. 295-302

Wallich H. 1977, Central Banks as Regulators and Lenders of Last Resort in an International Context: a View from the United States, in Key Issues in International Banking, Federal Reserve Bank of Boston Conference Series

Wijkman P. 1981, Seignorage, Financial Intermediation and the International Role of the Dollar, 1960-1971, Institute for International Economic Studies, seminar paper n.173

Willet T. and J. Mullen 1982, The Effects of Alternative International Monetary Systems on Macroeconomic Discipline and Inflationary Biases, in Lombra and Witte 1982

Williamson J. 1983, The Exchange Rate System, Institute for International Economics, Washington

Wionczeck M. (ed.) 1979, International Indebtedness and World Economic Stagnation, World Development, February

Wojinilower A. 1980, The Central Role of Credit Crunches in Recent Financial History, Brookings Papers on Economic Activity, n.2 pp. 277-339

Wood J. 1975, Commercial Bank Loan and Investment Behaviour, John Wiley and Sons

Woolley J. 1983, Political Factors in Monetary Policy, in D. Hodgman (ed.) The Political Economy of Monetary Policy: National and International Aspects, Federal Reserve Bank of Boston, Conference series

INDEX

Index

moral hazard 55, 59, 128,
    134, 144, 151, 155
multi-currency system 41,
    61
neomercantilism, <u>see</u>
    mercantilism

North Atlantic Treaty
Organization (NATO) 19,
32

oil crisis 67ff, 79
oligopolistic,
    interdependence 4, 10,
    49ff, 60, 107, 121,
    130, 144, 172, 184-6,
    191-2; and US policy
    52ff,
oligopolistic system 2,
    5, 8, 10ff, 23-4, 30ff
    38-9, 44, 190ff
oligopoly, leaders 3,
    10ff, 38-9, 49, 55,
    89, 102, 121, 152,
    200; and strong
    currency option 44;
    and managed float 40ff
Opec deposits 69, 79

parental responsibility
    61
peripheral Fordism 175
Peru 144
political business cycle
    9, 17, 47, 53, 56ff,
    62, 167ff, 177-8
political risk 154, 183
ponzi finance 110ff, 126,
    129, 154
prisoner dilemma 143,
    152-3
protectionistic policies
    17, 77, 181
public choice 23

regimes 12, 133-4, 143,
    176, 178, 190, 192;
    exchange rate 8, 38,
    40, 172; financing
    203ff

regulating mechanisms 7ff
    16, 176
reserve currency 9, 19ff,
    52, 193
residual country 19, 21,
    24ff, 37ff, 51-3, 119,
    178, 207

Saudi Arabia 100
seignorage 11, 19ff, 54
small country assumption
    4
small open economies 4
sovereign lending 78,
    100, 124, 151
Special Drawing Rights
    (SDR) 8, 144
speculative finance 110,
    116, 133
strong currency option
    44ff, 166
Substitution Account 8,
    186, 206
syndecated lending 68, 78
    100, 128
systemic risk 151-3, 159

transition theory 173ff
Triffin's dilemma 11,
    21ff; restatement 28ff

US banking system 20,
    53ff, 61, 89, 136, 199
    205-6
US budget deficit 92;
    and trade deficit 200

Venezuela 75, 83, 87, 102

World Bank 205

226

For Product Safety Concerns and Information please contact our EU
representative GPSR@taylorandfrancis.com
Taylor & Francis Verlag GmbH, Kaufingerstraße 24, 80331 München, Germany

www.ingramcontent.com/pod-product-compliance
Lightning Source LLC
Chambersburg PA
CBHW061156220326
41599CB00025B/4506

9 781032 954752